Human Nature

A Reader

Other Titles from
HACKETT READINGS

Certainty
Free Will
God
The Good Life
The Idea of Race
Justice
Life and Death
Materialism and the Mind-Body Problem
Reality
Time

Human Nature

A Reader

Edited by
Joel J. Kupperman

Hackett Publishing Company, Inc.
Indianapolis / Cambridge

Printed in the United States of America

16 15 14 13 12 1 2 3 4 5 6 7

For further information, please address
Hackett Publishing Company, Inc.
P.O. Box 44937
Indianapolis, Indiana 46244-0937

www.hackettpublishing.com

Composition by Innodata-Isogen, Inc.
Printed at Sheridan Books, Inc.

Library of Congress Cataloging-in-Publication Data

Human nature : a reader / edited by Joel J. Kupperman.
p. cm.
ISBN 978-1-60384-745-2 (pbk.) — ISBN 978-1-60384-746-9 (cloth)
1. Philosophical anthropology. I. Kupperman, Joel.
BD450.H8575 2012
128—dc23

2011041656

The paper used in this publication meets the minimum requirements of American National Standard for Information Sciences—Permanence of Paper for Printed Library Materials, ANSI Z39.48–1984.

∞

Contents

Introduction

This is a reader in philosophical accounts of human nature. It is a topic that has concerned many great philosophers, east and west. The subject is not only what human nature is but also what it is capable of. It is more complicated than it first may look. The initial temptation is to suppose that there is some quality (or set of qualities) that humans and only humans possess. Aristotle nominated rationality as the answer. But some chimpanzees are more rational than some mentally handicapped humans. Not all humans are alike or behave in the same way. We tend to say, "That's just human nature," when someone says or does something that *most* people would have said or done in her or his place.

Hence, the topic of human nature includes what we can often (or perhaps usually) expect of people. It also includes, among other things, the specific question of whether a tendency towards benevolence or sympathy is a feature of normal people. Both the Chinese philosopher Mencius (Mengzi) and the Scottish philosopher David Hume argued for an answer of "yes."

There are other issues. These include whether and how someone can modify her or his nature. This makes a central appearance in Indian and Chinese philosophies and also comes up in Book 2 of Hume's *Treatise of Human Nature*. There is also the question of whether there is some strong connection between being virtuous and being a happy or fulfilled person. The readings from Plato and Aristotle confront this issue.

There is a huge variety of views on these topics, and inevitably not all of them are represented in this reader. What are represented are distinctive views, most of them influential. They do not all agree. This is typical of philosophy, in which disagreement is rife. Much philosophy centers on disagreements and the arguments that they stimulate.

This feature of much philosophical writing is part of the reason five of the ten chapters of this book center on two philosophers rather than one. Since the very first philosophical works were written, almost all philosophy has been mindful of other philosophy. In some cases (e.g., Buddha and the Upanishads, or Mengzi and Xunzi) there is direct disagreement at least to a degree. Sometimes there is partial agreement (e.g., Plato and Aristotle). Occasionally a philosopher builds to some extent on the insights of a predecessor, as David Hume in his ethics built on Bishop Butler. Sometimes (as in the case of Kierkegaard and Sartre) a quirk in human nature is agreed upon but then is interpreted in different ways.

What a philosopher highlights in an account of human nature can depend very much on the philosopher's concerns. These might be primarily in arriving at a descriptive analysis of what distinguishes human beings from other organisms. Aristotle's claim that man is the rational animal has this character.

Alternatively, it could be in a descriptive analysis of what you can expect in human behavior—other people's or your own—which Hobbes attempts to provide. Those who are concerned with liberation, as the great Indian philosophers were, will focus on the elements in human nature that make liberation possible. Someone like Kierkegaard or Sartre, both of whom think that projects to improve one's life tend to be slippery, will focus on the features of human nature that make this the case.

Some accounts of human nature point toward a sense of what has most value as a part of human life. Aristotle clearly thinks that this is rationality. Plato's focus on the importance of reason points in the same direction, as does much of what Kant says about the categorical imperative.

The Upanishads and Buddha on the other hand are not only concerned with values (as these contribute to ultimate liberation) but also want to contrast what is central in human life with what is less central. The Upanishads offer us atman, which is like an impersonal inner soul. Buddha offers us our ability to control our emotions in order to avoid suffering.

Confucius and his followers are very concerned with the second nature that you can achieve, which will be the new (more finely developed) you, and will enable you to interact well with other people. Philosophers like Mengzi, Bishop Butler, and David Hume also want to focus on what they see to be especially important to human beings: the motivation to be sympathetic and benevolent to others. This is done to focus on capacities that may or may not be realized in a person.

In short, philosophical accounts of human nature can be mainly about, so to speak, facts on the ground. But, instead, they can also be mainly about capacities or values that are especially important in what someone is.

Part I

Some Ancient Views of Human Nature

1

Indian Philosophy: The Upanishads and Buddha

The Upanishads are a series of investigations into the nature of the human self that were written during the first millennium BCE (Before the Common Era). They are the oldest philosophy we have.

They do not agree with one another on every point, but there is a general convergence on a pair of central claims.

One of these is that there are two layers to the self. There is what we might think of as the personal level, which includes personality, a sense of one's connections, and bodily attributes. This is termed "jiva." It is subject to change in a person's life.

Think of the "jiva" as a superficial self. The persistent central claim in the Upanishads is that each of us has a deeper self, "atman," which is a purely spiritual nature and is impersonal. Not only do the Upanishads describe this two-level self, but they also recommend a path of life that can lead to fulfillment and liberation.

The liberation is from the seemingly endless cycle of reincarnations that we all have been in. Most contemporary Western readers will have an attitude toward reincarnation that is very different from that of the Upanishads. The current map of the afterlife usually presents two or three alternatives. These include heaven (desirable in a vague way) and hell (definitely undesirable). A traditional third alternative is limbo. As presented in works like Dante's *Divine Comedy*, limbo is reserved for virtuous pagans and others who are virtuous but have not gained salvation through Christ. It is not terrible but also is not really desirable and is in the suburbs of hell.

Given these alternatives, many of us might find the idea of reincarnation to be appealing. This is not the attitude presupposed by the Upanishads. The very idea of reincarnation inspired weariness.

They had been through it so many times. Getting off the wheel of rebirth seemed highly desirable. That would be true liberation.

The full nature of this liberation would be as follows. You had to get fully in touch with your deep spiritual self, your atman. To identify fully with it was to become impersonal and detached. This typically required many periods of quiet meditation that would lead to an impersonal identification with the universe.

The universe was thought of as Brahman, an impersonal divine reality. That atman is qualitatively the same as Brahman (much as a drop of ocean water is qualitatively the same stuff as the ocean) is the second of the two major claims of the Upanishads. Introspectively, to realize this fully is how you became detached and impersonal. This will be felt as liberating, as the concerns of life become progressively less pressing. It also is liberating in the sense that you will not be reincarnated but instead will merge with the cosmos, in a state termed "moksha." Moksha has much in common with the Buddhist nirvana, as we will see.

Buddha rejected the claim that each of us had an inner self, an atman. Buddha's view was termed "anatman," literally, no atman. Instead, Buddha contended, each of us is an ever changing mix of thoughts and of experiences in life. This "bundle" theory of the self has much in common with the view developed more than two thousand years later by the Scottish philosopher David Hume. In Buddha's version, it was important that you could manage elements in your bundle. Ideally you could eliminate your desires (i.e., strong preferences) and become more detached. This will prevent you from suffering. Suffering was regarded as a natural consequence of being given to having strong preferences because we cannot always get what we very much want.

Achieving this completely also would lead, Buddha held, to a fulfilling spiritual state, termed "nirvana." We might normally think of nirvana as a rewarding state after death. However, in at least one text Buddha (while still alive) claimed to be in nirvana. Like the moksha of the Upanishads, nirvana was a detached joyous state, involving unity with the cosmos.

Katha Upanishad

First Adhyâya

First Vallî

1. VÂGASRAVASA, desirous (of heavenly rewards), surrendered (at a sacrifice) all that he possessed. He had a son of the name of Na*k*iketas.

2. When the (promised) presents were being given (to the priests), faith entered into the heart of Na*k*iketas, who was still a boy, and he thought:

3. 'Unblessed, surely, are the worlds to which a man goes by giving (as his promised present at a sacrifice) cows which have drunk water, eaten hay, given their milk, and are barren.'

4. He (knowing that his father had promised to give up all that he possessed, and therefore his son also) said to his father: 'Dear father, to whom will you give me?'

He said it a second and a third time. Then the father replied (angrily):

'I shall give you unto Death.'

(The father, having once said so, though in haste, had to be true to his word and to sacrifice his son.)

5. The son said: 'I go as the first, at the head of many (who have still to die); I go in the midst of many (who are now dying). What will be the work of Yama (the ruler of the departed) which today he has to do unto me?'

6. 'Look back how it was with those who came before, look forward how it will be with those who come hereafter. A mortal ripens like corn, like corn he springs up again.'

(Na*k*iketas enters into the abode of Yama Vaivasvata, and there is no one to receive him. Thereupon one of the attendants of Yama is supposed to say:)

7. 'Fire enters into the houses, when a Brâhma*n*a enters as a guest. That fire is quenched by this peace-offering;—bring water, O Vaivasvata!'

8. 'A Brâhma*n*a that dwells in the house of a foolish man without receiving food to eat, destroys his hopes and expectations, his possessions, his righteousness, his sacred and his good deeds, and all his sons and cattle.'

(Yama, returning to his house after an absence of three nights, during which time Na*k*iketas had received no hospitality from him, says:)

Translated by F. Max Müller, 1884. Lightly revised.

9. 'O Brâhma*n*a, as you, a venerable guest, have dwelled in my house three nights without eating, therefore choose now three boons. Hail to you! and welfare to me!'

10. Na*k*iketas said: 'O Death, as the first of the three boons I choose that Gautama, my father, be pacified, kind, and free from anger towards me; and that he may know me and greet me, when I shall have been dismissed by you.'

11. Yama said: 'Through my favor Auddâlaki Âru*n*i, your father, will know you, and be again towards you as he was before. He shall sleep peacefully through the night, and free from anger, after having seen you freed from the mouth of death.'

12. Na*k*iketas said: 'In the heaven-world there is no fear; you are not there, O Death, and no one is afraid on account of old age. Leaving behind both hunger and thirst, and out of the reach of sorrow, all rejoice in the world of heaven.'

13. 'You know, O Death, the fire-sacrifice which leads us to heaven; tell it to me, for I am full of faith. Those who live in the heaven-world reach immortality,—this I ask as my second boon.'

14. Yama said: 'I tell it you, learn it from me, and when you understand that fire-sacrifice which leads to heaven, know, O Na*k*iketas, that it is the attainment of the endless worlds, and their firm support, hidden in darkness.'

15. Yama then told him that fire-sacrifice, the beginning of all the worlds, and what bricks are required for the altar, and how many, and how they are to be placed. And Na*k*iketas repeated all as it had been told to him. Then M*ri*tyu, being pleased with him, said again:

16. The generous, being satisfied, said to him: 'I give to you now another boon; that fire-sacrifice shall be named after you, take also this many-colored chain.'

17. 'He who has three times performed this Nâ*k*iketa rite, and has been united with the three (father, mother, and teacher), and has performed the three duties (study, sacrifice, almsgiving) overcomes birth and death. When he has learned and understood this fire, which knows (or makes us know) all that is born of Brahman, which is venerable and divine, then he obtains everlasting peace.'

18. 'He who knows the three Nâ*k*iketa fires, and knowing the three, piles up the Nâ*k*iketa sacrifice, he, having first thrown off the chains of death, rejoices in the world of heaven, beyond the reach of grief.'

19. 'This, O Na*k*iketas, is your fire which leads to heaven, and which you have chosen as your second boon. That fire all men will proclaim. Choose now, O Na*k*iketas, your third boon.'

20. Na*k*iketas said: 'There is that doubt, when a man is dead,—some saying, he is; others, he is not. This I should like to know, taught by you; this is the third of my boons.'

21. Death said: 'On this point even the gods have doubted formerly; it is not easy to understand. That subject is subtle. Choose another boon, O Na*k*iketas, do not press me, and let me off that boon.'

22. Na*k*iketas said: 'On this point even the gods have doubted indeed, and you, Death, have declared it to be not easy to understand, and another teacher like you is not to be found:—surely no other boon is like unto this.'

23. Death said: 'Choose sons and grandsons who shall live a hundred years, herds of cattle, elephants, gold, and horses. Choose the wide abode of the earth, and live yourself as many harvests as you desire.'

24. 'If you can think of any boon equal to that, choose wealth, and long life. Be (king), Na*k*iketas, on the wide earth. I make you the enjoyer of all desires.'

25. 'Whatever desires are difficult to attain among mortals, ask for them according to your wish;—these fair maidens with their chariots and musical instruments,—such are indeed not to be obtained by men,—be waited on by them whom I give to you, but do not ask me about dying.'

26. Na*k*iketas said: 'These things last till tomorrow, O Death, for they wear out this vigor of all the senses. Even the whole of life is short. Keep you your horses, keep dance and song for yourself.'

27. 'No man can be made happy by wealth. Shall we possess wealth, when we see you? Shall we live, as long as you rule? Only that boon (which I have chosen) is to be chosen by me.'

28. 'What mortal, slowly decaying here below, and knowing, after having approached them, the freedom from decay enjoyed by the immortals, would delight in a long life, after he has pondered on the pleasures which arise from beauty and love?'

29. 'No, that on which there is this doubt, O Death, tell us what there is in that great Hereafter. Na*k*iketas does not choose another boon but that which enters into the hidden world.'

Second Vallî

1. Death said: 'The good is one thing, the pleasant another; these two, having different objects, chain a man. It is well with him who clings to the good; he who chooses the pleasant, misses his end.'

2. 'The good and the pleasant approach man: the wise goes round about them and distinguishes them. Yes, the wise prefers the good

to the pleasant, but the fool chooses the pleasant through greed and avarice.'

3. 'You, O Na*k*iketas, after pondering all pleasures that are or seem delightful, have dismissed them all. You have not gone into the road that leads to wealth, in which many men perish.'

4. 'Wide apart and leading to different points are these two, ignorance, and what is known as wisdom. I believe Na*k*iketas to be one who desires knowledge, for even many pleasures did not tear you away.'

5. 'Fools dwelling in darkness, wise in their own conceit, and puffed up with vain knowledge, go round and round, staggering to and fro, like blind men led by the blind.'

6. 'The Hereafter never rises before the eyes of the careless child, deluded by the delusion of wealth. "This is the world," he thinks, "there is no other";—thus he falls again and again under my sway.'

7. 'He (the Self) of whom many are not even able to hear, whom many, even when they hear of him, do not comprehend; wonderful is a man, when found, who is able to teach him (the Self); wonderful is he who comprehends him, when taught by an able teacher.'

8. 'That (Self), when taught by an inferior man, is not easy to be known, even though often thought upon; unless it be taught by another, there is no way to it, for it is inconceivably smaller than what is small.'

9. 'That doctrine is not to be obtained by argument, but when it is declared by another, then, O dearest, it is easy to understand. You have obtained it now; you are truly a man of true resolve. May we have always an inquirer like you!'

10. Na*k*iketas said: 'I know that what is called a treasure is transient, for that eternal is not obtained by things which are not eternal. Hence the Nâ*k*iketa fire(-sacrifice) has been laid by me (first); then, by means of transient things, I have obtained what is not transient (the teaching of Yama).'

11. Yama said: 'Though you had seen the fulfillment of all desires, the foundation of the world, the endless rewards of good deeds, the shore where there is no fear, that which is magnified by praise, the wide abode, the rest, yet being wise you have with firm resolve dismissed it all.'

12. 'The wise who, by means of meditation on his Self, recognizes the Ancient, who is difficult to be seen, who has entered into the dark, who is hidden in the cave, who dwells in the abyss, as God, he indeed leaves joy and sorrow far behind.'

13. 'A mortal who has heard this and embraced it, who has separated from it all qualities, and has thus reached the subtle Being, rejoices, because he has obtained what is a cause for rejoicing. The house (of Brahman) is open, I believe, O Na*k*iketas.'

14. Na*k*iketas said: 'That which you see as neither this nor that, as neither effect nor cause, as neither past nor future, tell me that.'

15. Yama said: 'That word (or place) which all the Vedas record, which all penances proclaim, which men desire when they live as religious students, that word I tell you briefly, it is Om.'

16. 'That (imperishable) syllable means Brahman, that syllable means the highest (Brahman); he who knows that syllable, whatever he desires, is his.'

17. 'This is the best support, this is the highest support; he who knows that support is magnified in the world of Brahmâ.'

18. 'The knowing (Self) is not born, it dies not; it sprang from nothing, nothing sprang from it. The Ancient is unborn, eternal, everlasting; he is not killed, though the body is killed.'

19. 'If the killer thinks that he kills, if the killed thinks that he is killed, they do not understand; for this one does not kill, nor is that one killed.'

20. 'The Self, smaller than small, greater than great, is hidden in the heart of that creature. A man who is free from desires and free from grief, sees the majesty of the Self by the grace of the Creator.'

21. 'Though sitting still, he walks far; though lying down, he goes everywhere. Who, save myself, is able to know that God who rejoices and rejoices not?'

22. 'The wise who knows the Self as bodiless within the bodies, as unchanging among changing things, as great and omnipresent, does never grieve.'

23. 'That Self cannot be gained by the Veda, nor by understanding, nor by much learning. He whom the Self chooses, by him the Self can be gained. The Self chooses him (his body) as his own.'

24. 'But he who has not first turned away from his wickedness, who is not tranquil, and subdued, or whose mind is not at rest, he can never obtain the Self (even) by knowledge.'

25. 'Who then knows where He is, He to whom the Brahmans and Kshatriyas are (as it were) but food, and death itself a condiment?'

Third Vallî

1. 'There are the two, drinking their reward in the world of their own works, entered into the cave (of the heart), dwelling on the highest summit (the ether in the heart). Those who know Brahman call them shade and light; likewise, those householders who perform the Tri*n*â*k*iketa sacrifice.'

2. 'May we be able to master that Nâ*k*iketa rite which is a bridge for sacrificers; also that which is the highest, imperishable Brahman for those who wish to cross over to the fearless shore.'

3. 'Know the Self to be sitting in the chariot, the body to be the chariot, the intellect (buddhi) the charioteer, and the mind the reins.'

4. 'The senses they call the horses, the objects of the senses their roads. When he (the Highest Self) is in union with the body, the senses, and the mind, then wise people call him the Enjoyer.'

5. 'He who has no understanding and whose mind (the reins) is never firmly held, his senses (horses) are unmanageable, like vicious horses of a charioteer.'

6. 'But he who has understanding and whose mind is always firmly held, his senses are under control, like good horses of a charioteer.'

7. 'He who has no understanding, who is unmindful and always impure, never reaches that place, but enters into the round of births.'

8. 'But he who has understanding, who is mindful and always pure, reaches indeed that place, from whence he is not born again.'

9. 'But he who has understanding for his charioteer, and who holds the reins of the mind, he reaches the end of his journey, and that is the highest place of Vish*n*u.'

10. 'Beyond the senses there are the objects, beyond the objects there is the mind, beyond the mind there is the intellect, the Great Self is beyond the intellect.'

11. 'Beyond the Great there is the Undeveloped, beyond the Undeveloped there is the Person (purusha). Beyond the Person there is nothing—this is the goal, the highest road.'

12. 'That Self is hidden in all beings and does not shine forth, but it is seen by subtle seers through their sharp and subtle intellect.'

13. 'A wise man should keep down speech and mind; he should keep them within the Self which is knowledge; he should keep knowledge within the Self which is the Great; and he should keep that (the Great) within the Self which is the Quiet.'

14. 'Rise, awake! having obtained your boons, understand them! The sharp edge of a razor is difficult to pass over; thus the wise say the path (to the Self) is hard.'

15. 'He who has perceived that which is without sound, without touch, without form, without decay, without taste, eternal, without smell, without beginning, without end, beyond the Great, and unchangeable, is freed from the jaws of death.'

16. 'A wise man who has repeated or heard the ancient story of Na*k*iketas told by Death, is magnified in the world of Brahman.'

17. 'And he who repeats this greatest mystery in an assembly of Brâhmans, or full of devotion at the time of the Srâddha sacrifice, obtains thereby infinite rewards.'

Second Adhyâya

Fourth Vallî

1. Death said: 'The Self-existent pierced the openings (of the senses) so that they turn forward: therefore man looks forward, not backward into himself. Some wise man, however, with his eyes closed and wishing for immortality, saw the Self behind.'

2. 'Children follow after outward pleasures, and fall into the snare of widespread death. Wise men only, knowing the nature of what is immortal, do not look for anything stable here among things unstable.'

3. 'That by which we know form, taste, smell, sounds, and loving touches, by that also we know what exists besides. This is that (which you have asked for).'

4. 'The wise, when he knows that that by which he perceives all objects in sleep or in waking is the great omnipresent Self, grieves no more.'

5. 'He who knows this living soul which eats honey (perceives objects) as being the Self, always near, the Lord of the past and the future, henceforward fears no more. This is that.'

6. 'He who (knows) him who was born first from the brooding heat (for he was born before the water), who, entering into the heart, abides therein, and was perceived from the elements. This is that.'

7. '(He who knows) Aditi also, who is one with all deities, who arises with Prâ*n*a (breath or Hira*n*yagarbha), who, entering into the heart, abides therein, and was born from the elements. This is that.'

8. 'There is Agni (fire), the all-seeing, hidden in the two fire-sticks, well-guarded like a child (in the womb) by the mother, day after day to be adored by men when they awake and bring oblations. This is that.'

9. 'And that whence the sun rises, and whither it goes to set, there all the Devas are contained, and no one goes beyond. This is that.'

10. 'What is here (visible in the world), the same is there (invisible in Brahman); and what is there, the same is here. He who sees any difference here (between Brahman and the world), goes from death to death.'

11. 'Even by the mind this (Brahman) is to be obtained, and then there is no difference whatsoever. He goes from death to death who sees any difference here.'

12. 'The person (purusha), of the size of a thumb, stands in the middle of the Self (body?), as lord of the past and the future, and henceforward fears no more. This is that.'

13. 'That person, of the size of a thumb, is like a light without smoke, lord of the past and the future, he is the same today and tomorrow. This is that.'

The Buddhist *Dhamapada*

Chapter I

The Twin-Verses

All that we are is the result of what we have thought: it is founded on our thoughts, it is made up of our thoughts. If a man speaks or acts with an evil thought, pain follows him, as the wheel follows the foot of the ox that draws the carriage.

All that we are is the result of what we have thought: it is founded on our thoughts, it is made up of our thoughts. If a man speaks or acts with a pure thought, happiness follows him, like a shadow that never leaves him.

"He abused me, he beat me, he defeated me, he robbed me"—in those who harbor such thoughts hatred will never cease.

"He abused me, he beat me, he defeated me, he robbed me"—in those who do not harbor such thoughts hatred will cease.

For hatred does not cease by hatred at any time: hatred ceases by love—this is an old rule.

The world does not know that we must all come to an end here; but those who know it, their quarrels cease at once.

He who lives looking for pleasures only, his senses uncontrolled, immoderate in his food, idle, and weak, Mâra (the tempter) will certainly overthrow him, as the wind throws down a weak tree.

He who lives without looking for pleasures, his senses well controlled, moderate in his food, faithful and strong, him Mâra will certainly not overthrow, any more than the wind throws down a rocky mountain.

He who wishes to put on the yellow dress without having cleansed himself from sin, who disregards also temperance and truth, is unworthy of the yellow dress.

Translated by F. Max Müller

But he who has cleansed himself from sin, is well grounded in all virtues, and endowed also with temperance and truth: he is indeed worthy of the yellow dress.

They who imagine truth in untruth, and see untruth in truth, never arrive at truth, but follow vain desires.

They who know truth in truth, and untruth in untruth, arrive at truth, and follow true desires.

As rain breaks through an ill-thatched house, passion will break through an unreflecting mind.

As rain does not break through a well-thatched house, passion will not break through a well-reflecting mind.

The evil-doer mourns in this world, and he mourns in the next; he mourns in both. He mourns and suffers when he sees the evil result of his own work.

The virtuous man delights in this world, and he delights in the next; he delights in both. He delights and rejoices, when he sees the purity of his own work.

The evil-doer suffers in this world, and he suffers in the next; he suffers in both. He suffers when he thinks of the evil he has done; he suffers more when going on the evil path.

The virtuous man is happy in this world, and he is happy in the next; he is happy in both. He is happy when he thinks of the good he has done; he is still more happy when going on the good path.

The thoughtless man, even if he can recite a large portion of the law, but is not a doer of it, has no share in the priesthood, but is like a cowherd counting the cows of others.

The follower of the law, even if he can recite only a small portion of the law, but, having forsaken passion and hatred and foolishness, possesses true knowledge and serenity of mind, he, caring for nothing in this world or that to come, has indeed a share in the priesthood.

Chapter II

On Earnestness

Earnestness is the path of immortality (Nirvâna), thoughtlessness the path of death. Those who are in earnest do not die, those who are thoughtless are as if dead already.

Having understood this clearly, those who are advanced in earnestness delight in earnestness, and rejoice in the knowledge of the elect.

These wise people, meditative, steady, always possessed of strong powers, attain to Nirvâna, the highest happiness.

If an earnest person has roused himself, if he is not forgetful, if his deeds are pure, if he acts with consideration, if he restrains himself, and lives according to law—then his glory will increase.

By rousing himself, by earnestness, by restraint and control, the wise man may make for himself an island which no flood can overwhelm.

Fools follow after vanity. The wise man keeps earnestness as his best jewel.

Follow not after vanity, nor after the enjoyment of love and lust! He who is earnest and meditative, obtains ample joy.

When the learned man drives away vanity by earnestness, he, the wise, climbing the terraced heights of wisdom, looks down upon the fools: free from sorrow he looks upon the sorrowing crowd, as one that stands on a mountain looks down upon them that stand upon the plain.

Earnest among the thoughtless, awake among the sleepers, the wise man advances like a racer, leaving behind the hack.

By earnestness did Maghavan (Indra) rise to the lordship of the gods. People praise earnestness; thoughtlessness is always blamed.

A Bhikshu (mendicant) who delights in earnestness, who looks with fear on thoughtlessness, moves about like fire, burning all his fetters, small or large.

A Bhikshu (mendicant) who delights in reflection, who looks with fear on thoughtlessness, cannot fall away from his perfect state—he is close upon Nirvâna.

Chapter III

Thought

As a fletcher makes straight his arrow, a wise man makes straight his trembling and unsteady thought, which is difficult to guard, difficult to hold back.

As a fish taken from his watery home and thrown on the dry ground, our thought trembles all over in order to escape the dominion of Mâra, the tempter.

It is good to tame the mind, which is difficult to hold in and flighty, rushing wherever it listeth; a tamed mind brings happiness.

Let the wise man guard his thoughts, for they are difficult to perceive, very artful, and they rush wherever they list: thoughts well guarded bring happiness.

Those who bridle their mind which travels far, moves about alone, is without a body, and hides in the chamber of the heart, will be free from the bonds of Mâra, the tempter.

If a man's faith is unsteady, if he does not know the true law, if his peace of mind is troubled, his knowledge will never be perfect.

If a man's thoughts are not dissipated, if his mind is not perplexed, if he has ceased to think of good or evil, then there is no fear for him while he is watchful.

Knowing that this body is fragile like a jar, and making this thought firm like a fortress, one should attack Mâra, the tempter, with the weapon of knowledge, one should watch him when conquered, and should never rest.

Before long, alas! this body will lie on the earth, despised, without understanding, like a useless log.

Whatever a hater may do to a hater, or an enemy to an enemy, a wrongly-directed mind will do him greater mischief.

Not a mother, not a father, will do so much, nor any other relatives; a well-directed mind will do us greater service.

Chapter IV

Flowers

Who shall overcome this earth, and the world of Yama, the lord of the departed, and the world of the gods? Who shall find out the plainly shown path of virtue, as a clever man finds the right flower?

The disciple will overcome the earth, and the world of Yama, and the world of the gods. The disciple will find out the plainly shown path of virtue, as a clever man finds the right flower.

He who knows that this body is like froth, and has learned that it is as unsubstantial as a mirage, will break the flower-pointed arrow of Mâra, and never see the king of death.

Death carries off a man who is gathering flowers, and whose mind is distracted, as a flood carries off a sleeping village.

Death subdues a man who is gathering flowers, and whose mind is distracted, before he is satiated in his pleasures.

As the bee collects nectar and departs without injuring the flower, or its color or scent, so let a sage dwell in his village.

Not the perversities of others, not their sins of commission or omission, but his own misdeeds and negligences should a sage take notice of.

Like a beautiful flower, full of color, but without scent, are the fine but fruitless words of him who does not act accordingly.

But, like a beautiful flower, full of color and full of scent, are the fine and fruitful words of him who acts accordingly.

As many kinds of wreaths can be made from a heap of flowers, so many good things may be achieved by a mortal when once he is born.

The scent of flowers does not travel against the wind, nor that of sandalwood, or of Tagara and Mallikâ flowers, but the odor of good people travels even against the wind; a good man pervades every place.

Sandalwood or Tagara, a lotus-flower, or a Vassikî, among these sorts of perfumes, the perfume of virtue is unsurpassed.

Mean is the scent that comes from Tagara and sandalwood; the perfume of those who possess virtue rises up to the gods as the highest.

Of the people who possess these virtues, who live without thoughtlessness, and who are emancipated through true knowledge, Mâra, the tempter, never finds the way.

As on a heap of rubbish cast upon the highway the lily will grow full of sweet perfume and delight, thus among those who are mere rubbish the disciple of the truly enlightened Buddha shines forth by his knowledge among the blinded worldling.

Chapter V

The Fool

Long is the night to him who is awake; long is a mile to him who is tired; long is life to the foolish who do not know the true law.

If a traveller does not meet with one who is his better, or his equal, let him firmly keep to his solitary journey; there is no companionship with a fool.

"These sons belong to me, and this wealth belongs to me," with such thoughts a fool is tormented. He himself does not belong to himself; how much less sons and wealth?

The fool who knows his foolishness, is wise at least so far. But a fool who thinks himself wise, he is called a fool indeed.

If a fool be associated with a wise man even all his life, he will perceive the truth as little as a spoon perceives the taste of soup.

If an intelligent man be associated for one minute only with a wise man, he will soon perceive the truth, as the tongue perceives the taste of soup.

Fools of poor understanding have themselves for their greatest enemies, for they do evil deeds which bear bitter fruits.

That deed is not well done of which a man must repent, and the reward of which he receives crying and with a tearful face.

No, that deed is well done of which a man does not repent, and the reward of which he receives gladly and cheerfully.

As long as the evil deed done does not bear fruit, the fool thinks it is like honey; but when it ripens, then the fool suffers grief.

Let a fool month after month eat his food (like an ascetic) with the tip of a blade of Kuśa-grass, yet is he not worth the sixteenth particle of those who have well weighed the law.

An evil deed, like newly-drawn milk, does not turn suddenly; smouldering, like fire covered by ashes, it follows the fool.

And when the evil deed, after it has become known, turns to sorrow for the fool, then it destroys his bright lot, nay, it cleaves his head.

Let the fool wish for a false reputation, for precedence among the Bhikshus, for lordship in the convents, for worship among other people!

"May both the layman and he who has left the world think that this is done by me; may they be subject to me in everything which is to be done or is not to be done," thus is the mind of the fool, and his desire and pride increase.

"One is the road that leads to wealth, another the road that leads to Nirvâna"—if the Bhikshu, the disciple of Buddha, has learned this, he will not yearn for honor, he will strive after separation from the world.

Chapter VI

The Wise Man

If you see a man who shows you what is to be avoided, who administers reproofs, and is intelligent, follow that wise man as you would one who tells of hidden treasures; it will be better, not worse, for him who follows him.

Let him admonish, let him teach, let him forbid what is improper!—he will be beloved of the good, by the bad he will be hated.

Do not have evil-doers for friends, do not have low people for friends: have virtuous people for friends, have for friends the best of men.

He who drinks in the law lives happily with a serene mind: the sage rejoices always in the law, as preached by the elect.

Well-makers lead the water wherever they like; fletchers bend the arrow; carpenters bend a log of wood; wise people fashion themselves.

As a solid rock is not shaken by the wind, wise people falter not amidst blame and praise.

Wise people, after they have listened to the laws, become serene, like a deep, smooth, and still lake.

Good men indeed walk warily under all circumstances; good men speak not out of a desire for sensual gratification; whether touched by happiness or sorrow wise people never appear elated or depressed.

If, whether for his own sake, or for the sake of others, a man wishes neither for a son, nor for wealth, nor for lordship, and if he does not wish for his own success by unfair means, then he is good, wise, and virtuous.

Few are there among men who arrive at the other shore (become Arhats); the other people here run up and down the shore.

But those who, when the law has been well preached to them, follow the law, will pass over the dominion of death, however difficult to cross.

A wise man should leave the dark state of ordinary life, and follow the bright state of the Bhikshu. After going from his home to a homeless state, he should in his retirement look for enjoyment where enjoyment seemed difficult. Leaving all pleasures behind, and calling nothing his own, the wise man should purge himself from all the troubles of the mind.

Those whose mind is well grounded in the seven elements of knowledge, who without clinging to anything, rejoice in freedom from attachment, whose appetites have been conquered, and who are full of light, they are free even in this world.

2

Confucius

Confucius is the earliest Chinese philosopher of any standing that we know about. He lived from the late sixth century BCE until early in the fifth century. His philosophy was pioneering and created a template for much later Chinese thought. It remains a major influence not only on the culture of China but also on the cultures of Korea and Japan.

That said, the philosophy of Confucius—unlike modern Western philosophies—does not center on discrete theses that are argued for. *The Analects of Confucius,* which contains sayings of Confucius and of the inner circle of students who lived and traveled with Confucius, is ruminative. It displays a distinctive worldview centered on two parallel goals. One was the improvement and refinement of personal character. The other was the improvement of government. The two were linked as well as parallel. Confucius and his disciples thought that good government could be achieved only if truly virtuous people were in charge.

The background for this was a China that was disunited, consisting of a number of separate kingdoms that often were at war with each other. The rulers had absolute power and governed through officials who executed their commands. It will not surprise the reader that this government usually was highly selfish, with rulers taxing even the peasants and using what they got to finance luxuries for themselves. There were legends of very ancient emperors who had been very benevolent and helped develop civilization. What was prevalent during Confucius' time was very much the opposite. Most people, even if they had some education, had little to hope for apart from the possibility of being appointed a government official.

Students came to Confucius for a variety of reasons. In some cases, interest in the traditional culture of China (which Confucius taught about) was a factor. In some cases desire to improve one's nature was a factor. Confucius was very concerned with helping his students improve what they were like, and to make the transition from being sort of good to being deeply good.

For many there was also a mundane motive: studying with Confucius improved one's prospects of gaining a coveted position as an official.

This might seem surprising in light of the contrast between Confucius' moral earnestness and the general selfish corruptness of the rulers. But even rogues can desire intelligent and reliable people executing their commands. Further, Confucius taught skills that were essential for any bureaucrat. These included etiquette (useful in diplomatic contacts), awareness of the classics, and a sense of how things work.

The major features of Confucius' view that come through amount to a mixture of traditionalism and what we would consider liberalism. Confucius held strongly that a test of good government was how well the poorer elements in society would thrive. Confucius' liberalism came to the fore when a former student (who had become an official) increased taxes on the peasants. Confucius disowned him.

The traditionalism centered on the belief that there had been higher standards of behavior in the olden days, especially under the early emperors. But Confucius also believed that traditions of manners and ritual were civilizing and should be observed.

A further word should be said about ritual. Many people (including me) have mixed feelings about ritual. In a word association test, ritual would likely often be linked with "boring." But consider that many of the interactions of everyday life—including the ways we help others or make way for them—have a ritual quality. Think of the ritual of holding a door open for someone behind you, and the ritual of that person thanking you. Not everything that is ritual or ritual-like should be scorned, and much of it accomplishes useful social bonding.

The following passages are arranged by subject matter, and not in their sequence in The *Analects of Confucius.* That work, which was largely compiled after Confucius' death, has a quality that could be compared to what you would get if you took a continuous narrative, put it on a deck of cards, and then shuffled the deck.

Analects

Becoming Good

"As if cut, as if polished; As if carved, as if ground." *Analects* 1.15

"People are true to type with regard to what sort of mistakes they make. Observe closely the sort of mistakes a person makes—then you will know his character." *Analects* 4.7

"I should just give up! I have yet to meet someone who is able to perceive his own faults and then take himself to task inwardly." *Analects* 5.27

"Find inspiration in the *Odes*, take your place through ritual, and achieve perfection with music." *Analects* 8.8

"The common people can be made to follow it (the way), but they cannot be made to understand it." *Analects* 8.9

"A gentleman's cultural refinement resembles his native substance, and his native substance resembles his cultural refinement. The skin of a tiger or leopard, shorn of its fur, is no different from the skin of a dog or sheep." *Analects* 12.8

What It Is to Be Good

"Without Goodness, one cannot remain constant in adversity and cannot enjoy enduring happiness." *Analects* 4.2

"The gentleman is self-possessed and relaxed, while the petty man is perpetually full of worry." *Analects* 7.37

"The wise are not confused, the Good do not worry, and the courageous do not fear." *Analects* 9.29

Confucius, commenting on some very high-minded and exceptionally principled officials, "I, however, am different from all of them in that I have no preconceived ideas of what is permissible and what is not." *Analects* 18.8. Southill's translation has "But I am different from these. With me there is no inflexible thou shalt or thou shalt not."

Government and the Role of Laws

"One who rules through the power of Virtue is analogous to the Pole Star: it simply remains in its place and receives the homage of the myriad lesser stars." *Analects* 2.1

"If you try to guide the common people with coercive regulations and keep them in line with punishments, the common people will become evasive and will have no sense of shame. If, however, you guide them with Virtue, and keep them in line by means of ritual, the people will have a sense of shame and will rectify themselves." *Analects* 2.3

"Ji Kangzi (the local ruler) was concerned about the prevalence of robbers in Lu. Confucius said, 'If you could just get rid of your own excessive desires, the people would not steal even if you rewarded them for it.'" *Analects* 12.18

3

Plato and Aristotle, and Freudian Echoes of Plato

Plato is generally thought of as the first great "Western" philosopher. The word "Western" here is in quotation marks because the Greek heritage influenced not only European and then New World philosophies but also Islamic philosophies in the Middle East. Aristotle, who followed Plato and differed from him in some respects, was a major influence in both areas.

Plato and Aristotle agreed on the general importance in life of intellectual abilities and of moral virtues but gave somewhat different pictures of this. Plato strongly emphasized timeless truths. Aristotle was more focused on details of the world around us and of our lives.

There is a strong link between Plato's philosophy and the rise of modern science in the West. As noted, Plato emphasized the importance of truths that are unchanging, such as truths about the essence ("the form") of things and of course mathematical truths. There is a report that Plato gave a lecture about "The Good" and that the lecture was all mathematics. Modern science has focused on laws, such as the law of gravity, that capture relations in nature that are timeless truths, always the same.

Aristotle's philosophical work is far more diverse, and much of it is focused on various phenomena in the natural world. There is a definite contrast between Plato's portrayal of the good life and Aristotle's. Plato emphasizes the requirement that reason should govern (and where appropriate override) the emotions. Aristotle would certainly go along with this but gives a much more complex account of what would make a kind of life highly desirable.

The major factor in *eudaemonia*—which is sometimes translated as "happiness" but is better translated as "well-being"—is, according to Aristotle, the possession and exercise of virtues. The virtues are not much good if they are not applied as part of life. There are moral virtues, but there are also intellectual virtues: cognitive abilities of various sorts.

This is not the whole Aristotelian story of the good life, although it is the most important part. Also relevant are satisfactions connected with friendly or loving relations and such things as prosperity and good reputation. There are many different things that can matter, at least slightly. If Plato's philosophy led to a cultural preoccupation with rational unchanging elements in pictures of the world, Aristotle's philosophy promoted carefulness with details and complications.

Freudian Echoes of Plato

Freud, like Plato, believed that reason should dominate our thought and behavior. A Platonic dialogue that especially spells this out is the *Phaedrus*. The central image is that of a chariot driven by a rational figure. It controls two horses—a good horse and a bad one. This, Plato suggests, is how our mind is constituted, and, if we are rational, rationality will dominate.

The Freudian ego is analogous to this rational decider. The good horse corresponds to the superego and the bad horse (that especially must be controlled) to the id.

Republic

I went down to the Piraeus yesterday with Glaucon, the son of Ariston. I wanted to say a prayer to the goddess, and I was also curious to see how [327] they would manage the festival, since they were holding it for the first time. I thought the procession of the local residents was a fine one and that the one conducted by the Thracians was no less outstanding. After we had said our prayer and seen the procession, we started back towards Athens. Polemarchus saw us from a distance as we were setting off for home and told his slave to run and ask us to wait for him. The slave caught hold of my cloak from behind: Polemarchus wants you to wait, he said. I turned around and asked where Polemarchus was. He's coming up behind you, he said, please wait for him. And Glaucon replied: All right, we will.

Just then Polemarchus caught up with us. Adeimantus, Glaucon's brother, was with him and so were Niceratus, the son of Nicias, and some others, all of whom were apparently on their way from the procession.

Polemarchus said: It looks to me, Socrates, as if you two are starting off for Athens.

It looks the way it is, then, I said.

Do you see how many we are? he said.

I do.

From Plato, *Republic*, trans. G. M. A. Grube, rev. C. D. C. Reeve (Indianapolis: Hackett Publishing Co., 1992). Reprinted by permission of the publisher.

Well, you must either prove stronger than we are, or you will have to stay here.

Isn't there another alternative, namely, that we persuade you to let us go?

But could you persuade us, if we won't listen?

Certainly not, Glaucon said.

Well, we won't listen; you'd better make up your mind to that.

Don't you know, Adeimantus said, that there is to be a torch race on horseback for the goddess tonight? [328]

On horseback? I said. That's something new. Are they going to race on horseback and hand the torches on in relays, or what?

In relays, Polemarchus said, and there will be an all-night festival that will be well worth seeing. After dinner, we'll go out to look at it. We'll be joined there by many of the young men, and we'll talk. So don't go; stay.

It seems, Glaucon said, that we'll have to stay.

If you think so, I said, then we must.

So we went to Polemarchus' house, and there we found Lysias and Euthydemus, the brothers of Polemarchus, Thrasymachus of Chalcedon, Charmantides of Paiania, and Cleitophon the son of Aristonymus. Polemarchus' father, Cephalus, was also there, and I thought he looked quite old, as I hadn't seen him for some time. He was sitting on a sort of cushioned chair with a wreath on his head, as he had been offering a sacrifice in the courtyard. There was a circle of chairs, and we sat down by him.

As soon as he saw me, Cephalus welcomed me and said: Socrates, you don't come down to the Piraeus to see us as often as you should. If it were still easy for me to walk to town, you wouldn't have to come here; we'd come to you. But, as it is, you ought to come here more often, for you should know that as the physical pleasures wither away, my desire for conversation and its pleasures grows. So do as I say: Stay with these young men now, but come regularly to see us, just as you would to friends or relatives.

Indeed, Cephalus, I replied, I enjoy talking with the very old, for we should ask them, as we might ask those who have travelled a road that we too will probably have to follow, what kind of road it is, whether rough and difficult or smooth and easy. And I'd gladly find out from you what you think about this, as you have reached the point in life the poets call "the threshold of old age." Is it a difficult time? What is your report about it?

By god, Socrates, I'll tell you exactly what I think. A number of us, who [329] are more or less the same age, often get together in accordance with the old saying. When we meet, the majority complain about the lost pleasures they remember from their youth, those of sex, drinking parties, feasts, and the other things that go along with them, and they get angry as if they had been deprived of important things and had lived well then but are now hardly living at all. Some others moan about the abuse heaped on old people by their relatives, and because of this they repeat over and over that old age is the cause of many evils. But I don't think they blame the real cause, Socrates, for if old age were really the cause, I should have suffered in the same way and so should everyone else of my age. But as it is, I've met some who don't feel like that in the least. Indeed, I was once present when someone asked the poet Sophocles: "How are you as far as sex goes, Sophocles? Can you still make love with a woman?" "Quiet, man," the poet replied, "I am very glad to have escaped from all that, like a slave who has escaped from a savage and tyrannical master." I thought at the time that he was right, and I still do, for old age brings peace and freedom from all such things. When the appetites relax and cease to importune us, everything Sophocles said comes to pass, and we escape from many mad masters. In these matters and in those concerning relatives, the real cause isn't old age, Socrates, but the way people live. If they are moderate and contented, old age, too, is only moderately onerous; if they aren't, both old age and youth are hard to bear.

I admired him for saying that and I wanted him to tell me more, so I urged him on: When you say things like that, Cephalus, I suppose that the majority of people don't agree, they think that you bear old age more easily not because of the way you live but because you're wealthy, for the wealthy, they say, have many consolations.

That's true; they don't agree. And there is something in what they say, though not as much as they think. Themistocles' retort is relevant here. When someone from Seriphus insulted him by saying that his high reputation was due to his city and not to himself, he replied that, had he been [330] a Seriphian, he wouldn't be famous, but neither would the other even if he had been an Athenian. The same applies to those who aren't rich and find old age hard to bear: A good person wouldn't easily bear old age if he were poor, but a bad one wouldn't be at peace with himself even if he were wealthy.

Did you inherit most of your wealth, Cephalus, I asked, or did you make it for yourself?

What did I make for myself, Socrates, you ask. As a money-maker I'm in a sort of mean between my grandfather and my father. My grandfather and namesake inherited about the same amount of wealth as I possess but multiplied it many times. My father, Lysanias, however, diminished that amount to even less than I have now. As for me, I'm satisfied to leave my sons here not less but a little more than I inherited.

The reason I asked is that you don't seem to love money too much. And those who haven't made their own money are usually like you. But those who have made it for themselves are twice as fond of it as those who haven't. Just as poets love their poems and fathers love their children, so those who have made their own money don't just care about it because it's useful, as other people do, but because it's something they've made themselves. This makes them poor company, for they haven't a good word to say about anything except money.

That's true.

It certainly is. But tell me something else. What's the greatest good you've received from being very wealthy?

What I have to say probably wouldn't persuade most people. But you know, Socrates, that when someone thinks his end is near, he becomes frightened and concerned about things he didn't fear before. It's then that the stories we're told about Hades, about how people who've been unjust here must pay the penalty there—stories he used to make fun of—twist his soul this way and that for fear they're true. And whether because of the weakness of old age or because he is now closer to what happens in Hades and has a clearer view of it, or whatever it is, he is filled with foreboding and fear, and he examines himself to see whether he has been unjust to anyone. If he finds many injustices in his life, he awakes from sleep in terror, as children do, and lives in anticipation of bad things to come. But someone who knows that he hasn't been unjust has sweet good [331] hope as his constant companion—a nurse to his old age, as Pindar says, for he puts it charmingly, Socrates, when he says that when someone lives a just and pious life

> *Sweet hope is in his heart,*
> *Nurse and companion to his age.*
> *Hope, captain of the ever-twisting*
> *Minds of mortal men.*

How wonderfully well he puts that. It's in this connection that wealth is most valuable, I'd say, not for every man but for a decent and orderly one. Wealth can do a lot to save us from having to cheat or deceive someone against our will and from having to depart for that other place in fear because we owe sacrifice to a god or money to a person. It has many other uses, but, benefit for benefit, I'd say that this is how it is most useful to a man of any understanding.

A fine sentiment, Cephalus, but, speaking of this very thing itself, namely, justice, are we to say unconditionally that it is speaking the truth and paying whatever debts one has incurred? Or is doing these things sometimes just, sometimes unjust? I mean this sort of thing, for example: Everyone would surely agree that if a sane man lends weapons to a friend and then asks for them back when he is out of his mind, the friend shouldn't return them, and wouldn't be acting justly if he did. Nor should anyone be willing to tell the whole truth to someone who is out of his mind.

That's true.

Then the definition of justice isn't speaking the truth and repaying what one has borrowed.

It certainly is, Socrates, said Polemarchus, interrupting, if indeed we're to trust Simonides at all.

Well, then, Cephalus said, I'll hand over the argument to you, as I have to look after the sacrifice.

So, Polemarchus said, am I then to be your heir in everything?

You certainly are, Cephalus said, laughing, and off he went to the sacrifice.

Then tell us, heir to the argument, I said, just what Simonides stated about justice that you consider correct.

He stated that it is just to give to each what is owed to him. And it's a fine saying, in my view.

Well, now, it isn't easy to doubt Simonides, for he's a wise and godlike man. But what exactly does he mean? Perhaps you know, Polemarchus, but I don't understand him. Clearly, he doesn't mean what we said a moment ago, that it is just to give back whatever a person has lent to you, even if he's out of his mind when he asks for it. And yet what he has lent to you is surely something that's owed to him, isn't it? [332]

Yes.

But it is absolutely not to be given to him when he's out of his mind?

That's true.

Then it seems that Simonides must have meant something different when he says that to return what is owed is just.

Something different indeed, by god. He means that friends owe it to their friends to do good for them, never harm.

I follow you. Someone doesn't give a lender back what he's owed by giving him gold, if doing so would be harmful, and both he and the lender are friends. Isn't that what you think Simonides meant?

It is.

But what about this? Should one also give one's enemies whatever is owed to them?

By all means, one should give them what is owed to them. And in my view what enemies owe to each other is appropriately and precisely—something bad.

It seems then that Simonides was speaking in riddles—just like a poet!—when he said what justice is, for he thought it just to give to each what is appropriate to him, and this is what he called giving him what is owed to him.

What else did you think he meant?

Then what do you think he'd answer if someone asked him: "Simonides, which of the things that are owed or that are appropriate for someone or something to have does the craft we call medicine give, and to whom or what does it give them?"

It's clear that it gives medicines, food, and drink to bodies.

And what owed or appropriate things does the craft we call cooking give, and to whom or what does it give them?

It gives seasonings to food.

Good. Now, what does the craft we call justice give, and to whom or what does it give it?

If we are to follow the previous answers, Socrates, it gives benefits to friends and does harm to enemies.

Simonides means, then, that to treat friends well and enemies badly is justice?

I believe so.

And who is most capable of treating friends well and enemies badly in matters of disease and health?

A doctor.

And who can do so best in a storm at sea?

A ship's captain.

What about the just person? In what actions and what work is he most capable of benefiting friends and harming enemies?

In wars and alliances, I suppose.

All right. Now, when people aren't sick, Polemarchus, a doctor is useless to them?

True.

And so is a ship's captain to those who aren't sailing?

Yes.

And to people who aren't at war, a just man is useless?

No, I don't think that at all.

Justice is also useful in peacetime, then?

It is. [333]

And so is farming, isn't it?

Yes.

For getting produce?

Yes.

And shoemaking as well?

Yes.

For getting shoes, I think you'd say?

Certainly.

Well, then, what is justice useful for getting and using in peacetime?

Contracts, Socrates.

And by contracts do you mean partnerships, or what?

I mean partnerships.

Is someone a good and useful partner in a game of checkers because he's just or because he's a checkers player?

Because he's a checkers player.

And in laying bricks and stones, is a just person a better and more useful partner than a builder?

Not at all.

In what kind of partnership, then, is a just person a better partner than a builder or a lyre-player, in the way that a lyre-player is better than a just person at hitting the right notes?

In money matters, I think.

Except perhaps, Polemarchus, in using money, for whenever one needs to buy a horse jointly, I think a horse breeder is a more useful partner, isn't he?

Apparently.

And when one needs to buy a boat, it's a boatbuilder or a ship's captain?

Probably.

In what joint use of silver or gold, then, is a just person a more useful partner than the others?

When it must be deposited for safekeeping, Socrates.

You mean whenever there is no need to use them but only to keep them?

That's right.

Then it is when money isn't being used that justice is useful for it?

I'm afraid so.

And whenever one needs to keep a pruning knife safe, but not to use it, justice is useful both in partnerships and for the individual. When you need to use it, however, it is skill at vine pruning that's useful?

Apparently.

You'll agree, then, that when one needs to keep a shield or a lyre safe and not to use them, justice is a useful thing, but when you need to use them, it is soldiery or musicianship that's useful?

Necessarily.

And so, too, with everything else, justice is useless when they are in use but useful when they aren't?

It looks that way.

In that case, justice isn't worth much, since it is only useful for useless things. But let's look into the following point. Isn't the person most able to land a blow, whether in boxing or any other kind of fight, also most able to guard against it?

Certainly.

And the one who is most able to guard against disease is also most able to produce it unnoticed?

So it seems to me, anyway.

And the one who is the best guardian of an army is the very one who can steal the enemy's plans and dispositions? [334]

Certainly.

Whenever someone is a clever guardian, then, he is also a clever thief.

Probably so.

If a just person is clever at guarding money, therefore, he must also be clever at stealing it.

According to our argument, at any rate.

A just person has turned out then, it seems, to be a kind of thief. Maybe you learned this from Homer, for he's fond of Autolycus, the maternal grandfather of Odysseus, whom he describes as better than everyone at lying and stealing. According to you, Homer, and Simonides, then, justice seems to be some sort of craft of stealing, one that benefits friends and harms enemies. Isn't that what you meant?

No, by god, it isn't. I don't know any more what I did mean, but I still believe that to benefit one's friends and harm one's enemies is justice.

Speaking of friends, do you mean those a person believes to be good and useful to him or those who actually are good and useful, even if he doesn't think they are, and similarly with enemies?

Probably, one loves those one considers good and useful and hates those one considers bad and harmful.

But surely people often make mistakes about this, believing many people to be good and useful when they aren't, and making the opposite mistake about enemies?

They do indeed.

And then good people are their enemies and bad ones their friends?

That's right.

And so it's just to benefit bad people and harm good ones?

Apparently.

But good people are just and able to do no wrong?

True.

Then, according to your account, it's just to do bad things to those who do no injustice.

No, that's not just at all, Socrates; my account must be a bad one.

It's just, then, is it, to harm unjust people and benefit just ones?

That's obviously a more attractive view than the other one, anyway.

Then, it follows, Polemarchus, that it is just for the many, who are mistaken in their judgment, to harm their friends, who are bad, and benefit their enemies, who are good. And so we arrive at a conclusion opposite to what we said Simonides meant.

That certainly follows. But let's change our definition, for it seems that we didn't define friends and enemies correctly.

How did we define them, Polemarchus?

We said that a friend is someone who is believed to be useful.

And how are we to change that now?

Someone who is both believed to be useful and is useful is a friend; someone who is believed to be useful but isn't, is believed to be a friend but isn't. And the same for the enemy. [335]

According to this account, then, a good person will be a friend and a bad one an enemy.

Yes.

So you want us to add something to what we said before about justice, when we said that it is just to treat friends well and enemies badly. You want us to add to this that it is just to treat well a friend who is good and to harm an enemy who is bad?

Right. That seems fine to me.

Is it, then, the role of a just man to harm anyone?

Certainly, he must harm those who are both bad and enemies.

Do horses become better or worse when they are harmed?

Worse.

With respect to the virtue that makes dogs good or the one that makes horses good?

The one that makes horses good.

And when dogs are harmed, they become worse in the virtue that makes dogs good, not horses?

Necessarily.

Then won't we say the same about human beings, too, that when they are harmed they become worse in human virtue?

Indeed.

But isn't justice human virtue?

Yes, certainly.

Then people who are harmed must become more unjust?

So it seems.

Can musicians make people unmusical through music?

They cannot.

Or horsemen make people unhorsemanlike through horsemanship?

No.

Well, then, can those who are just make people unjust through justice? In a word, can those who are good make people bad through virtue?

They cannot.

It isn't the function of heat to cool things but of its opposite?

Yes.

Nor the function of dryness to make things wet but of its opposite?

Indeed.

Nor the function of goodness to harm but of its opposite?

Apparently.

And a just person is good?

Indeed.

Then, Polemarchus, it isn't the function of a just person to harm a friend or anyone else, rather it is the function of his opposite, an unjust person?

In my view that's completely true, Socrates.

If anyone tells us, then, that it is just to give to each what he's owed and understands by this that a just man should harm his enemies and benefit his friends, he isn't wise to say it, since what he says isn't true, for it has become clear to us that it is never just to harm anyone?

I agree.

You and I shall fight as partners, then, against anyone who tells us that Simonides, Bias, Pittacus, or any of our other wise and blessedly happy men said this.

I, at any rate, am willing to be your partner in the battle.

Do you know to whom I think the saying belongs that it is just to benefit friends and harm enemies? [336]

Who?

I think it belongs to Periander, or Perdiccas, or Xerxes, or Ismenias of Corinth, or some other wealthy man who believed himself to have great power.

That's absolutely true.

All right, since it has become apparent that justice and the just aren't what such people say they are, what else could they be?

While we were speaking, Thrasymachus had tried many times to take over the discussion but was restrained by those sitting near him, who wanted to hear our argument to the end. When we paused after what I'd just said, however, he couldn't keep quiet any longer. He coiled himself up like a wild beast about to spring, and he hurled himself at us as if to tear us to pieces.

Polemarchus and I were frightened and flustered as he roared into our midst: What nonsense have you two been talking, Socrates? Why do you act like idiots by giving way to one another? If you truly want to know what justice is, don't just ask questions and then refute the answers simply to satisfy your competitiveness or love of honor. You know very well that it is easier to ask questions than answer them. Give an answer yourself, and tell us what you say the just is. And don't tell me that it's the right, the beneficial, the profitable, the gainful, or the advantageous, but tell me clearly and exactly what you mean; for I won't accept such nonsense from you.

His words startled me, and, looking at him, I was afraid. And I think that if I hadn't seen him before he stared at me, I'd have been dumbstruck. But as it was, I happened to look at him just as our discussion began to exasperate him, so I was able to answer, and, trembling a little, I said: Don't be too hard on us, Thrasymachus, for if Polemarchus and I made an error in our investigation, you should know that we did so unwillingly. If we were searching for gold, we'd never willingly give way to each other, if by doing so we'd destroy our chance of finding it. So don't think that in searching for justice, a thing more valuable than even a large quantity of gold, we'd mindlessly give way to one another or be less than completely serious about finding it. You surely mustn't think that, but rather—as I do—that we're incapable of finding it. Hence it's surely far more appropriate for us to be pitied by you clever people than to be given rough treatment. [337]

When he heard that, he gave a loud, sarcastic laugh. By Heracles, he said, that's just Socrates' usual irony. I knew, and I said so to these people earlier, that you'd be unwilling to answer and that, if someone questioned *you*, you'd be ironical and do anything rather than give an answer.

That's because you're a clever fellow, Thrasymachus. You knew very well that if you ask someone how much twelve is, and, as you ask, you warn him by saying "Don't tell me, man, that twelve is twice six, or three times four, or six times two, or four times three, for I won't accept such nonsense," then you'll see clearly, I think, that no one could answer a question framed like that. And if he said to you: "What are you saying, Thrasymachus, am I not to give any of the answers you mention, not even if twelve happens to be one of those things? I'm amazed. Do you want me to say something other than the truth? Or do you mean something else?" What answer would you give him?

Well, so you think the two cases are alike?

Why shouldn't they be alike? But even if they aren't alike, yet seem so to the person you asked, do you think him any less likely to give the answer that seems right to him, whether we forbid him to or not?

Is that what you're going to do, give one of the forbidden answers?

I wouldn't be surprised—provided that it's the one that seems right to me after I've investigated the matter.

What if I show you a different answer about justice than all these—and a better one? What would you deserve then?

What else than the appropriate penalty for one who doesn't know, namely, to learn from the one who does know? Therefore, that's what I deserve.

You amuse me, but in addition to learning, you must pay a fine.

I will as soon as I have some money.

He has some already, said Glaucon. If it's a matter of money, speak, Thrasymachus, for we'll all contribute for Socrates.

I know, he said, so that Socrates can carry on as usual. He gives no answer himself, and then, when someone else does give one, he takes up the argument and refutes it.

How can someone give an answer, I said, when he doesn't know it and doesn't claim to know it, and when an eminent man forbids him to express the opinion he has? It's much more appropriate for you to answer, since you say you know and can tell us. So do it as a favor to me, and don't [338] begrudge your teaching to Glaucon and the others.

While I was saying this, Glaucon and the others begged him to speak. It was obvious that Thrasymachus thought he had a fine answer and that he wanted to earn their admiration by giving it, but he pretended that he wanted to indulge his love of victory by forcing me to answer. However, he agreed in the end, and then said: There you have Socrates' wisdom; he himself isn't willing to teach, but he goes around learning from others and isn't even grateful to them.

When you say that I learn from others you are right, Thrasymachus, but when you say that I'm not grateful, that isn't true. I show what gratitude I can, but since I have no money, I can give only praise. But just how enthusiastically I give it when someone seems to me to speak well, you'll know as soon as you've answered, for I think that you will speak well.

Listen, then. I say that justice is nothing other than the advantage of the stronger. Well, why don't you praise me? But then you'd do anything to avoid having to do that.

I must first understand you, for I don't yet know what you mean. The advantage of the stronger, you say, is just. What do you mean, Thrasymachus? Surely you don't mean something like this: Polydamus, the pancratist, is stronger than we are; it is to his advantage to eat beef to build up his physical strength; therefore, this food is also advantageous and just for us who are weaker than he is?

You disgust me, Socrates. Your trick is to take hold of the argument at the point where you can do it the most harm.

Not at all, but tell us more clearly what you mean.

Don't you know that some cities are ruled by a tyranny, some by a democracy, and some by an aristocracy?

Of course.

And in each city this element is stronger, namely, the ruler?

Certainly.

And each makes laws to its own advantage. Democracy makes democratic laws, tyranny makes tyrannical laws, and so on with the others. And they declare what they have made—what is to their own advantage—to be just for their subjects, and they punish anyone who goes against this as lawless and unjust. This, then, is what I say justice is, the same in all cities, the advantage of the established rule. Since the established rule is [339] surely stronger, anyone who reasons correctly will conclude that the just is the same everywhere, namely, the advantage of the stronger.

Now I see what you mean. Whether it's true or not, I'll try to find out. But you yourself have answered that the just is the advantageous, Thrasymachus, whereas you forbade that answer to me. True, you've added "of the stronger" to it.

And I suppose you think that's an insignificant addition.

It isn't clear yet whether it's significant. But it is clear that we must investigate to see whether or not it's true. I agree that the just is some kind of advantage. But you add that it's *of the stronger.* I don't know about that. We'll have to look into it.

Go ahead and look.

We will. Tell me, don't you also say that it is just to obey the rulers?

I do.

And are the rulers in all cities infallible, or are they liable to error?

No doubt they are liable to error.

When they undertake to make laws, therefore, they make some correctly, others incorrectly?

I suppose so.

And a law is correct if it prescribes what is to the rulers' own advantage and incorrect if it prescribes what is to their disadvantage? Is that what you mean?

It is.

And whatever laws they make must be obeyed by their subjects, and this is justice?

Of course.

Then, according to your account, it is just to do not only what is to the advantage of the stronger, but also the opposite, what is not to their advantage.

What are you saying?

The same as you. But let's examine it more fully. Haven't we agreed that, in giving orders to their subjects, the rulers are sometimes in error as to what is best for themselves, and yet that it is just for their subjects to do whatever their rulers order? Haven't we agreed to that much?

I think so.

Then you must also think that you have agreed that it is just to do what is disadvantageous to the rulers and those who are stronger, whenever they unintentionally order what is bad for themselves. But you also say that it is just for the others to obey the orders they give. You're terribly clever, Thrasymachus, but doesn't it necessarily follow that it is just to do the opposite of what you said, since the weaker are then ordered to do what is disadvantageous to the stronger?

By god, Socrates, said Polemarchus, that's quite clear. [340]

If you are to be his witness anyway, said Cleitophon, interrupting.

Who needs a witness? Polemarchus replied. Thrasymachus himself agrees that the rulers sometimes order what is bad for themselves and that it is just for the others to do it.

That, Polemarchus, is because Thrasymachus maintained that it is just to obey the orders of the rulers.

He also maintained, Cleitophon, that the advantage of the stronger is just. And having maintained both principles he went on to agree that the stronger sometimes gives orders to those who are weaker than he is—in other words, to his subjects—that are disadvantageous to the stronger himself. From these agreements it follows that what is to the advantage of the stronger is no more just than what is not to his advantage.

But, Cleitophon responded, he said that the advantage of the stronger is what the stronger believes to be his advantage. This is what the weaker must do, and this is what he maintained the just to be.

That isn't what he said, Polemarchus replied.

It makes no difference, Polemarchus, I said. If Thrasymachus wants to put it that way now, let's accept it. Tell me, Thrasymachus, is this what you wanted to say the just is, namely, what the stronger believes to be to his advantage, whether it is in fact to his advantage or not? Is that what we are to say you mean?

Not at all. Do you think I'd call someone who is in error stronger at the very moment he errs?

I did think that was what you meant when you agreed that the rulers aren't infallible but are liable to error.

That's because you are a false witness in arguments, Socrates. When someone makes an error in the treatment of patients, do you call him a doctor in regard to that very error? Or when someone makes an error in accounting, do you call him an accountant in regard to that very error in calculation? I think that we express ourselves in words that, taken literally, do say that a doctor is in error, or an accountant, or a grammarian. But each of these, insofar as he is what we call him, never errs, so that, according to the precise account (and you are a stickler for precise accounts), no craftsman ever errs. It's when his knowledge fails him that he makes an error, and in regard to that error he is no craftsman. No craftsman, expert, or ruler makes an error at the moment when he is ruling, even though everyone will say that a physician or a ruler makes errors. It's in this loose way that you must also take the answer I gave earlier. But the most precise answer is this. A ruler, insofar as he is a [341] ruler, never makes errors and unerringly decrees what is best for himself, and this his subject must do. Thus, as I said from the first, it is just to do what is to the advantage of the stronger.

All right, Thrasymachus, so you think I'm a false witness?

You certainly are.

And you think that I asked the questions I did in order to harm you in the argument?

I know it very well, but it won't do you any good. You'll never be able to trick me, so you can't harm me that way, and without trickery you'll never be able to overpower me in argument.

I wouldn't so much as try, Thrasymachus. But in order to prevent this sort of thing from happening again, define clearly whether it is the ruler and stronger in the ordinary sense or in the precise sense whose advantage you said it is just for the weaker to promote as the advantage of the stronger.

I mean the ruler in the most precise sense. Now practice your harmdoing and false witnessing on that if you can—I ask no concessions from you—but you certainly won't be able to.

Do you think that I'm crazy enough to try to shave a lion or to bear false witness against Thrasymachus?

You certainly tried just now, though you were a loser at that too.

Enough of this. Tell me: Is a doctor in the precise sense, whom you mentioned before, a money-maker or someone who treats the sick? Tell me about the one who is really a doctor.

He's the one who treats the sick.

What about a ship's captain? Is a captain in the precise sense a ruler of sailors or a sailor?

A ruler of sailors.

We shouldn't, I think, take into account the fact that he sails in a ship, and he shouldn't be called a sailor for that reason, for it isn't because of his sailing that he is called a ship's captain, but because of his craft and his rule over sailors?

That's true.

And is there something advantageous to each of these, that is, to bodies and to sailors?

Certainly.

And aren't the respective crafts by nature set over them to seek and provide what is to their advantage?

They are.

And is there any advantage for each of the crafts themselves except to be as complete or perfect as possible?

What are you asking?

This: If you asked me whether our bodies are sufficient in themselves, or whether they need something else, I'd answer: "They certainly have needs. And because of this, because our bodies are deficient rather than self-sufficient, the craft of medicine has now been discovered. The craft of medicine was developed to provide what is advantageous for a body." Do you think that I'm right in saying this or not?

You are right.

Now, is medicine deficient? Does a craft need some further virtue, as [342] the eyes are in need of sight, and the ears of hearing, so that another craft is needed to seek and provide what is advantageous to them? Does a craft itself have some similar deficiency, so that each craft needs another, to seek out what is to its advantage? And does the craft that does the seeking need still another, and so on without end? Or does each seek out what is to its own advantage by itself? Or does it need neither itself nor another craft to seek out what is advantageous to it, because of its own deficiencies? Or is it that there is no deficiency or error in any craft? That it isn't appropriate for any craft to seek what is to the advantage of anything except that of which it is the craft? And that, since it is itself correct, it is without either fault or impurity, as long as it is wholly and precisely the craft that it is?

Apparently so.

Medicine doesn't seek its own advantage, then, but that of the body?

Yes.

And horse-breeding doesn't seek its own advantage, but that of horses? Indeed, no other craft seeks its own advantage—for it has no further needs—but the advantage of that of which it is the craft?

Apparently so.

Now, surely, Thrasymachus, the crafts rule over and are stronger than the things of which they are the crafts?

Very reluctantly, he conceded this as well.

No kind of knowledge seeks or orders what is advantageous to itself, then, but what is advantageous to the weaker, which is subject to it.

He tried to fight this conclusion, but he conceded it in the end. And after he had, I said: Surely, then, no doctor, insofar as he is a doctor, seeks or orders what is advantageous to himself, but what is advantageous to his patient? We agreed that a doctor in the precise sense is a ruler of bodies, not a money-maker. Wasn't that agreed?

Yes.

So a ship's captain in the precise sense is a ruler of sailors, not a sailor?

That's what we agreed.

Doesn't it follow that a ship's captain or ruler won't seek and order what is advantageous to himself, but what is advantageous to a sailor?

He reluctantly agreed.

So, then, Thrasymachus, no one in any position of rule, insofar as he is a ruler, seeks or orders what is advantageous to himself, but what is advantageous to his subjects; the ones of whom he is himself the craftsman. It is to his subjects and what is advantageous and proper to them that he looks, and everything he says and does he says and does for them.

When we reached this point in the argument, and it was clear to all that his account of justice had turned into its opposite, instead of answering, [343] Thrasymachus said: Tell me, Socrates, do you still have a wet nurse?

What's this? Hadn't you better answer *my* questions rather than asking *me* such things?

Because she's letting you run around with a snotty nose, and doesn't wipe it when she needs to! Why, for all she cares, you don't even know about sheep and shepherds.

Just what is it I don't know?

You think that shepherds and cowherds seek the good of their sheep and cattle, and fatten them and take care of them, looking to something other than their master's good and their own. Moreover, you believe that rulers in cities—true rulers, that is—think about their subjects differently than one does about sheep, and that night and day they think of something besides their own advantage. You are so far from understanding about justice and what's just, about injustice and what's unjust, that you don't realize that justice is really the good of another, the advantage of the stronger and the ruler, and harmful to the one who obeys and serves. Injustice is the opposite, it rules the truly simple and just, and those it rules do what is to the advantage of the other and stronger, and they make the one they serve happy, but themselves not at all. You must look at it as follows, my most simple Socrates: A just man always gets less than an unjust one. First, in their contracts with one another, you'll never find, when the partnership ends, that a just partner has got more than an unjust one, but less. Second, in matters relating to the city, when taxes are to be paid, a just man pays more on the same property, an unjust one less, but when the city is giving out refunds, a just man gets nothing, while an unjust one makes a large profit. Finally, when each of them holds a ruling position in some public office, a just person, even if he isn't penalized in other ways, finds that his private affairs deteriorate because he has to neglect them, that he gains no advantage from the public purse because of his justice, and that he's hated by his relatives and acquaintances when he's unwilling to do them an unjust favor. The opposite is true of an unjust man in every respect. Therefore, I repeat what I said before: A person of great power outdoes everyone else. Consider him if you want to figure [344] out how much more advantageous it is for the individual to be just rather than unjust. You'll understand this most easily if you turn your thoughts to the most complete injustice, the one that makes the doer of injustice happiest and the sufferers of it, who are unwilling to do injustice, most wretched. This is tyranny, which through stealth or force appropriates the property of others, whether sacred or profane, public or private, not little by little, but all at once. If someone commits only one part of injustice and is caught, he's punished and greatly reproached—such partly unjust people are called temple-robbers, kidnappers, housebreakers, robbers, and thieves when they commit these crimes. But when someone, in addition to appropriating their possessions, kidnaps and enslaves the citizens as well, instead of these shameful names he is called happy and blessed, not only by the citizens themselves, but by all who learn that he has done the whole of injustice. Those who reproach injustice do so because they are afraid not of doing it but of suffering it. So, Socrates, injustice, if it is on a large enough scale, is stronger, freer, and more masterly than justice. And, as I said from the first, justice is what is advantageous to the stronger, while injustice is to one's own profit and advantage.

Having emptied this great flood of words into our ears all at once like a bath attendant, Thrasymachus intended to leave. But those present didn't let him and made him stay to give an account of what he had said. I too begged him to stay, and I said to him: After hurling such a speech at us, Thrasymachus, do you intend to leave before adequately instructing us or finding out whether you are right or not? Or do you think it a small matter to determine which whole way of life would make living most worthwhile for each of us?

Is *that* what I seem to you to think? Thrasymachus said.

Either that, or else you care nothing for us and aren't worried about whether we'll live better or worse lives because of our ignorance of what you say you know. So show some willingness to teach it to us. It wouldn't be a bad investment for you to be the benefactor of a group as large as ours. For my own part, I'll tell you that I am not persuaded. I don't believe [345] that injustice is more profitable than justice, not even if you give it full scope and put no obstacles in its way. Suppose that there *is* an unjust person, and suppose he *does* have the power to do injustice, whether by trickery or open warfare; nonetheless, he doesn't persuade me that injustice is more profitable than justice. Perhaps someone here, besides myself, feels the same as I do. So come now, and persuade us that we are wrong to esteem justice more highly than injustice in planning our lives.

And how am I to persuade you, if you aren't persuaded by what I said just now? What more can I do? Am I to take my argument and pour it into your very soul?

God forbid! Don't do that! But, first, stick to what you've said, and then, if you change your position, do it openly and don't deceive us. You see, Thrasymachus, that having defined the true doctor—to continue examining the things you said before—you didn't consider it necessary later to keep a precise guard on the true shepherd. You think that, insofar as he's a shepherd, he fattens sheep, not looking to what is best for the sheep but to a banquet, like a guest about to be entertained at a feast, or to a future sale, like a money-maker rather than a shepherd. Shepherding is concerned only to provide what is best for the things it is set over, and it is itself adequately provided with all it needs to be at its best when it doesn't fall short in any way of being the craft of shepherding. That's why I thought it necessary for us to agree before that every kind of rule, insofar as it rules, doesn't seek anything other than what is best for the things it rules and cares for, and this is true both of public and private kinds of rule. But do you think that those who rule cities, the true rulers, rule willingly?

I don't think it, by god, I know it.

But, Thrasymachus, don't you realize that in other kinds of rule no one wants to rule for its own sake, but they ask for pay, thinking that their ruling will benefit not themselves but their subjects? Tell me, doesn't every craft differ from every other in having a different function? Please [346] don't answer contrary to what you believe, so that we can come to some definite conclusion.

Yes, that's what differentiates them.

And each craft benefits us in its own peculiar way, different from the others. For example, medicine gives us health, navigation gives us safety while sailing, and so on with the others?

Certainly.

And wage-earning gives us wages, for this is its function? Or would you call medicine the same as navigation? Indeed, if you want to define matters precisely, as you proposed, even if someone who is a ship's captain becomes healthy because sailing is advantageous to his health, you wouldn't for that reason call his craft medicine?

Certainly not.

Nor would you call wage-earning medicine, even if someone becomes healthy while earning wages?

Certainly not.

Nor would you call medicine wage-earning, even if someone earns pay while healing?

No.

We are agreed, then, that each craft brings its own peculiar benefit?

It does.

Then whatever benefit all craftsmen receive in common must clearly result from their joint practice of some additional craft that benefits each of them?

So it seems.

And we say that the additional craft in question, which benefits the craftsmen by earning them wages, is the craft of wage-earning?

He reluctantly agreed.

Then this benefit, receiving wages, doesn't result from their own craft, but rather, if we're to examine this precisely, medicine provides health, and wage-earning provides wages; house-building provides a house, and wage-earning, which accompanies it, provides a wage; and so on with the other crafts. Each of them does its own work and benefits the things it is set over. So, if wages aren't added, is there any benefit that the craftsman gets from his craft?

Apparently none.

But he still provides a benefit when he works for nothing?

Yes, I think he does.

Then, it is clear now, Thrasymachus, that no craft or rule provides for its own advantage, but, as we've been saying for some time, it provides and orders for its subject and aims at its advantage, that of the weaker, not of the stronger. That's why I said just now, Thrasymachus, that no one willingly chooses to rule and to take other people's troubles in hand and straighten them out, but each asks for wages; for anyone who intends [347] to practice his craft well never does or orders what is best for himself—at least not when he orders as his craft prescribes—but what is best for his subject. It is because of this, it seems, that wages must be provided to a person if he's to be willing to rule, whether in the form of money or honor or a penalty if he refuses.

What do you mean, Socrates? said Glaucon. I know the first two kinds of wages, but I don't understand what penalty you mean or how you can call it a wage.

Then you don't understand the best people's kind of wages, the kind that moves the most decent to rule, when they are willing to rule at all. Don't you know that the love of honor and the love of money are despised, and rightly so?

I do.

Therefore good people won't be willing to rule for the sake of either money or honor. They don't want to be paid wages openly for ruling and get called hired hands, nor to take them in secret from their rule and be called thieves. And they won't rule for the sake of honor, because they aren't ambitious honor-lovers. So, if they're to be willing to rule, some compulsion or punishment must be brought to bear on them—perhaps that's why it is thought shameful to seek to rule before one is compelled to. Now, the greatest punishment, if one isn't willing to rule, is to be ruled by someone worse than oneself. And I think that it's fear of this that makes decent people rule when they do. They approach ruling not as something good or something to be enjoyed, but as something necessary, since it can't be entrusted to anyone better than—or even as good as—themselves. In a city of good men, if it came into being, the citizens would fight in order *not to rule,* just as they do now in order to rule. There it would be quite clear that anyone who is really a true ruler doesn't by nature seek his own advantage but that of his subjects. And everyone, knowing this, would rather be benefited by others than take the trouble to benefit them. So I can't at all agree with Thrasymachus that justice is the advantage of the stronger—but we'll look further into that another time. What Thrasymachus is now saying—that the life of an unjust person is better than that of a just one—seems to be of far greater importance. Which life would you choose, Glaucon? And which of our views do you consider truer?

I certainly think that the life of a just person is more profitable.

Did you hear all of the good things Thrasymachus listed a moment ago for the unjust life? [348]

I heard, but I wasn't persuaded.

Then, do you want us to persuade him, if we're able to find a way, that what he says isn't true?

Of course I do.

If we oppose him with a parallel speech about the blessings of the just life, and then he replies, and then we do, we'd have to count and measure the good things mentioned on each side, and we'd need a jury to decide the case. But if, on the other hand, we investigate the question, as we've been doing, by seeking agreement with each other, we ourselves can be both jury and advocates at once.

Certainly.

Which approach do you prefer? I asked.

The second.

Come, then, Thrasymachus, I said, answer us from the beginning. You say that complete injustice is more profitable than complete justice?

I certainly do say that, and I've told you why.

Well, then, what do you say about this? Do you call one of the two a virtue and the other a vice?

Of course.

That is to say, you call justice a virtue and injustice a vice?

That's hardly likely, since I say that injustice is profitable and justice isn't.

Then, what exactly do you say?

The opposite.

That justice is a vice?

No, just very high-minded simplicity.

Then do you call being unjust being low-minded?

No, I call it good judgment.

You consider unjust people, then, Thrasymachus, to be clever and good?

Yes, those who are completely unjust, who can bring cities and whole communities under their power. Perhaps, you think I meant pickpockets? Not that such crimes aren't also profitable, if they're not found out, but they aren't worth mentioning by comparison to what I'm talking about.

I'm not unaware of what you want to say. But I wonder about this: Do you really include injustice with virtue and wisdom, and justice with their opposites?

I certainly do.

That's harder, and it isn't easy now to know what to say. If you had declared that injustice is more profitable, but agreed that it is a vice or shameful, as some others do, we could have discussed the matter on the basis of conventional beliefs. But now, obviously, you'll say that injustice is fine and strong and apply to it all the attributes we used to apply to justice, since you dare to include it with virtue and wisdom. [349]

You've divined my views exactly.

Nonetheless, we mustn't shrink from pursuing the argument and looking into this, just as long as I take you to be saying what you really think. And I believe that you aren't joking now, Thrasymachus, but are saying what you believe to be the truth.

What difference does it make to you, whether *I* believe it or not? It's *my account* you're supposed to be refuting.

It makes no difference. But try to answer this further question: Do you think that a just person wants to outdo someone else who's just?

Not at all, for he wouldn't then be as polite and innocent as he is.

Or to outdo someone who does a just action?

No, he doesn't even want to do that.

And does he claim that he deserves to outdo an unjust person and believe that it is just for him to do so, or doesn't he believe that?

He'd want to outdo him, and he'd claim to deserve to do so, but he wouldn't be able.

That's not what I asked, but whether a just person wants to outdo an unjust person but not a just one, thinking that this is what he deserves?

He does.

What about an unjust person? Does he claim that he deserves to outdo a just person or someone who does a just action?

Of course he does; he thinks he deserves to outdo everyone.

Then will an unjust person also outdo an *unjust* person or someone who does an *unjust* action, and will he strive to get the most he can for himself from everyone?

He will.

Then, let's put it this way: A just person doesn't outdo someone like himself but someone unlike himself, whereas an unjust person outdoes both like and unlike.

Very well put.

An unjust person is clever and good, and a just one is neither?

That's well put, too.

It follows, then, that an unjust person is like clever and good people, while the other isn't?

Of course that's so. How could he fail to be like them when he has their qualities, while the other isn't like them?

Fine. Then each of them has the qualities of the people he's like?

Of course.

All right, Thrasymachus. Do you call one person musical and another nonmusical?

I do.

Which of them is clever in music, and which isn't?

The musical one is clever, of course, and the other isn't.

And the things he's clever in, he's good in, and the things he isn't clever in, he's bad in?

Yes.

Isn't the same true of a doctor?

It is.

Do you think that a musician, in tuning his lyre and in tightening and loosening the strings, wants to outdo another musician, claiming that this is what he deserves?

I do not.

But he does want to outdo a nonmusician?

Necessarily.

What about a doctor? Does he, when prescribing food and drink, want to outdo another doctor or someone who does the action that medicine prescribes? [350]

Certainly not.

But he does want to outdo a nondoctor?

Yes.

In any branch of knowledge or ignorance, do you think that a knowledgeable person would intentionally try to outdo other knowledgeable people or say something better or different than they do, rather than doing or saying the very same thing as those like him?

Well, perhaps it must be as you say.

And what about an ignorant person? Doesn't he want to outdo both a knowledgeable person and an ignorant one?

Probably.

A knowledgeable person is clever?

I agree.

And a clever one is good?

I agree.

Therefore, a good and clever person doesn't want to outdo those like himself but those who are unlike him and his opposite.

So it seems.

But a bad and ignorant person wants to outdo both his like and his opposite.

Apparently.

Now, Thrasymachus, we found that an unjust person tries to outdo those like him and those unlike him? Didn't you say that?

I did.

And that a just person won't outdo his like but his unlike?

Yes.

Then, a just person is like a clever and good one, and an unjust is like an ignorant and bad one.

It looks that way.

Moreover, we agreed that each has the qualities of the one he resembles.

Yes, we did.

Then, a just person has turned out to be good and clever, and an unjust one ignorant and bad.

Thrasymachus agreed to all this, not easily as I'm telling it, but reluctantly, with toil, trouble, and—since it was summer—a quantity of sweat that was a wonder to behold. And then I saw something I'd never seen before—Thrasymachus blushing. But, in any case, after we'd agreed that justice is virtue and wisdom and that injustice is vice and ignorance, I said: All right, let's take that as established. But we also said that injustice is powerful, or don't you remember that, Thrasymachus?

I remember, but I'm not satisfied with what you're now saying. I could make a speech about it, but, if I did, I know that you'd accuse me of engaging in oratory. So either allow me to speak, or, if you want to ask questions, go ahead, and I'll say, "All right," and nod yes and no, as one does to old wives' tales.

Don't do that, contrary to your own opinion.

I'll answer so as to please you, since you won't let me make a speech. What else do you want?

Nothing, by god. But if that's what you're going to do, go ahead and do it. I'll ask my questions.

Ask ahead.

I'll ask what I asked before, so that we may proceed with our argument [351] about justice and injustice in an orderly fashion, for surely it was claimed that injustice is stronger and more powerful than justice. But, now, if justice is indeed wisdom and virtue, it will easily be shown to be stronger than injustice, since injustice is ignorance (no one could now be ignorant of that). However, I don't want to state the matter so unconditionally, Thrasymachus, but to look into it in some such way as this. Would you say that it is unjust for a city to try to enslave other cities unjustly and to hold them in subjection when it has enslaved many of them?

Of course, that's what the best city will especially do, the one that is most completely unjust.

I understand that's your position, but the point I want to examine is this: Will the city that becomes stronger than another achieve this power without justice, or will it need the help of justice?

If what you said a moment ago stands, and justice is cleverness or wisdom, it will need the help of justice, but if things are as I stated, it will need the help of injustice.

I'm impressed, Thrasymachus, that you don't merely nod yes or no but give very fine answers.

That's because I'm trying to please you.

You're doing well at it, too. So please me some more by answering this question: Do you think that a city, an army, a band of robbers or thieves, or any other tribe with a common unjust purpose would be able to achieve it if they were unjust to each other?

No, indeed.

What if they weren't unjust to one another? Would they achieve more?

Certainly.

Injustice, Thrasymachus, causes civil war, hatred, and fighting among themselves, while justice brings friendship and a sense of common purpose. Isn't that so?

Let it be so, in order not to disagree with you.

You're still doing well on that front. So tell me this: If the effect of injustice is to produce hatred wherever it occurs, then, whenever it arises, whether among free men or slaves, won't it cause them to hate one another, engage in civil war, and prevent them from achieving any common purpose?

Certainly.

What if it arises between two people? Won't they be at odds, hate each other, and be enemies to one another and to just people?

They will.

Does injustice lose its power to cause dissension when it arises within a single individual, or will it preserve it intact?

Let it preserve it intact.

Apparently, then, injustice has the power, first, to make whatever it arises in—whether it is a city, a family, an army, or anything else—incapable of achieving anything as a unit, because of the civil wars and [352] differences it creates, and, second, it makes that unit an enemy to itself and to what is in every way its opposite, namely, justice. Isn't that so?

Certainly.

And even in a single individual, it has by its nature the very same effect. First, it makes him incapable of achieving anything, because he is in a state of civil war and not of one mind; second, it makes him his own enemy, as well as the enemy of just people. Hasn't it that effect?

Yes.

And the gods too are just?

Let it be so.

So an unjust person is also an enemy of the gods, Thrasymachus, while a just person is their friend?

Enjoy your banquet of words! Have no fear, I won't oppose you. That would make these people hate me.

Come, then, complete the banquet for me by continuing to answer as you've been doing. We have shown that just people are cleverer and more capable of doing things, while unjust ones aren't even able to act together, for when we speak of a powerful achievement by unjust men acting together, what we say isn't altogether true. They would never have been able to keep their hands off each other if they were completely unjust. But clearly there must have been some sort of justice in them that at least prevented them from doing injustice among themselves at the same time as they were doing it to others. And it was this that enabled them to achieve what they did. When they started doing unjust things, they were only halfway corrupted by their injustice (for those who are all bad and completely unjust are completely incapable of accomplishing anything). These are the things I understand to hold, not the ones you first maintained. We must now examine, as we proposed before, whether just people also live better and are happier than unjust ones. I think it's clear already that this is so, but we must look into it further, since the argument concerns no ordinary topic but the way we ought to live.

Go ahead and look.

I will. Tell me, do you think there is such a thing as the function of a horse?

I do.

And would you define the function of a horse or of anything else as that which one can do only with it or best with it?

I don't understand.

Let me put it this way: Is it possible to see with anything other than eyes?

Certainly not.

Or to hear with anything other than ears?

No.

Then, we are right to say that seeing and hearing are the functions of eyes and ears?

Of course.

What about this? Could you use a dagger or a carving knife or lots of other things in pruning a vine? [353]

Of course.

But wouldn't you do a finer job with a pruning knife designed for the purpose than with anything else?

You would.

Then shall we take pruning to be its function?

Yes.

Now, I think you'll understand what I was asking earlier when I asked whether the function of each thing is what it alone can do or what it does better than anything else.

I understand, and I think that this is the function of each.

All right. Does each thing to which a particular function is assigned also have a virtue? Let's go over the same ground again. We say that eyes have some function?

They do.

So there is also a virtue of eyes?

There is.

And ears have a function?

Yes.

So there is also a virtue of ears?

There is.

And all other things are the same, aren't they?

They are.

And could eyes perform their function well if they lacked their peculiar virtue and had the vice instead?

How could they, for don't you mean if they had blindness instead of sight?

Whatever their virtue is, for I'm not now asking about that but about whether anything that has a function performs it well by means of its own peculiar virtue and badly by means of its vice?

That's true, it does.

So ears, too, deprived of their own virtue, perform their function badly?

That's right.

And the same could be said about everything else?

So it seems.

Come, then, and let's consider this: Is there some function of a soul that you couldn't perform with anything else, for example, taking care of things, ruling, deliberating, and the like? Is there anything other than a soul to which you could rightly assign these, and say that they are its peculiar function?

No, none of them.

What of living? Isn't that a function of a soul?

It certainly is.

And don't we also say that there is a virtue of a soul?

We do.

Then, will a soul ever perform its function well, Thrasymachus, if it is deprived of its own peculiar virtue, or is that impossible?

It's impossible.

Doesn't it follow, then, that a bad soul rules and takes care of things badly and that a good soul does all these things well?

It does.

Now, we agreed that justice is a soul's virtue, and injustice its vice?

We did.

Then, it follows that a just soul and a just man will live well, and an unjust one badly.

Apparently so, according to your argument.

And surely anyone who lives well is blessed and happy, and anyone who doesn't is the opposite. [354]

Of course.

Therefore, a just person is happy, and an unjust one wretched.

So be it.

It profits no one to be wretched but to be happy.

Of course.

And so, Thrasymachus, injustice is never more profitable than justice.

Let that be your banquet, Socrates, at the feast of Bendis.

Given by you, Thrasymachus, after you became gentle and ceased to give me rough treatment. Yet I haven't had a fine banquet. But that's my fault not yours. I seem to have behaved like a glutton, snatching at every dish that passes and tasting it before properly savoring its predecessor. Before finding the answer to our first inquiry about what justice is, I let that go and turned to investigate whether it is a kind of vice and ignorance or a kind of wisdom and virtue. Then an argument came up about injustice being more profitable than justice, and I couldn't refrain from abandoning the previous one and following up on that. Hence the result of the discussion, as far as I'm concerned, is that I know nothing, for when I don't know what justice is, I'll hardly know whether it is a kind of virtue or not, or whether a person who has it is happy or unhappy.

Nicomachean Ethics

Book I

[Happiness]

1
[Ends and Goods]

Every craft and every line of inquiry, and likewise every action and decision, seems to seek some good; that is why some people were right to describe the good as what everything seeks. But the ends [that are sought] appear to differ; some are activities, and others are products apart from the activities. Wherever there are ends apart from the actions, the products are by nature better than the activities.

Since there are many actions, crafts, and sciences, the ends turn out to be many as well; for health is the end of medicine, a boat of boat building, victory of generalship, and wealth of household management. But some of these pursuits are subordinate to some

From Aristotle, *Nicomachean Ethics*, 2nd ed., trans. T. H. Irwin (Indianapolis: Hackett Publishing Co., 1999). Reprinted by permission of the publisher.

one capacity; for instance, bridle making and every other science producing equipment for horses are subordinate to horsemanship, while this and every action in warfare are, in turn, subordinate to generalship, and in the same way other pursuits are subordinate to further ones. In all such cases, then, the ends of the ruling sciences are more choiceworthy than all the ends subordinate to them, since the lower ends are also pursued for the sake of the higher. Here it does not matter whether the ends of the actions are the activities themselves, or something apart from them, as in the sciences we have mentioned.

2
[The Highest Good and Political Science]

Suppose, then, that the things achievable by action have some end that we wish for because of itself, and because of which we wish for the other things, and that we do not choose everything because of something else—for if we do, it will go on without limit, so that desire will prove to be empty and futile. Clearly, this end will be the good, that is to say, the best good.

Then surely knowledge of this good also carries great weight for [determining the best] way of life; if we know it, we are more likely, like archers who have a target to aim at, to hit the right mark. If so, we should try to grasp, in outline at any rate, what the good is, and which is its proper science or capacity.

It seems proper to the most controlling science—the highest ruling science. And this appears characteristic of political science. For it is the one that prescribes which of the sciences ought to be studied in cities, and which ones each class in the city should learn, and how far; indeed we see that even the most honored capacities—generalship, household management, and rhetoric, for instance—are subordinate to it. And since it uses the other sciences concerned with action, and moreover legislates what must be done and what avoided, its end will include the ends of the other sciences, and so this will be the human good. For even if the good is the same for a city as for an individual, still the good of the city is apparently a greater and more complete good to acquire and preserve. For while it is satisfactory to acquire and preserve the good even for an individual, it is finer and more divine to acquire and preserve it for a people and for cities. And so, since our line of inquiry seeks these [goods, for an individual and for a community], it is a sort of political science.

3
[The Method of Political Science]

Our discussion will be adequate if we make things perspicuous enough to accord with the subject matter; for we would not seek the same degree of exactness in all sorts of arguments alike, any more than in the products of different crafts. Now, fine and just things, which political science examines, differ and vary so much as to seem to rest on convention only, not on nature. But [this is not a good reason, since] goods also vary in the same way, because they result in harm to many people—for some have been destroyed because of their wealth, others because of their bravery. And so, since this is our subject and these are our premises, we shall be satisfied to indicate the truth roughly and in outline; since our subject and our premises are things that hold good usually [but not universally], we shall be satisfied to draw conclusions of the same sort.

Each of our claims, then, ought to be accepted in the same way [as claiming to hold good usually]. For the educated person seeks exactness in each area to the extent that the nature of the subject allows; for apparently it is just as mistaken to demand demonstrations from a rhetorician as to accept [merely] persuasive arguments from a mathematician. Further, each person judges rightly what he knows, and is a good judge about that; hence the good judge in a given area is the person educated in that area, and the unqualifiedly good judge is the person educated in every area.

This is why a youth is not a suitable student of political science; for he lacks experience of the actions in life, which are the subject and premises of our arguments. Moreover, since he tends to follow his feelings, his study will be futile and useless; for the end [of political science] is action, not knowledge. It does not matter whether he is young in years or immature in character, since the deficiency does not depend on age, but results from following his feelings in his life and in a given pursuit; for an immature person, like an incontinent person, gets no benefit from his knowledge. But for those who accord with reason in forming their desires and in their actions, knowledge of political science will be of great benefit.

These are the preliminary points about the student, about the way our claims are to be accepted, and about what we propose to do.

4
[Common Beliefs]

Let us, then, begin again. Since every sort of knowledge and decision pursues some good, what is the good that we say political science seeks? What, [in other words,] is the highest of all the goods achievable in action?

As far as its name goes, most people virtually agree; for both the many and the cultivated call it happiness, and they suppose that living well and doing well are the same as being happy. But they disagree about what happiness is, and the many do not give the same answer as the wise.

For the many think it is something obvious and evident—for instance, pleasure, wealth, or honor. Some take it to be one thing, others another. Indeed, the same person often changes his mind; for when he has fallen ill, he thinks happiness is health, and when he has fallen into poverty, he thinks it is wealth. And when they are conscious of their own ignorance, they admire anyone who speaks of something grand and above their heads. [Among the wise,] however, some used to think that besides these many goods there is some other good that exists in its own right and that causes all these goods to be goods.

Presumably, then, it is rather futile to examine all these beliefs, and it is enough to examine those that are most current or seem to have some argument for them.

We must notice, however, the difference between arguments from principles and arguments toward principles. For indeed Plato was right to be puzzled about this, when he used to ask if [the argument] set out from the principles or led toward them—just as on a race course the path may go from the starting line to the far end, or back again. For we should certainly begin from things known, but things are known in two ways; for some are known to us, some known without qualification. Presumably, then, *we* ought to begin from things known to *us*.

That is why we need to have been brought up in fine habits if we are to be adequate students of fine and just things, and of political questions generally. For we begin from the [belief] that [something is true]; if this is apparent enough to us, we can begin without also [knowing] why [it is true]. Someone who is well brought up has the beginnings, or can easily acquire them. Someone who neither has them nor can acquire them should listen to Hesiod: "He who grasps everything himself is best of all; he is noble also who listens to one who has spoken well; but he who neither grasps it himself nor takes to heart what he hears from another is a useless man."

5
[The Three Lives]

But let us begin again from the point from which we digressed. For, it would seem, people quite reasonably reach their conception of the good, i.e., of happiness, from the lives [they lead]; for there are roughly three most favored lives: the lives of gratification, of political activity, and, third, of study.

The many, the most vulgar, would seem to conceive the good and happiness as pleasure, and hence they also like the life of gratification. In this they appear completely slavish, since the life they decide on is a life for grazing animals. Still, they have some argument in their defense, since many in positions of power feel as Sardanapallus felt, [and also choose this life].

The cultivated people, those active [in politics], conceive the good as honor, since this is more or less the end [normally pursued] in the political life. This, however, appears to be too superficial to be what we are seeking; for it seems to depend more on those who honor than on the one honored, whereas we intuitively believe that the good is something of our own and hard to take from us. Further, it would seem, they pursue honor to convince themselves that they are good; at any rate, they seek to be honored by prudent people, among people who know them, and for virtue. It is clear, then, that—in their view at any rate—virtue is superior [to honor].

Perhaps, indeed, one might conceive virtue more than honor to be the end of the political life. However, this also is apparently too incomplete [to be the good]. For it seems possible for someone to possess virtue but be asleep or inactive throughout his life, and, moreover, to suffer the worst evils and misfortunes. If this is the sort of life he leads, no one would count him happy, except to defend a philosopher's paradox. Enough about this, since it has been adequately discussed in the popular works as well.

The third life is the life of study, which we shall examine in what follows.

The moneymaker's life is in a way forced on him [not chosen for itself]; and clearly wealth is not the good we are seeking, since it is [merely] useful, [choiceworthy only] for some other end. Hence one would be more inclined to suppose that [any of] the goods mentioned earlier is the end, since they are liked for themselves. But apparently they are not [the end] either; and many arguments have been presented against them. Let us, then, dismiss them.

6

[The Platonic Form of the Good]

Presumably, though, we had better examine the universal good, and puzzle out what is meant in speaking of it. This sort of inquiry is, to be sure, unwelcome to us, because those who introduced the Forms were friends of ours; still, it presumably seems better, indeed only right, to destroy even what is close to us if that is the way to preserve truth. We must especially do this as philosophers, [lovers of wisdom]; for though we love both the truth and our friends, reverence is due to the truth first.

Those who introduced this view did not mean to produce an Idea for any [series] in which they spoke of prior and posterior [members]; that was why they did not mean to establish an Idea [of number] for [the series of] numbers. But the good is spoken of both in what-it-is [that is, substance], and in quality and relative; and what exists in its own right, that is, substance, is by nature prior to the relative, since a relative would seem to be an appendage and coincident of being. And so there is no common Idea over these.

Further, good is spoken of in as many ways as being [is spoken of]: in what-it-is, as god and mind; in quality, as the virtues; in quantity, as the measured amount; in relative, as the useful; in time, as the opportune moment; in place, as the [right] situation; and so on. Hence it is clear that the good cannot be some common and single universal; for if it were, it would be spoken of in only one [of the types of] predication, not in them all.

Further, if a number of things have a single Idea, there is also a single science of them; hence [if there were an Idea of good] there would also be some single science of all goods. But, in fact, there are many sciences even of the goods under one [type of] predication; for the science of the opportune moment, for instance, in war is generalship, in disease medicine. And similarly the science of the measured amount in food is medicine, in exertion gymnastics. [Hence there is no single science of the good, and so no Idea.]

One might be puzzled about what [the believers in Ideas] really mean in speaking of the So-and-So Itself, since Man Itself and man have one and the same account of man; for insofar as each is man, they will not differ at all. If that is so, then [Good Itself and good have the same account of good]; hence they also will not differ at all insofar as each is good, [hence there is no point in appealing to Good Itself].

Moreover, Good Itself will be no more of a good by being eternal; for a white thing is no whiter if it lasts a long time than if it lasts a day.

The Pythagoreans would seem to have a more plausible view about the good, since they place the One in the column of goods. Indeed, Speusippus seems to have followed them. But let us leave this for another discussion.

A dispute emerges, however, about what we have said, because the arguments [in favor of the Idea] are not concerned with every sort of good. Goods pursued and liked in their own right are spoken of as one species of goods, whereas those that in some way tend to produce or preserve these goods, or to prevent their contraries, are spoken of as goods because of these and in a different way. Clearly, then, goods are spoken of in two ways, and some are goods in their own right, and others goods because of these. Let us, then, separate the goods in their own right from the [merely] useful goods, and consider whether goods in their own right correspond to a single Idea.

But what sorts of goods may we take to be goods in their own right? Are they the goods that are pursued even on their own—for instance, prudence, seeing, some types of pleasures, and honors? For even if we also pursue these because of something else, we may nonetheless take them to be goods in their own right. Alternatively, is nothing except the Idea good in its own right, so that the Form will be futile? But if these other things are also goods in their own right, then, [if there is an Idea of good,] the same account of good will have to turn up in all of them, just as the same account of whiteness turns up in snow and in chalk. In fact, however, honor, prudence, and pleasure have different and dissimilar accounts, precisely insofar as they are goods. Hence the good is not something common corresponding to a single Idea.

But how, then, is good spoken of? For it is not like homonyms resulting from chance. Is it spoken of from the fact that goods derive from one thing or all contribute to one thing? Or is it spoken of more by analogy? For as sight is to body, so understanding is to soul, and so on for other cases.

Presumably, though, we should leave these questions for now, since their exact treatment is more appropriate for another [branch of] philosophy. And the same is true about the Idea. For even if there is some one good predicated in common, or some separable good, itself in its own right, clearly that is not the sort of good a human being can achieve in action or possess; but that is the sort we are looking for now.

Perhaps, however, someone might think it is better to get to know the Idea with a view to the goods that we can possess and achieve in action; for [one might suppose that] if we have this as a sort of pattern, we shall also know better about the goods that are goods for us, and if we know about them, we shall hit on them. This argument certainly has some plausibility, but it would seem to clash with the sciences. For each of these, though it aims at some good and seeks to supply what is lacking, leaves out knowledge of the Idea; but if the Idea were such an important aid, surely it would not be reasonable for all craftsmen to know nothing about it and not even to look for it.

Moreover, it is a puzzle to know what the weaver or carpenter will gain for his own craft from knowing this Good Itself, or how anyone will be better at medicine or generalship from having gazed on the Idea Itself. For what the doctor appears to consider is not even health [universally, let alone good universally], but human health, and presumably the health of this human being even more, since he treats one particular patient at a time.

So much, then, for these questions.

7

[An Account of the Human Good]

But let us return once again to the good we are looking for, and consider just what it could be. For it is apparently one thing in one action or craft, and another thing in another; for it is one thing in medicine, another in generalship, and so on for the rest. What, then, is the good of each action or craft? Surely it is that for the sake of which the other things are done; in medicine this is health, in generalship victory, in house-building a house, in another case something else, but in every action and decision it is the end, since it is for the sake of the end that everyone does the other actions. And so, if there is some end of everything achievable in action, the good achievable in action will be this end; if there are more ends than one, [the good achievable in action] will be these ends.

Our argument, then, has followed a different route to reach the same conclusion. But we must try to make this still more perspicuous. Since there are apparently many ends, and we choose some of them (for instance, wealth, flutes, and, in general, instruments) because of something else, it is clear that not all ends are complete. But the best good is apparently something complete. And so, if only one end is complete, the good we are looking for will be this end; if more ends than one are complete, it will be the most complete end of these.

We say that an end pursued in its own right is more complete than an end pursued because of something else, and that an end that is never choiceworthy because of something else is more complete than ends that are choiceworthy both in their own right and because of this end. Hence an end that is always choiceworthy in its own right, never because of something else, is complete without qualification.

Now happiness, more than anything else, seems complete without qualification. For we always choose it because of itself, never because of something else. Honor, pleasure, understanding, and every virtue we certainly choose because of themselves, since we would choose each of them even if it had no further result; but we also choose them for the sake of happiness, supposing that through them we shall be happy. Happiness, by contrast, no one ever chooses for their sake, or for the sake of anything else at all.

The same conclusion [that happiness is complete] also appears to follow from self-sufficiency. For the complete good seems to be self-sufficient. What we count as self-sufficient is not what suffices for a solitary person by himself, living an isolated life, but what suffices also for parents, children, wife, and, in general, for friends and fellow citizens, since a human being is a naturally political [animal]. Here, however, we must impose some limit; for if we extend the good to parents' parents and children's children and to friends of friends, we shall go on without limit; but we must examine this another time. Anyhow, we regard something as self-sufficient when all by itself it makes a life choiceworthy and lacking nothing; and that is what we think happiness does.

Moreover, we think happiness is most choiceworthy of all goods, [since] it is not counted as one good among many. [If it were] counted as one among many, then, clearly, we think it would be more choiceworthy if the smallest of goods were added; for the good that is added becomes an extra quantity of goods, and the larger of two goods is always more choiceworthy. Happiness, then, is apparently something complete and self-sufficient, since it is the end of the things achievable in action.

But presumably the remark that the best good is happiness is apparently something [generally] agreed, and we still need a clearer statement of what the best good is. Perhaps, then, we shall find this if we first grasp the function of a human being. For just as the good, i.e., [doing] well, for a flautist, a sculptor, and every craftsman, and, in general, for whatever has a function and [characteristic] action, seems to depend on its function, the same seems to be true for a human being, if a human being has some function.

Then do the carpenter and the leather worker have their functions and actions, but has a human being no function? Is he by nature idle, without any function? Or, just as eye, hand, foot, and, in general, every [bodily] part apparently has its function, may we likewise ascribe to a human being some function apart from all of these?

What, then, could this be? For living is apparently shared with plants, but what we are looking for is the special function of a human being; hence we should set aside the life of nutrition and growth. The life next in order is some sort of life of sense perception; but this too is apparently shared with horse, ox, and every animal.

The remaining possibility, then, is some sort of life of action of the [part of the soul] that has reason. One [part] of it has reason as obeying reason; the other has it as itself having reason and thinking. Moreover, life is also spoken of in two ways [as capacity and as activity], and we must take [a human being's special function to be] life as activity, since this seems to be called life more fully. We have found, then, that the human function is activity of the soul in accord with reason or requiring reason.

Now we say that the function of a [kind of thing]—of a harpist, for instance—is the same in kind as the function of an excellent individual of the kind—of an excellent harpist, for instance. And the same is true without qualification in every case, if we add to the function the superior achievement in accord with the virtue; for the function of a harpist is to play the harp, and the function of a good harpist is to play it well. Moreover, we take the human function to be a certain kind of life, and take this life to be activity and actions of the soul that involve reason; hence the function of the excellent man is to do this well and finely.

Now each function is completed well by being completed in accord with the virtue proper [to that kind of thing]. And so the human good proves to be activity of the soul in accord with virtue, and indeed with the best and most complete virtue, if there are more virtues than one. Moreover, it must be in a complete life. For one swallow does not make a spring, nor does one day; nor, similarly, does one day or a short time make us blessed and happy.

This, then, is a sketch of the good; for, presumably, we must draw the outline first, and fill it in later. If the sketch is good, anyone, it seems, can advance and articulate it, and in such cases time discovers more, or is a good partner in discovery. That is also how the crafts have improved, since anyone can add what is lacking [in the outline].

We must also remember our previous remarks, so that we do not look for the same degree of exactness in all areas, but the degree that accords with a given subject matter and is proper to a given line of inquiry. For the carpenter's and the geometer's inquiries about the right angle are different also; the carpenter restricts himself to what helps his work, but the geometer inquires into what, or what sort of thing, the right angle is, since he studies the truth. We must do the same, then, in other areas too, [seeking the proper degree of exactness], so that digressions do not overwhelm our main task.

Nor should we make the same demand for an explanation in all cases. On the contrary, in some cases it is enough to prove rightly that [something is true, without also explaining why it is true]. This is so, for instance, with principles, where the fact that [something is true] is the first thing, that is to say, the principle.

Some principles are studied by means of induction, some by means of perception, some by means of some sort of habituation, and others by other means. In each case we should try to find them out by means suited to their nature, and work hard to define them rightly. For they carry great weight for what follows; for the principle seems to be more than half the whole, and makes evident the answer to many of our questions.

8
[Defense of the Account of the Good]

We should examine the principle, however, not only from the conclusion and premises [of a deduction], but also from what is said about it; for all the facts harmonize with a true account, whereas the truth soon clashes with a false one.

Goods are divided, then, into three types, some called external, some goods of the soul, others goods of the body. We say that the goods of the soul are goods most fully, and more than the others, and we take actions and activities of the soul to be [goods] of the soul. And so our account [of the good] is right, to judge by this belief anyhow—and it is an ancient belief, and accepted by philosophers.

Our account is also correct in saying that some sort of actions and activities are the end; for in that way the end turns out to be a good of the soul, not an external good.

The belief that the happy person lives well and does well also agrees with our account, since we have virtually said that the end is a sort of living well and doing well.

Further, all the features that people look for in happiness appear to be true of the end described in our account. For to some people happiness seems to be virtue; to others prudence; to others some sort of wisdom; to others again it seems to be these, or one of these, involving pleasure or requiring it to be added; others add in external prosperity as well. Some of these views are traditional, held by many, while others are held by a few men who are widely esteemed. It is reasonable for each group not to be completely wrong, but to be correct on one point at least, or even on most points.

First, our account agrees with those who say happiness is virtue [in general] or some [particular] virtue; for activity in accord with virtue is proper to virtue. Presumably, though, it matters quite a bit whether we suppose that the best good consists in possessing or in using—that is to say, in a state or in an activity [that actualizes the state]. For someone may be in a state that achieves no good—if, for instance, he is asleep or inactive in some other way—but this cannot be true of the activity; for it will necessarily act and act well. And just as Olympic prizes are not for the finest and strongest, but for the contestants—since it is only these who win—the same is true in life; among the fine and good people, only those who act correctly win the prize.

Moreover, the life of these active people is also pleasant in itself. For being pleased is a condition of the soul, [and hence is included in the activity of the soul]. Further, each type of person finds pleasure in whatever he is called a lover of; a horse, for instance, pleases the horse-lover, a spectacle the lover of spectacles. Similarly, what is just pleases the lover of justice, and in general what accords with virtue pleases the lover of virtue.

Now the things that please most people conflict, because they are not pleasant by nature, whereas the things that please lovers of the fine are things pleasant by nature. Actions in accord with virtue are pleasant by nature, so that they both please lovers of the fine and are pleasant in their own right.

Hence these people's life does not need pleasure to be added [to virtuous activity] as some sort of extra decoration; rather, it has its pleasure within itself. For besides the reasons already given, someone who does not enjoy fine actions is not good; for no one would call a person just, for instance, if he did not enjoy doing just actions, or generous if he did not enjoy generous actions, and similarly for the other virtues.

If this is so, actions in accord with the virtues are pleasant in their own right. Moreover, these actions are good and fine as well as pleasant; indeed, they are good, fine, and pleasant more than anything else is, since on this question the excellent person judges rightly, and his judgment agrees with what we have said.

Happiness, then, is best, finest, and most pleasant, and the Delian inscription is wrong to distinguish these things: "What is most just is finest; being healthy is most beneficial; but it is most pleasant to win our heart's desire." For all three features are found in the best activities, and we say happiness is these activities, or [rather] one of them, the best one.

Nonetheless, happiness evidently also needs external goods to be added, as we said, since we cannot, or cannot easily, do fine actions if we lack the resources. For, first of all, in many actions we use friends, wealth, and political power just as we use instruments. Further, deprivation of certain [externals]—for instance, good birth, good children, beauty—mars our blessedness. For we do not altogether have the character of happiness if we look utterly repulsive or are ill-born, solitary, or childless; and we have it even less, presumably, if our children or friends are totally bad, or were good but have died.

And so, as we have said, happiness would seem to need this sort of prosperity added also. That is why some people identify happiness with good fortune, and others identify it with virtue.

9
[How Is Happiness Achieved?]

This also leads to a puzzle: Is happiness acquired by learning, or habituation, or by some other form of cultivation? Or is it the result of some divine fate, or even of fortune?

First, then, if the gods give any gift at all to human beings, it is reasonable for them to give us happiness more than any other human good, insofar as it is the best of human goods. Presumably, however, this question is more suitable for a different inquiry.

But even if it is not sent by the gods, but instead results from virtue and some sort of learning or cultivation, happiness appears to be one of the most divine things, since the prize and goal of virtue appears to be the best good, something divine and blessed. Moreover [if happiness comes in this way] it will be widely shared; for anyone who is not deformed [in his capacity] for virtue will be able to achieve happiness through some sort of learning and attention.

And since it is better to be happy in this way than because of fortune, it is reasonable for this to be the way [we become] happy. For whatever is natural is naturally in the finest state possible. The same is true of the products of crafts and of every other cause, especially the best cause; and it would be seriously inappropriate to entrust what is greatest and finest to fortune.

The answer to our question is also evident from our account. For we have said that happiness is a certain sort of activity of the soul in accord with virtue, [and hence not a result of fortune]. Of the other goods, some are necessary conditions of happiness, while others are naturally useful and cooperative as instruments [but are not parts of it].

Further, this conclusion agrees with our opening remarks. For we took the goal of political science to be the best good; and most of its attention is devoted to the character of the citizens, to make them good people who do fine actions.

It is not surprising, then, that we regard neither ox, nor horse, nor any other kind of animal as happy; for none of them can share in this sort of activity. For the same reason a child is not happy either, since his age prevents him from doing these sorts of actions. If he is called happy, he is being congratulated [simply] because of anticipated blessedness; for, as we have said, happiness requires both complete virtue and a complete life.

It needs a complete life because life includes many reversals of fortune, good and bad, and the most prosperous person may fall into a terrible disaster in old age, as the Trojan stories tell us about Priam. If someone has suffered these sorts of misfortunes and comes to a miserable end, no one counts him happy.

10
[Can We Be Happy during Our Lifetime?]

Then should we count no human being happy during his lifetime, but follow Solon's advice to wait to see the end? But if we agree with Solon, can someone really be happy during the time after he has died? Surely that is completely absurd, especially when we say happiness is an activity.

We do not say, then, that someone is happy during the time he is dead, and Solon's point is not this [absurd one], but rather that when a human being has died, we can safely pronounce [that he was] blessed [before he died], on the assumption that he is now finally beyond evils and misfortunes. But this claim is also disputable. For if a living person has good or evil of which he is not aware, a dead person also, it seems, has good or evil, if, for instance, he receives honors or dishonors, and his children, and descendants in general, do well or suffer misfortune.

However, this conclusion also raises a puzzle. For even if someone has lived in blessedness until old age, and has died appropriately, many fluctuations of his descendants' fortunes may still happen to him; for some may be good people and get the life they deserve, while the contrary may be true of others, and clearly they may be as distantly related to their ancestor as you please. Surely, then, it would be an absurd result if the dead person's condition changed along with the fortunes of his descendants, so that at one time he would turn out to have been happy [in his lifetime] and at another time he would turn out to have been miserable. But it would also be absurd if the condition of descendants did not affect their ancestors at all or for any length of time.

But we must return to the previous puzzle, since that will perhaps also show us the answer to our present question. Let us grant that we must wait to see the end, and must then count someone blessed, not as now being blessed [during the time he is dead] but because he previously was blessed. Would it not be absurd, then, if, at the very time when he is happy, we refused to ascribe truly to him the happiness he has? Such refusal results from reluctance to call him happy during his lifetime, because of its ups and downs; for we suppose happiness is enduring and definitely not prone to fluctuate, but the same person's fortunes often turn to and fro. For clearly, if we take our cue from his fortunes, we shall often call him happy and then miserable again, thereby representing the happy person as a kind of chameleon, insecurely based.

But surely it is quite wrong to take our cue from someone's fortunes. For his doing well or badly does not rest on them. A human life, as we said, needs these added, but activities in accord with virtue control happiness, and the contrary activities control its contrary. Indeed, the present puzzle is further evidence for our account [of happiness]. For no human achievement has the stability of activities in accord with virtue, since these seem to be more enduring even than our knowledge of the sciences. Indeed, the most honorable among the virtues themselves are more enduring than the other virtues, because blessed people devote their lives to them more fully and more continually than to anything else—for this continual activity would seem to be the reason we do not forget them.

It follows, then, that the happy person has the [stability] we are looking for and keeps the character he has throughout his life. For always, or more than anything else, he will do and study the actions in accord with virtue, and will bear fortunes most finely, in every way and in all conditions appropriately, since he is truly "good, foursquare, and blameless."

Many events, however, are subject to fortune; some are minor, some major. Hence, minor strokes of good or ill fortune clearly will not carry any weight for his life. But many major strokes of good fortune will make it more blessed; for in themselves they naturally add adornment to it, and his use of them proves to be fine and excellent. Conversely, if he suffers many major misfortunes, they oppress and spoil his blessedness, since they involve pain and impede many activities. And yet, even here what is fine shines through, whenever someone bears many severe misfortunes with good temper, not because he feels no distress, but because he is noble and magnanimous.

And since it is activities that control life, as we said, no blessed person could ever become miserable, since he will never do hateful and base actions. For a truly good and prudent person, we suppose, will bear strokes of fortune suitably, and from his resources at any time will do the finest actions, just as a good general will make the best use of his forces in war, and a good shoemaker will make the finest shoe from the hides given to him, and similarly for all other craftsmen.

If this is so, the happy person could never become miserable, but neither will he be blessed if he falls into misfortunes as bad as Priam's. Nor, however, will he be inconstant and prone to fluctuate, since he will neither be easily shaken from his happiness nor shaken by just any misfortunes. He will be shaken from it, though, by many serious misfortunes, and from these a return to happiness will take no short time. At best, it will take a long and complete length of time that includes great and fine successes.

Then why not say that the happy person is the one whose activities accord with complete virtue, with an adequate supply of external goods, not for just any time but for a complete life? Or should we add that he will also go on living this way and will come to an appropriate end, since the future is not apparent to us, and we take happiness to be the end, and altogether complete in every way? Given these facts [about the future and about happiness], we shall say that a living person who has, and will keep, the goods we mentioned is blessed, but blessed as a human being is. So much for a determination of this question.

11

[How Happiness Can Be Affected after One's Death]

Still, it is apparently rather unfriendly and contrary to the [common] beliefs to claim that the fortunes of our descendants and all our friends contribute nothing. But since they can find themselves in many and various circumstances, some of which affect us more, some less, it is apparently a long—indeed endless—task to differentiate all the particular cases. Perhaps a general outline will be enough of an answer.

Misfortunes, then, even to the person himself, differ, and some have a certain gravity and weight for his life, whereas others would seem to be lighter. The same is true for the misfortunes of his friends; and it matters whether they happen to living or to dead people—much more than it matters whether lawless and terrible crimes are committed before a tragic drama begins or in the course of it.

In our reasoning, then, we should also take account of this difference, but even more account, presumably, of the puzzle about whether the dead share in any good or evil. For if we consider this, anything good or evil penetrating to the dead would seem to be weak and unimportant, either without qualification or for them. Even if the good or evil is not so weak and unimportant, still its importance and character are not enough to make people happy who are not already happy, or to take away the blessedness of those who are happy. And so, when friends do well, and likewise when they do badly, it appears to contribute something to the dead, but of a character and size that neither makes happy people not happy nor anything of this sort.

12
[Praise and Honor]

Now that we have determined these points, let us consider whether happiness is something praiseworthy, or instead something honorable; for clearly it is not a capacity [which is neither praiseworthy nor honorable].

Whatever is praiseworthy appears to be praised for its character and its state in relation to something. We praise the just and the brave person, for instance, and in general the good person and virtue, because of their actions and achievements; and we praise the strong person, the good runner, and each of the others because he naturally has a certain character and is in a certain state in relation to something good and excellent. This is clear also from praises of the gods; for these praises appear ridiculous because they are referred to us, but they are referred to us because, as we said, praise depends on such a reference.

If praise is for these sorts of things, then clearly for the best things there is no praise, but something greater and better. And indeed this is how it appears. For the gods and the most godlike of men are [not praised, but] congratulated for their blessedness and happiness. The same is true of goods; for we never praise happiness, as we praise justice, but we count it blessed, as something better and more godlike [than anything that is praised].

Indeed, Eudoxus seems to have used the right sort of argument in defending the supremacy of pleasure. By not praising pleasure, though it is a good, we indicate—so he thought—that it is superior to everything praiseworthy; [only] the god and the good have this superiority since the other goods are [praised] by reference to them.

[Here he seems to have argued correctly.] For praise is given to virtue, since it makes us do fine actions; but celebrations are for achievements, either of body or of soul. But an exact treatment of this is presumably more proper for specialists in celebrations. For us, anyhow, it is clear from what has been said that happiness is something honorable and complete.

A further reason why this would seem to be correct is that happiness is a principle; for [the principle] is what we all aim at in all our other actions; and we take the principle and cause of goods to be something honorable and divine.

13
[Introduction to the Virtues]

Since happiness is a certain sort of activity of the soul in accord with complete virtue, we must examine virtue; for that will perhaps also be a way to study happiness better. Moreover, the true politician seems to have put more effort into virtue than into anything else, since he wants to make the citizens good and law-abiding. We find an example of this in the Spartan and Cretan legislators and in any others who share their concerns. Since, then, the examination of virtue is proper for political science, the inquiry clearly suits our decision at the beginning.

It is clear that the virtue we must examine is human virtue, since we are also seeking the human good and human happiness. By human virtue we mean virtue of the soul, not of the body, since we also say that happiness is an activity of the soul. If this is so, it is clear that the politician must in some way know about the soul, just as someone setting out to heal the eyes must know about the whole body as well. This is all the more true to the extent that political science is better and more honorable than medicine; even among doctors, the cultivated ones devote a lot of effort to finding out about the body. Hence the politician as well [as the student of nature] must study the soul. But he must study it for his specific purpose, far enough for his inquiry [into virtue]; for a more exact treatment would presumably take more effort than his purpose requires.

[We] have discussed the soul sufficiently [for our purposes] in [our] popular works as well [as our less popular], and we should use this discussion. We have said, for instance, that one [part] of the soul is nonrational, while one has reason. Are these distinguished as parts of a body and everything divisible into parts are? Or are they two [only] in definition, and inseparable by nature, as the convex and the concave are in a surface? It does not matter for present purposes.

Consider the nonrational [part]. One [part] of it, i.e., the cause of nutrition and growth, would seem to be plantlike and shared [with all living things]; for we can ascribe this capacity of the soul to everything that is nourished, including embryos, and the same capacity to full-grown living things, since this is more reasonable than to ascribe another capacity to them.

Hence the virtue of this capacity is apparently shared, not [specifically] human. For this part and this capacity more than others seem to be active in sleep, and here the good and the bad person are least distinct; hence happy people are said to be no better off than miserable people for half their lives. This lack of distinction is not surprising, since sleep is inactivity of the soul insofar as it is called excellent or base, unless to some small extent some movements penetrate [to our awareness], and in this way the decent person comes to have better images [in dreams] than just any random person has. Enough about this, however, and let us leave aside the nutritive part, since by nature it has no share in human virtue.

Another nature in the soul would also seem to be nonrational, though in a way it shares in reason. For in the continent and the incontinent person we praise their reason, that is to say, the [part] of the soul that has reason, because it exhorts them correctly and toward what is best; but they evidently also have in them some other [part] that is by nature something apart from reason, clashing and struggling with reason. For just as paralyzed parts of a body, when we decide to move them to the right, do the contrary and move off to the left, the same is true of the soul; for incontinent people have impulses in contrary directions. In bodies, admittedly, we see the part go astray, whereas we do not see it in the soul; nonetheless, presumably, we should suppose that the soul also has something apart from reason, countering and opposing reason. The [precise] way it is different does not matter.

However, this [part] as well [as the rational part] appears, as we said, to share in reason. At any rate, in the continent person it obeys reason; and in the temperate and the brave person it presumably listens still better to reason, since there it agrees with reason in everything.

The nonrational [part], then, as well [as the whole soul] apparently has two parts. For while the plantlike [part] shares in reason not at all, the [part] with appetites and in general desires shares in reason in a way, insofar as it both listens to reason and obeys it. This is the way in which we are said to "listen to reason" from father or friends, as opposed to the way in which [we "give the reason"] in mathematics. The nonrational part also [obeys and] is persuaded in some way by reason, as is shown by correction, and by every sort of reproof and exhortation.

If, then, we ought to say that this [part] also has reason, then the [part] that has reason, as well [as the nonrational part], will have two parts. One will have reason fully, by having it within itself; the other will have reason by listening to reason as to a father.

The division between virtues accords with this difference. For some virtues are called virtues of thought, others virtues of character; wisdom, comprehension, and prudence are called virtues of thought, generosity and temperance virtues of character. For when we speak of someone's character we do not say that he is wise or has good comprehension, but that he is gentle or temperate. And yet, we also praise the wise person for his state, and the states that are praiseworthy are the ones we call virtues.

The Ego and the Id

We shall now look upon the mind of an individual as an unknown and unconscious id, upon whose surface rests the ego, developed from its nucleus. . . . If we make an effort to conceive of this pictorially, we may add that the ego does not envelop the whole of the id, but only does so to the extent to which the system . . . forms its surface, more or less as the germinal layer rests upon the ovum. The ego is not sharply separated from the id; its lower portion merges into it.

But the repressed merges into the id as well, and is simply a part of it. The repressed is only cut off sharply from the ego by the resistances of repression; it can communicate with the ego through the id. We at once realize that almost all the delimitations we have been led into outlining by our study of pathology relate only to the superficial levels of the mental apparatus—the only ones known to us.

From Sigmund Freud, *The Ego and the Id*, trans. Joan Riviere (London: Hogarth Press and the Institute of Psychoanalysis, 1927).

4

Mengzi and Xunzi: The Capacity for True Benevolence

Mengzi (usually referred to as Mencius) and Xunzi (in early translations referred to as Hsun Tzu) are both Confucians. Mencius lived in the fourth century BCE. Xunzi came later and was born sometime around 310 BCE. They both subscribe to the central Confucian project: that of enabling sort-of-good people to perfect and polish themselves into being reliably very good people. But they give somewhat different accounts of the starting points.

The two of them are often contrasted in brief accounts of Chinese philosophy that are akin to CliffsNotes. Mencius, it is said, held that human nature is good, and Xunzi held that it was evil. Both capsule descriptions are wrong and misleading.

Mencius held that it was human nature to have occasional benevolent urges. If a child were crawling toward a well, risking falling in and drowning, it was normal human nature to wish that the child not fall in. We, however, could have this benevolent wish but not be benevolent in much of the rest of our life. Mencius' project was to get people to be benevolent in their entire lives.

This comes out in a conversation between Mencius and a ruler, many of whose people are precariously poor. Mencius begins by saying that he had heard that the ruler had spared an ox that was about to be sacrificed. He had seen the fear in the animal's eyes and saved him, the ruler says. (A sheep then was substituted; presumably the ruler did not look in the sheep's eyes.)

Mencius takes the ruler's benevolent impulse in sparing the ox as showing that the ruler has the psychological wherewithal to become a really benevolent person. What about your people, some of whom are near starvation? he asks. Why can't the benevolence be extended to them? The obvious answer, of course, is that the ruler hardly sees them, but he did look at the ox. If one made the effort to think about unseen suffering beings, things might be different.

Xunzi also is easily misrepresented. He did not think that people are naturally evil. Evil is normally linked to a perverse desire to inflict harm. In Xunzi's account, the initial human nature that we have as children involves what is merely a crude and careless attitude toward harmfulness. With any luck this initial human nature will be succeeded by a more circumspect one, in which there will be an awareness of potential harm and of ways to avoid it. The civilization and culture of the past make this development possible. Xunzi shares Mencius' ideal of people who are thoughtful, considerate, and benevolent. It is their images of the starting points that are different.

It should be remarked that Mencius' philosophy is similar in some respects to one two thousand years later: that of the Scottish philosopher David Hume. (There is no evidence that I know of that Hume was aware of Mencius' philosophy, although he did spend some time in France, where there was a dawning interest in Chinese philosophy.) Both Mencius and Hume believe that there is a widespread element of benevolence in human nature. Hume's example—akin to Mencius' of the child about to fall into the well—is our tendency not to step on the foot of a man afflicted with gout, a painful disease of the feet. Both believe also that this element can be worn away in misguided paths of life. Mencius uses the image of a grassy hill that is overgrazed, so that the grass ultimately disappears and the hill is bare. Hume refers to the life and career of the wicked Roman emperor Nero.

It should be added that this claim that there is an element of benevolence in normal human nature plays different roles in the philosophies of Mencius and Hume. For Mencius, it supports the suggestion that it might be psychologically possible to extend broadly this benevolent impulse and to become systematically benevolent. For Hume, the element of benevolence provides the key to an explanation of how it is that morality exists in the world. The sympathy that goes along with benevolent inclination allows us to identify with someone who is (or might be) harmed or mistreated. This contributes to a sense that such things should not be permitted, which is translated into the formation of moral rules.

Mengzi

Book One

1A1 Mengzi had an audience with King Hui of Liang. The King said, "Sir, you have come, not regarding one thousand *li* as too far. Surely you will have something to profit my state?"

From Philip J. Ivanhoe and Bryan W. Van Norden, eds., Chapter 3, "Mengzi," trans. Bryan W. Van Norden, in *Readings in Classical Chinese Philosophy,* 2nd ed. (Indianapolis: Hackett Publishing Co., 2005). Reprinted by permission of the publisher.

Mengzi said in response, "Why must Your Majesty say, 'profit'? Let there be benevolence and righteousness and that is all. Your Majesty says, 'How can my state be profited?' The Counsellors say, 'How can my family be profited?' The scholars and commoners say, 'How can I be profited?' Those above and those below mutually compete for profit and the state is endangered.

"In a case where the ruler of a state that can field ten thousand chariots is murdered, it must be by a family that can field a thousand chariots. In a case where the ruler of a state that can field a thousand chariots is murdered, it must be by a family that can field a hundred chariots. One thousand out of ten thousand, or one hundred out of a thousand, cannot be considered to not be a lot. But if righteousness is put behind and profit is put ahead, one will not be satisfied without grasping from others.

"There have never been those who were benevolent who abandoned their parents. There have never been those who were righteous who put their ruler last. Let Your Majesty say, 'Benevolence and righteousness,' and that is all. Why must you say 'profit'?"

1A3 King Hui of Liang said, "In relation to the state, We exert our heart to the utmost. When there is a famine in the region inside the river, then We move people to the region east of the river, and move grain to the region inside the river. When there is a famine in the region east of the river, We do the converse. When We examine the government of neighboring states, there is none that exerts itself as We do. Yet the people of neighboring states do not grow fewer, and Our people do not grow more numerous. How is this?"

Mengzi responded, "Your Majesty is fond of war. Allow me to use an illustration from warfare: Thunderingly, the drums beat the soldiers forward; their swords have already clashed; casting aside their armor and trailing their weapons they run away. Some run a hundred paces and then stop; others run fifty paces and then stop. How would it be if those who ran fifty paces laughed at those who ran a hundred paces?"

He responded, "That is unacceptable. They simply did not run a hundred paces. But what they did is running away too."

Mengzi said, "If Your Majesty understands this, then you will not expect your people to be more numerous than those of neighboring states.". . .

1A7 King Xuan of Qi asked, "May I hear from you of the actions of the Lord Protectors Huan of Qi and Wen of Jin?"

Mengzi said in response, "The disciples of Zhongni [i.e., Kongzi] did not give accounts of the actions of Huan and Wen. Because of this, they were not passed on to later generations, and I, your servant, have not heard of them. But, if you insist, then may we talk about being a genuine king?"

Xuan said, "What must one's Virtue be like so that one can become a king?"

Mengzi said, "One cares for the people and becomes a king. This is something no one can stop."

Xuan said, "Can one such as I care for the people?"

Mengzi said, "He can."

Xuan said, "How do you know that I can?"

Mengzi said, "I heard your attendant Hu He say,

> The King was sitting up in his hall. There was an ox being led past below. The King saw it and said, 'Where is the ox going?' Someone responded, 'We are about to consecrate a bell with its blood.' The King said, 'Spare it. I cannot bear its frightened appearance, like an innocent going to the execution ground.' Someone responded, 'So should we abandon the consecrating of the bell?' The King said, 'How can that be abandoned? Exchange it for a sheep.'"

Mengzi continued, "I do not know if this happened."

Xuan said, "It happened."

Mengzi said, "This feeling is sufficient to be a king. The commoners all thought Your Majesty was being stingy. But I knew that Your Majesty could not bear the frightened appearance of the ox."

The King said, "That is so. There really were commoners like that. Although Qi is a small state, how could I be stingy about one ox? It was just that I could not bear its frightened appearance, like an innocent going to the execution ground. Hence, I exchanged it for a sheep."

Mengzi said, "Let Your Majesty not be surprised at the commoners' taking you to be stingy. You took a small thing and exchanged it for a big thing. How could they understand? If Your Majesty were pained at its being innocent and going to the execution ground, then what is there to choose between an ox and a sheep?"

The King laughed, saying, "What was this feeling really?! It's not the case that I grudged its value and exchanged it for a sheep. But it makes sense that the commoners would say I was stingy."

Mengzi said, "There is no harm. This is just the way benevolence works. You saw the ox but had not seen the sheep. As for the relation of gentlemen to birds and beasts, if they see them living, they cannot bear to see them die. If they hear their cries, they cannot bear to eat their flesh. Hence, gentlemen keep their distance from the kitchen."

The King was pleased and said, "The *Odes* say,

> Another person had the heart,
> But I measured it.

This describes you. I was the one who did it. I reflected and sought it out, but did not understand my heart. You spoke, and in my heart there was a feeling of compassion. In what way does this heart accord with being a king?"

Mengzi said, "Suppose there were someone who reported to Your Majesty, saying, 'My strength is sufficient to lift five hundred pounds, but not sufficient to lift one feather. My eyesight is sufficient to examine the tip of an autumn hair,[1] but I cannot see a wagon of firewood.' Would Your Majesty accept that?"

Xuan said, "No."

Mengzi said, "In the present case your kindness is sufficient to reach birds and beasts, but the benefits do not reach the commoners. Why is this case alone different? Hence, not lifting one feather is due to not using one's strength. Not seeing a wagon of firewood is due to not using one's eyesight. The commoners not receiving care is due to not using one's kindness. Hence, Your Majesty's not being a genuine king is due to not acting; it is not due to not being able."

Xuan said, "What is the difference between concrete cases of not doing and not being able?"

Mengzi said, "'Pick up Mount Tai and leap over the North Sea.' If you say, 'I cannot,' this is truly not being able. 'Massage the stiff joints of an elderly person.' If you say, 'I cannot,' this is not acting; it is not a case of not being able. So Your Majesty's not being a king is not in the category of picking up Mount Tai and leaping over the North Sea. Your Majesty's not being a king is in the category of massaging the stiff joints of an elderly person.

"Treat your elders as elders, and extend it to the elders of others; treat your young ones as young ones,[2] and extend it to the young ones of others; then you can turn the whole world in the palm of your hand. The *Odes* say,

1. An animal's hair is fine (and hence thin) during autumn.

2. That is, "Treat your elders and young ones as elders and young ones *should* be treated."

> He set an example for his wife,
> It extended to his brothers,
> And so he controlled his family and state.

This means that he simply took this feeling and applied it to that. Hence, if one extends one's kindness, it will be sufficient to care for all within the Four Seas. If one does not extend one's kindness, one will lack the wherewithal to care for one's wife and children. That in which the ancients greatly exceeded others was no other than this. They were simply good at extending what they did. In the present case your kindness is sufficient to reach birds and beasts, but the benefits do not reach the commoners. Why is this case alone different? Weigh, and then you will distinguish the light and the heavy. Measure, and then you will distinguish the long and the short. Things are all like this, the heart most of all. Let Your Majesty measure it.

"Perhaps Your Majesty can only be happy in his heart by rallying soldiers, endangering his scholars and ministers, and incurring the resentment of the other lords?"

Xuan said, "No. How could I be happy about these things?"

Mengzi said, "Could I hear Your Majesty's greatest desire?" The King smiled and did not speak.

Mengzi said, "Is it because your hearty and sweet foods are insufficient for your mouth? Are your light and warm clothes insufficient for your body? Or yet because the beautiful and charming sights are insufficient for your eyes to look at? The melodies are insufficient for your ears to listen to? The servants are insufficient to order about in front of you? Your Majesty's various ministers *are* sufficient to serve you. Does Your Majesty actually do what you do for these things?!"

Xuan said, "No. It is not for the sake of these things."

Mengzi said, "Then Your Majesty's greatest desire can be known. You desire to govern the land, bring to your court the states of Qin and Chu, oversee the Central Kingdom, and dominate the barbarians. By means of such things as you do, to seek such things as you desire, is like climbing a tree in search of a fish."

The King said, "Is it as extreme as that?"

Mengzi said, "The danger is greater than that! If one climbs a tree in search of a fish, although one will not get a fish, there will not be any disaster afterward. By means of such things as you do, to seek such things as you desire, if one exhausts the strength of one's heart in doing it, afterward there must be disaster."

Xuan said, "Could I hear of this?"

Mengzi said, "If the people of Zou and the people of Chu fought, who does Your Majesty think would win?"

Xuan said, "The people of Chu would win."

Mengzi said, "So the small definitely cannot match the big, the few definitely cannot match the many, the weak definitely cannot match the strong. The region within the seas is nine thousand square *li*. Qi amounts to one thousand. To take on eight with one, how is this different from Zou matching Chu?!

"Simply return to the fundamentals. Suppose Your Majesty were to bestow benevolence in governing. This would cause all under Heaven who serve others to all want to take their place in Your Majesty's court, those who plough to all want to plough in Your Majesty's uncultivated fields, merchants to all want to place their goods in Your Majesty's markets, those who travel to all wish to use Your Majesty's roads. All under Heaven who wish to complain of their rulers would all desire to report to Your Majesty. If it were like this, who could stop it?"[3]

The King said, "I am ignorant and unable to undertake this. But I am willing for you, Master, to redirect my resolution, enlighten, and instruct me. Although I am not clever, please let me try."

Mengzi said, "To lack a constant livelihood, yet to have a constant heart—only a scholar is capable of this. As for the people, if they lack a constant livelihood, it follows that they will lack a constant heart. And if one simply fails to have a constant heart, dissipation and evil will not be avoided. When they thereupon sink into crime, to go and punish them is to trap the people. When there are benevolent people in positions of authority, how is it possible to trap the people? For this reason, an enlightened ruler, in regulating the people's livelihood, must ensure that it is sufficient, on the one hand, to serve one's father and mother, and on the other hand, to nurture wife and children. In good years, one is always full. In years of famine, one escapes death. Only when the people have a regulated livelihood do they rush toward the good, and thus the people follow the ruler easily.

"Nowadays, in regulating the people's livelihood, on the one hand it is insufficient to serve one's father and mother, on the other it is insufficient to nurture wife and children. In good years, one is always bitter. In years of famine, one cannot escape death. This is a case in which one fears not having the means to save people from death. How could one have leisure for teaching ritual and righteousness?

"If Your Majesty wishes to put benevolent government into effect, then simply return to the fundamentals. Plant every household

3. That is, who could stop such a ruler from eventually becoming king of all the world?

of five *mu* with mulberry trees, and fifty-year-olds can wear silk. Let the nurturing of chickens, pigs, and dogs not be neglected, and seventy-year-olds can eat meat. If you do not disturb the seasonal work in each field of one hundred *mu*, a household with eight mouths to feed need not go hungry. If you are careful about the teachings of the schools, explaining the righteousness of filial piety and fraternal respect, then those with gray hair will not be carrying loads on the roads. For the old to wear silk and eat meat, and the black-haired people[4] to be neither hungry nor cold, yet for their ruler not to become a king—such a thing has never happened."

1B5 . . . King Xuan of Qi said, "Your teachings are excellent!"

Mengzi responded, "If Your Majesty regards them as excellent, then why do you not put them into practice?"

The King said, "We have a weakness. We are fond of wealth."

He responded, "In former times, Duke Liu was fond of wealth. The *Odes* say,

> He stacked, he stored,
> He bundled up dried meat and grain,
> In bags, in sacks,
> Thinking to gather together and bring glory."

2A6 Mengzi said, "Humans all have hearts that are not unfeeling toward others. The former kings had hearts that were not unfeeling toward others, so they had governments that were not unfeeling toward others. If one puts into practice a government that is not unfeeling toward others by means of a heart that is not unfeeling toward others, bringing order to the whole world is in the palm of your hand.

"The reason why I say that humans all have hearts that are not unfeeling toward others is this. Suppose someone suddenly saw a child about to fall into a well: everyone in such a situation would have a feeling of alarm and compassion—not because one sought to get in good with the child's parents, not because one wanted fame among their neighbors and friends, and not because one would dislike the sound of the child's cries.

"From this we can see that if one is without the heart of compassion, one is not a human. If one is without the heart of disdain, one is not a human. If one is without the heart of deference, one is not a human. If one is without the heart of approval and disapproval, one is not a

4. That is, the Chinese people.

human. The heart of compassion is the sprout of benevolence. The heart of disdain is the sprout of righteousness. The heart of deference is the sprout of propriety. The heart of approval and disapproval is the sprout of wisdom.

"People having these four sprouts is like their having four limbs. To have these four sprouts but to say of oneself that one is unable to be virtuous is to steal from oneself. To say that one's ruler is unable to be virtuous is to steal from one's ruler. In general, having these four sprouts within oneself, if one knows to fill them all out, it will be like a fire starting up, a spring breaking through! If one can merely fill them out, they will be sufficient to care for all within the Four Seas. If one merely fails to fill them out, they will be insufficient to serve one's parents."

Xunzi

Chapter Twenty-Three: Human Nature Is Bad

People's nature is bad. Their goodness is a matter of deliberate effort. Now people's nature is such that they are born with a fondness for profit. If they follow along with this, then struggle and contention will arise, and yielding and deference will perish therein. They are born with feelings of hate and dislike. If they follow along with these, then cruelty and villainy will arise, and loyalty and trustworthiness will perish therein. They are born with desires of the eyes and ears, a fondness for beautiful sights and sounds. If they follow along with these, then lasciviousness and chaos will arise, and ritual and the standards of righteousness, proper form and good order, will perish therein. Thus, if people follow along with their inborn nature and dispositions, they are sure to come to struggle and contention, turn to disrupting social divisions and disorder, and end up in violence. So, it is necessary to await the transforming influence of teachers and models and the guidance of ritual and the standards of righteousness, and only then will they come to yielding and deference, turn to culture and order, and end up under control. Looking at it in this way, it is clear that people's nature is bad, and their goodness is a matter of deliberate effort.

Thus, crooked wood must await steaming and straightening on the shaping frame, and only then does it become straight. Blunt metal

From Philip J. Ivanhoe and Bryan W. Van Norden, eds., Chapter 6, "Xunzi," trans. Eric L. Hutton, in *Readings in Classical Chinese Philosophy,* 2nd ed. (Hackett Publishing Co., 2005). Reprinted by permission of the publisher.

must await honing and grinding, and only then does it become sharp. Now since people's nature is bad, they must await teachers and proper models, and only then do they become correct in their behavior. They must obtain ritual and the standards of righteousness, and only then do they become well ordered. Now without teachers or proper models for people, they will be deviant, dangerous, and incorrect in their behavior. Without ritual and the standards of righteousness, they will be unruly, chaotic, and not well ordered. In ancient times, the sage-kings saw that because people's nature is bad, they were deviant, dangerous, and not correct in their behavior, and they were unruly, chaotic, and not well-ordered. Therefore, for their sake they set up ritual and standards of righteousness, and established proper models and measures. They did this in order to straighten out and beautify people's nature and inborn dispositions and thereby correct them, and in order to train and transform people's nature and inborn dispositions and thereby guide them. Then for the first time they were well ordered and conformed to the Way. Among people of today, those who are transformed by teachers and proper models, who accumulate culture and learning, and who make ritual and the standards of righteousness their path become gentlemen. Those who give rein to their nature and inborn dispositions, who take comfort in being utterly unrestrained, and who violate ritual and the standards of righteousness become petty men. Looking at it in this way, it is clear that people's nature is bad, and their goodness is a matter of deliberate effort.

Mengzi says: When people engage in learning, this manifests the goodness of their nature. I say: This is not so. This is a case of not attaining knowledge of people's nature and of not inspecting clearly the division between people's nature and their deliberate efforts. In every case, the nature of a thing is the accomplishment of Heaven. It cannot be learned. It cannot be worked at. Ritual and the standards of righteousness are what the sage produces. They are things that people become capable of through learning, things that are achieved through working at them. Those things in people that cannot be learned and cannot be worked at are called their "nature." Those things in people that they become capable of through learning and that they achieve through working at them are called their "deliberate efforts." This is the division between nature and deliberate effort.

Now people's nature is such that their eyes can see, and their ears can hear. The keenness by which they see does not depart from their eyes, and the acuity by which they hear does not depart from their ears. Their eyes are simply keen, and their ears are simply acute; it is clear that one does not learn these things. Mengzi says: People's nature is good, but they all wind up losing their nature and original state. I say: If it is like this, then he is simply mistaken. People's nature is such that they are born and then depart from their original simplicity and their original material; they are sure to lose these things. Looking at it in this way, it is clear that people's nature is bad. The so-called goodness of people's nature would mean that one would not depart from one's original simplicity but would instead beautify it, would not depart from one's original material but instead make use of it. It would be to cause the relation of one's original simplicity and original material to beauty, and the relation of the heart's thoughts to goodness, to be like the way the keenness by which one sees does not depart from one's eyes, and the acuity by which one hears does not depart from one's ears, so that one can say [being good] is just like the way the eyes are bright and the ears are acute. . . .

Someone asks: If people's nature is bad, then from what are ritual and the standards of righteousness produced? I answer: In every case, ritual and the standards of righteousness are produced from the deliberate effort of the sage; they are not produced from people's nature. Thus, when the potter mixes clay and makes vessels, the vessels are produced from the deliberate efforts of the craftsman; they are not produced from people's nature. Thus, when the craftsman carves wood and makes utensils, the utensils are produced from the deliberate efforts of the craftsman; they are not produced from people's nature. The sage accumulates reflections and deliberations and practices deliberate efforts and reasoned activities in order to produce ritual and standards of righteousness and to establish proper models and measures. So, ritual and the standards of righteousness and proper models and measures are produced from the deliberate efforts of the sage; they are not produced from people's nature.

As for the way that the eyes like pretty colors, the ears like beautiful sounds, the mouth likes good flavors, the heart likes what is beneficial, and the bones and flesh like what is comfortable—these are produced from people's inborn dispositions and nature. These are things that come about of themselves in response to stimulation, things that do not need to await being worked at before being produced. Those things that are not immediate responses to stimulation, that must await being worked at before they are so, are said to be produced from deliberate effort. These are the things that nature and deliberate effort produce, and their different signs.

So, the sage transforms his nature and establishes deliberate effort. In establishing deliberate effort, he produces ritual and the standards of righteousness. In producing ritual and the standards of righteousness, he institutes proper models and measures. Thus, ritual and the standards of righteousness and proper models and measures are produced by the sage. Thus, that in which the sage is like the masses, that in which he is no different than the masses, is his nature. That in which he differs from and surpasses the masses is his deliberate efforts.

Liking what is beneficial and desiring gain are people's inborn dispositions and nature. Suppose there were brothers who had some property to divide, and that they followed the fondness for benefit and desire for gain in their inborn dispositions and nature. If they were to do so, then the brothers would conflict and contend with each other for it. However, let them be transformed by the proper form and good order of ritual and the standards of righteousness. If so, then they would even give it over to their countrymen. Thus, following along with inborn dispositions and nature, even brothers will struggle with each other. If transformed by ritual and the standards of righteousness, then they will even give it over to their countrymen.

In every case, people desire to become good because their nature is bad. The person who has little longs to have much. The person of narrow experience longs to be broadened. The ugly person longs to be beautiful. The poor person longs to be rich. The lowly person longs to be noble. That which one does not have within oneself, one is sure to seek for outside. Thus, when one is rich, one does not long for wealth. When one is noble, one does not long for power. That which one has within oneself, one is sure not to go outside oneself for it. Looking at it in this way, people desire to become good because their nature is bad.

Now people's nature is originally without ritual and without the standards of righteousness. Thus, they must force themselves to engage in learning and seek to possess them. Their nature does not know of ritual and the standards of righteousness, and so they must reflect and deliberate and seek to know them. So, going only by what they have from birth, people lack ritual and the standards of righteousness and do not know of ritual and the standards of righteousness. If people lack ritual and the standards of righteousness, then they will be chaotic. If they do not know of ritual and the standards of righteousness, then they will be unruly. So, going only by what they have from birth, unruliness and disorder are within them. Looking at it in this way, it is clear that people's nature is bad, and their goodness is a matter of deliberate effort.

Mengzi says: People's nature is good. I say: This is not so. In every case, both in ancient times and in the present, what everyone under Heaven calls good is being correct, ordered, peaceful, and controlled. What they call bad is being deviant, dangerous, unruly, and chaotic.

This is the division between good and bad. Now does he really think that people's nature is originally correct, ordered, peaceful, and controlled? Then what use would there be for sage-kings? What use for ritual and the standards of righteousness? Even though there might exist sage-kings and ritual and the standards of righteousness, whatever could these add to the nature's correctness, order, peacefulness, and self-control? Now, such is not the case, because people's nature is bad. Thus, in ancient times the sage-kings saw that because their nature is bad, people were deviant, dangerous, and not correct in their behavior, and they were unruly, chaotic, and not well ordered. Therefore, for their sake they set up the power of rulers and superiors in order to control them. They made clear ritual and the standards of righteousness in order to transform them. They set up laws and standards in order to manage them. They multiplied punishments and fines in order to restrain them. As a result, they caused all under Heaven to become well ordered and conform to the Way. This is the order of the sage-kings, and the transformation from ritual and the standards of righteousness.

Now suppose one were to try doing away with the power of rulers and superiors, try doing without the transformation from ritual and the standards of righteousness, try doing away with the order of laws and standards, try doing without the restraint of punishments and fines. Then stand aside and observe how all the people of the world would treat each other. If it were like this, then the strong would harm the weak and take from them. The many would tyrannize the few and shout them down. One would not have to wait even a moment for all under Heaven to arrive at unruliness and chaos and perish. Looking at it in this way, it is clear that people's nature is bad, and that their goodness is a matter of deliberate effort.

So, those who are good at speaking of ancient times are sure to have some measure from the present. Those who are good at speaking of Heaven are sure to have some evidence from among mankind. For any discourse, one values it if things conform to its distinctions, and if it matches the test of experience. Thus, one sits and propounds it, but when one stands up then one can implement it, and when one unfolds it then one can put it into practice. Now Mengzi says: People's nature is good. Nothing conforms to his distinctions, and this does not match the test of experience. He sits and propounds it, but when he stands up then he cannot implement it, and when he unfolds it then he cannot put it into practice. Is his error not great indeed! Thus, if human nature is good then one may do away with the sage-kings and put ritual and the standards of righteousness to rest. If human nature is bad, then one simply must side with the sage-kings and honor ritual and the standards of righteousness. . . .

Someone suggests: Ritual and the standards of righteousness and the accumulation of deliberate effort are people's nature, and that is why the sage is able to produce them. I answer: This is not so. The potter mixes clay and produces tiles. Yet, how could the clay of the tiles be the potter's nature? The craftsman carves wood and makes utensils. Yet, how could the wood of the utensils be the craftsman's nature? The relationship of the sage to ritual and the standards of righteousness can be compared to mixing clay and producing things. So, how could ritual and the standards of righteousness and the accumulation of deliberate effort be people's original nature? In every respect, the nature of Yao and Shun was one and the same as that of Jie and Robber Zhi. The nature of the gentleman is one and the same as that of the petty man. Now will you take ritual and the standards of righteousness and the accumulation of deliberate effort to be a matter of human nature? Then for what do you value Yao and Shun? For what do you value the gentleman? Everything that one values in Yao and Shun and the gentleman exists because they were able to transform their nature and to establish deliberate effort. In establishing deliberate effort, they produced ritual and the standards of righteousness. Thus, the relationship of the sage to ritual and the standards of righteousness and the accumulation of deliberate effort is like mixing clay and producing things. Looking at it in this way, then how could ritual and the standards of righteousness and the accumulation of deliberate effort be people's nature? What one finds base in Jie and Robber Zhi and the petty man is that they follow along with their nature and inborn dispositions and find comfort in utter lack of restraint, so that they turn to greed for profit and struggle and contention. Thus, it is clear that people's nature is bad, and that their goodness is a matter of deliberate effort. Heaven did not favor Zengzi, Minzi Qian, and Xiao Yi and exclude the masses. Then why is it that only Zengzi, Minzi Qian, and Xiao Yi were rich in the true substance of filial piety and were perfect in their reputation for filial piety? It is because they exerted themselves to the utmost in ritual and the standards of righteousness. Heaven does not favor the people of Qi and Lu and exclude the people of Qin. Then why is it that with regard to the standards of righteousness for father and son, and the proper distinction between husband and wife, they are not as good at filial reverence and respectful good form as those of Qi and Lu? It is because the people of Qin follow along with their inborn dispositions and nature, take comfort in utter lack of restraint, and are lax in regard to ritual and the standards of righteousness. How could it be because their natures are different?

Anyone on the streets could become a Yu. How do I mean this? I say: That by which Yu was Yu was that he was benevolent, righteous, lawful, and correct. Thus, benevolence, righteousness, lawfulness, and correctness have patterns that can be known and can be practiced. However, people on the streets all have the material for knowing benevolence, righteousness, lawfulness, and correctness, and they all have the equipment for practicing benevolence, righteousness, lawfulness, and correctness. Thus, it is clear that they could become a Yu. Now if benevolence, righteousness, lawfulness, and correctness originally had no patterns that could be known or practiced, then even Yu would not know benevolence, righteousness, lawfulness, and correctness, nor would he be able to practice benevolence, righteousness, lawfulness, and correctness. Shall we suppose that people on the streets originally do not have the material to know benevolence, righteousness, lawfulness, and correctness, and that they originally do not have the equipment for practicing benevolence, righteousness, lawfulness, and correctness? If so, then within the family, the people on the streets could not know the standards of righteousness for father and son, and outside the family, they could not know the proper relations of ruler and minister. This is not so. Now it is the case that the people on the streets can all know the standards of righteousness for father and son within the family, and can know the proper relations of ruler and minister outside the family. Thus, it is clear that the material for understanding these things and the equipment for practicing them is present in the people on the streets. Now if the people on the streets were to use their material for understanding these things and the equipment for practicing them to base themselves upon the knowable patterns and practicable aspects of benevolence and righteousness, then it is clear that the people on the streets could become a Yu. Now if the people on the streets were to submit themselves to the proper arts and practice learning, if they were to concentrate their heart and make single-minded their intentions, if they were to ponder, query, and thoroughly investigate—then if they add to this days upon days and connect to this a long period of time, if they accumulate goodness without stopping, then they will achieve spiritlike powers and understanding, and will form a triad with Heaven and earth.

Thus, becoming a sage is something that people achieve through accumulation. Someone says: Sageliness is achieved through accumulation, but why is it that not everyone can accumulate in this way? I say: They could do it, but they cannot be made to do it. Thus, the petty man could become a gentleman, but is not willing to become a gentleman. The gentleman could become a petty man, but is not willing to become a petty man. It has never been that the petty man and gentleman are incapable of becoming each other. However, the reason they do not become each other is that while they could do so, they cannot be made to do so. Thus, it is the case that the people in the streets could become a Yu, but it is not necessarily the case that the people in the streets will be able to become a Yu. Even if one is not able to become a Yu, this does not harm the fact that one could become a Yu. One's feet could walk over every place under Heaven. Even so, there has not yet been anyone who has been able to walk everywhere under Heaven. It has never been that craftsmen, carpenters, farmers, and merchants could not do each other's business. However, none have ever been able to do each other's business. Looking at it in this way, one is not always able to do what one could do. Even if one is not able to do it, this is no harm to the fact that one could do it. Thus, the difference between being able and being unable, on the one hand, and could and could not, on the other, is far indeed. It is clear, then, that [the gentleman and the petty man] could become one another.

Yao asked Shun, "What are people's inborn dispositions like?" Shun answered, "People's inborn dispositions are most unlovely! Why ask about them? When one has a wife and son, then one's filial piety to one's parents declines. When one's appetites and desires are fulfilled, then one's faithfulness to friends declines. When one's rank and salary are full, then one's loyalty to one's ruler declines. People's inborn dispositions? People's inborn dispositions? They are most unlovely! Why ask about them? Only the worthy man is not like that."

5

Human Imperfection in the Judeo-Christian Tradition: From Adam to St. Augustine

Both the Old and New Testaments testify to the prevalence of harmful or inappropriate impulses in human life. Some philosophers have suggested that this is simply a fact about human nature: none of us is perfect. Be that as it may, explanations—some of them grounded in scripture—abound. One line of thought is that this imperfection is inherited from Adam, who ate the forbidden fruit from the tree of knowledge. This is often referred to as "original sin" and is often held to have marked the lives of Adam's descendants.

The theme of inherited guilt is carried forward in the account of what happened to Noah after the flood. Noah planted a vineyard, then made wine out of the grapes and became intoxicated after drinking it. One of his three sons, Ham, saw his father lying naked on the ground. This was an improper experience and was made worse when Ham told his brothers (Shem and Japheth). These behaved properly. They took a sheet and walked backward with it toward their father, so that he was covered before they looked at him. There is a beautiful fresco of this in the Romanesque church of St. Savin sur Gartempe in France.

When Noah recovered and found out what had happened, he uttered a curse. The curse was not on Ham, but on Ham's son Canaan and all his descendants. They all would pay for this inherited guilt. Note that this was a very convenient curse, placed in the Old Testament at about the time the Hebrews invaded the land of Canaan and killed Canaanites and expropriated from them what they wanted.

It should be noted in passing that the idea of inherited guilt is rejected later in the Old Testament, specifically in Jeremiah 31:29–30: "In those days they shall say no more, The fathers have eaten a sour grape, and the children's teeth are set on edge. But every one shall die for his own iniquity: every man that eateth the sour grape, his teeth shall be set on edge."

Despite this, the idea of inherited sin persisted. Specifically, the idea of original sin, stemming from Adam's fault, became a major element in early Christianity. It plays a prominent role in the *Confessions* of the great early Christian philosopher St. Augustine, much of which is presented below.

He regarded his early life as a demonstration of the power of original sin.

The biblical passages that precede St. Augustine in what follows are from the King James Version.

The King James Bible

"The Lord God commanded the man, saying, Of every tree in the garden thou mayest freely eat; But of the tree of knowledge of good and evil, thou shalt not eat of it: for in the day that thou eatest thereof thou shalt surely die." (Genesis 2:16–17) "And when the woman saw that the tree was good for food, and that it was pleasant to the eyes, and a tree to be desired to make one wise, she took of the fruit thereof, and did eat, and gave also to her husband with her; and he did eat." (Genesis 3:6)

"And Noah began to be a husbandman, and he planted a vineyard. And he drank of the wine, and was drunken, and was uncovered within his tent. And Ham, the father of Canaan, saw the nakedness of his father, and told his two brethren without. And Shem and Japheth took a garment, and laid it upon both their shoulders, and went backward, and covered the nakedness of their father; and their faces were backward, and they saw not their father's nakedness.

"And Noah awoke from his wine, and knew what his youngest son had done unto him. And he said, Cursed be Canaan; a servant of servants shall he be unto his brethren. And he said, Blessed be the Lord God of Shem, God shall enlarge Japheth, and he shall dwell in the tents of Shem; and Canaan shall be his servant." (Genesis 9:20–27)

". . . So will I watch over them, to build, and to plant, saieth the Lord. In those days they shall say no more, The fathers have eaten a sour grape, and the children's teeth are set on edge. But every one shall die for his own iniquity; every man that eateth the sour grape, his teeth shall be set on edge." (Jeremiah 31:28–30)

"And, behold, one came and said unto him, Good Master, what good thing should I do, that I may have eternal life? And he said unto him, Why callest thou me good? There is none good but one, that is, God; but if thou wilt enter into life, keep the commandments. . . . The young man saith unto him, All these things have I kept from my youth up: what lack I yet? Jesus said unto him, If thou wilt be perfect, go and sell that thou hast, and give to the poor, and thou shalt have treasure in heaven; and come and follow me. But when the young man heard that saying, he went away sorrowful, for he had great possessions. Then said Jesus unto his disciples, Verily I say unto you, that a rich man shall hardly enter into the kingdom of heaven. And again I say onto you, It is easier for a camel to go through the eye of a needle, than for a rich man to enter the kingdom of God." (Gospel According to St. Matthew 19:16–24)

Confessions

Book Two

I

I propose now to set down my past wickedness and the carnal corruptions of my soul, not for love of them but that I may love Thee, O my God. I do it for love of Thy love, passing again in the bitterness of remembrance over my most evil ways that Thou mayest thereby grow ever lovelier to me, O Loveliness that dost not deceive, Loveliness happy and abiding: and I collect my self out of that broken state in which my very being was torn asunder because I was turned away from Thee, the One, and wasted myself upon the many.

Arrived now at adolescence I burned for all the satisfactions of hell, and I sank to the animal in a succession of dark lusts: my beauty consumed away, and I stank in Thine eyes, yet was pleasing in my own and anxious to please the eyes of men.

II

My one delight was to love and to be loved. But in this I did not keep the measure of mind to mind, which is the luminous line of friendship; but from the muddy concupiscence of the flesh and the hot imagination of puberty mists steamed up to becloud and darken my heart so that I could not distinguish the white light of love from the fog of lust. Both love and lust boiled within me, and swept my youthful immaturity over the precipice of evil desires to leave me half

From Augustine, *Confessions*, 2nd ed., trans. F. J. Sheed (Indianapolis: Hackett Publishing Co., 2006). Reprinted by permission of the publisher.

drowned in a whirlpool of abominable sins. Your wrath had grown mighty against me and I knew it not. I had grown deaf from the clanking of the chain of my mortality, the punishment for the pride of my soul: and I departed further from You, and You left me to myself: and I was tossed about and wasted and poured out and boiling over in my fornications: and You were silent, O my late-won Joy. You were silent, and I, arrogant and depressed, weary and restless, wandered further and further from You into more and more sins which could bear no fruit save sorrows.

If only there had been some one then to bring relief to the wretchedness of my state, and turn to account the fleeting beauties of these new temptations and bring within bounds their attractions for me: so that the tides of my youth might have driven in upon the shore of marriage: for then they might have been brought to calm with the having of children as Your Law prescribes, O Lord, for in this way You form the offspring of this our death, able with gentle hand to blunt the thorns that You would not have in Your paradise. For Your omnipotence is not far from us, even when we are far from You. Or, on the other hand, I might well have listened more heedfully to the voice from the clouds: *Nevertheless such [as marry] shall have tribulation of the flesh; but I spare you;* and, *It is good for a man not to touch a woman;* and, *He that is without a wife is solicitous for the things that belong to the Lord, how he may please God: but he that is with a wife is solicitous for the things of the world, how he may please his wife.* I should have listened more closely to these words and made myself a eunuch for the kingdom of heaven; and so in all tranquillity awaited Your embraces.

Instead I foamed in my wickedness, following the rushing of my own tide, leaving You and going beyond all Your laws. Nor did I escape Your scourges. No mortal can. You were always by me, mercifully hard upon me, and besprinkling all my illicit pleasures with certain elements of bitterness, to draw me on to seek for pleasures in which no bitterness should be. And where was I to find such pleasures save in You O Lord, You who use sorrow to teach, and wound us to heal, and kill us lest we die to You. Where then was I, and how far from the delights of Your house, in that sixteenth year of my life in this world, when the madness of lust—needing no licence from human shamelessness, receiving no licence from Your laws—took complete control of me, and I surrendered wholly to it? My family took no care to save me from this moral destruction by marriage: their only concern was that I should learn to make as fine and persuasive speeches as possible.

III

In that year my studies were interrupted. I had come back from Madaura, a neighbouring city to which I had been sent to study grammar and rhetoric, and the money was being got together for the longer journey to Carthage, where I was to go because my father was set upon it—not that he was rich, for he was only a poor citizen of Thagaste. But to whom am I telling this? Not to Thee, O my God, but in Thy presence I am telling it to my own kind, to the race of men, or rather to that small part of the human race that may come upon these writings. And to what purpose do I tell it? Simply that I and any other who may read may realise out of what depths we must cry to Thee. For nothing is more surely heard by Thee than a heart that confesses Thee and a life in Thy faith.

Everyone of course praised my father because, although his means did not allow it, he had somehow provided the wherewithal for his son to travel so far for the sake of his studies. Many a very much richer citizen did no such thing for his children. Yet this same father never bothered about how I was growing towards You or how chaste or unchaste I might be, so long as I grew in eloquence, however much I might lack of Your cultivation O God, who are the one true and good Lord of your field, my heart.

But during that sixteenth year between Madaura and Carthage, owing to the narrowness of the family fortunes I did not go to school, but lived idly at home with my parents. The briars of unclean lusts grew so that they towered over my head, and there was no hand to root them out. On the contrary my father saw me one day in the public baths, now obviously growing towards manhood and showing the turbulent signs of adolescence. The effect upon him was that he already began to look forward to grandchildren, and went home in happy excitement to tell my mother. He rejoiced, indeed, through that intoxication in which the world forgets You its Creator and loves what You have created instead of You, the intoxication of the invisible wine of a will perverted and turned towards baseness. But in my mother's breast You had already laid the foundation of Your temple and begun Your holy habitation: whereas my father was still only a catechumen, and a new catechumen at that. So that she was stricken with a holy fear. And though I was not as yet baptised, she was in terror of my walking in the crooked ways of those who walk with their backs towards You and not their faces.

I have dared to say that You were silent, my God, when I went afar from You. But was it truly so? Whose but Yours were the words You dinned into my ears through the voice of my mother, Your faithful servant? Not that at that time any of it sank into my heart to make me do it. I still remember her anxiety and how earnestly she urged upon me not to sin with women, above all not with any man's wife. All this sounded to me womanish and I should have blushed to obey. Yet it was from You, though I did not know it and thought that You were silent and she speaking: whereas You were speaking to me through her, and in ignoring her I was ignoring You: I, her son, the son of Your handmaid, Your servant. But I realised none of this and went headlong on my course, so blinded that I was ashamed among the other youths that my viciousness was less than theirs; I heard them boasting of their exploits, and the viler the exploits the louder the boasting; and I set about the same exploits not only for the pleasure of the act but for the pleasure of the boasting. Nothing is utterly condemnable save vice: yet I grew in vice through desire of praise; and when I lacked opportunity to equal others in vice, I invented things I had not done, lest I might be held cowardly for being innocent, or contemptible for being chaste.

With the basest companions I walked the streets of Babylon and wallowed in its filth as if it had been a bed of spices and precious ointments. To make me cleave closer to that city's very centre, the invisible Enemy trod me down and seduced me, for I was easy to seduce. My mother had by now fled out of the centre of Babylon, but she still lingered in its outskirts. She had urged me to chastity but she did not follow up what my father had told her of me: and though she saw my sexual passions as most evil now and full of peril for the future, she did not consider that if they could not be pared down to the quick, they had better be brought under control within the bounds of married love. She did not want me married because she feared that a wife might be a hindrance to my prospects—not those hopes of the world to come which my mother had in You, O God, but my prospects as a student. Both my parents were unduly set upon the success of my studies, my father because he had practically no thought of You and only vain ambition for me, my mother because she thought that the usual course of studies would be not only no hindrance to my coming to You but an actual help. Recalling the past as well as I can, that is how I read my parents' characters. Anyhow, I was left to do pretty well as I liked, and go after pleasure not only beyond the limit of reasonable discipline but to sheer dissoluteness in many kinds of evil. And in all this, O God, a mist hung between my eyes and the brightness of Your Truth: *and mine iniquity had come forth as it were from fatness.*

IV

Your Law, O Lord, punishes theft; and this law is so written in the hearts of men that not even the breaking of it blots it out: for no thief bears calmly being stolen from—not even if he is rich and the other steals through want. Yet I chose to steal, and not because want drove me to it—unless a want of justice and contempt for it and an excess of iniquity. For I stole things which I already had in plenty and of better quality. Nor had I any desire to enjoy the things I stole, but only the stealing of them and the sin. There was a pear tree near our vineyard, heavy with fruit, but fruit that was not particularly tempting either to look at or to taste. A group of young blackguards, and I among them, went out to knock down the pears and carry them off late one night, for it was our bad habit to carry on our games in the streets till very late. We carried off an immense load of pears, not to eat—for we barely tasted them before throwing them to the hogs. Our only pleasure in doing it was that it was forbidden. Such was my heart, O God, such was my heart: yet in the depth of the abyss You had pity on it. Let that heart now tell You what it sought when I was thus evil for no object, having no cause for wrongdoing save my wrongness. The malice of the act was base and I loved it—that is to say I loved my own undoing, I loved the evil in me—not the thing for which I did the evil, simply the evil: my soul was depraved, and hurled itself down from security in You into utter destruction, seeking no profit from wickedness but only to be wicked.

V

There is an appeal to the eye in beautiful things, in gold and silver and all such; the sense of touch has its own powerful pleasures; and the other senses find qualities in things suited to them. Worldly success has its glory, and the power to command and to overcome: and from this springs the thirst for revenge. But in our quest of all these things, we must not depart from You, Lord, or deviate from Your Law. This life we live here below has its own attractiveness, grounded in the measure of beauty it has and its harmony with the beauty of all lesser things. The bond of human friendship is admirable, holding many souls as one. Yet in the enjoyment of all such things we commit sin if through immoderate inclination to them—for though they are good, they are of the lowest order of good—things higher and better are forgotten, even You, O Lord our God, and Your Truth and Your Law. These lower things have their delights but not such as my God has, for He made them all: *and in Him doth the righteous delight, and He is the joy of the upright of heart.*

Now when we ask why this or that particular evil act was done, it is normal to assume that it could not have been done save through the desire of gaining or the fear of losing some one of these lower goods. For they have their own charm and their own beauty, though compared with the higher values of heaven they are poor and mean enough. Such a man has committed a murder. Why? He wanted the other man's wife or his property; or he had chosen robbery as a means of livelihood; or he feared to lose this or that through his victim's act; or he had been wronged and was aflame for vengeance. Would any man commit a murder for no cause, for the sheer delight of murdering? The thing would be incredible. There is of course the case of the man [Catiline] who was said to be so stupidly and savagely cruel that he practised cruelty and evil even when he had nothing to gain by them. But even there a cause was stated—he did it, he said, lest through idleness his hand or his resolution should grow slack. And why did he want to prevent that? So that one day by the multiplication of his crimes the city should be his, and he would have gained honours and authority and riches, and would no longer be in fear of the law or in the difficulties that want of money and the awareness of his crimes had brought him. So that not even Catiline loved his crimes as crimes: he loved some other thing which was his reason for committing them.

VI

What was it then that in my wretched folly I loved in you, O theft of mine, deed wrought in that dark night when I was sixteen? For you were not lovely: you were a theft. Or are you anything at all, that I should talk with you? The pears that we stole were beautiful for they were created by Thee, Thou most Beautiful of all, Creator of all, Thou good God, my Sovereign and true Good. The pears were beautiful but it was not pears that my empty soul desired. For I had any number of better pears of my own, and plucked those only that I might steal. For once I had gathered them I threw them away, tasting only my own sin and savouring that with delight; for if I took so much as a bite of any one of those pears, it was the sin that sweetened it. And now, Lord my God, I ask what was it that attracted me in that theft, for there was no beauty in it to attract. I do not mean merely that it lacked the beauty that there is in justice and prudence, or in the mind of man or his senses and vegetative life: or even so much as the beauty and glory of the stars in the heavens, or of earth and sea with their oncoming of new life to replace the generations that pass. It had not even that false show or shadow of beauty by which sin tempts us.

[For there is a certain show of beauty in sin.] Thus pride wears the mask of loftiness of spirit, although You alone, O God, are high over all. Ambition seeks honour and glory, although You alone are to be honoured before all and glorious forever. By cruelty the great seek to be feared, yet who is to be feared but God alone: from His power what can be wrested away, or when or where or how or by whom? The caresses by which the lustful seduce are a seeking for love: but nothing is more caressing than Your charity, nor is anything more healthfully loved than Your supremely lovely, supremely luminous Truth. Curiosity may be regarded as a desire for knowledge, whereas You supremely know all things. Ignorance and sheer stupidity hide under the names of simplicity and innocence: yet no being has simplicity like to Yours: and none is more innocent than You, for it is their own deeds that harm the wicked. Sloth pretends that it wants quietude: but what sure rest is there save the Lord? Luxuriousness would be called abundance and completeness; but You are the fullness and inexhaustible abundance of incorruptible delight. Wastefulness is a parody of generosity: but You are the infinitely generous giver of all good. Avarice wants to possess overmuch: but You possess all. Enviousness claims that it strives to excel: but what can excel before You? Anger clamours for just vengeance: but whose vengeance is so just as Yours? Fear is the recoil from a new and sudden threat to something one holds dear, and a cautious regard for one's own safety: but nothing new or sudden can happen to You, nothing can threaten Your hold upon things loved, and where is safety secure save in You? Grief pines at the loss of things in which desire delighted: for it wills to be like to You from whom nothing can be taken away.

Thus the soul is guilty of fornication when she turns from You and seeks from any other source what she will nowhere find pure and without taint unless she returns to You. Thus even those who go from You and stand up against You are still perversely imitating You. But by the mere fact of their imitation, they declare that You are the creator of all that is, and that there is nowhere for them to go where You are not.

So once again what did I enjoy in that theft of mine? Of what excellence of my Lord was I making perverse and vicious imitation? Perhaps it was the thrill of acting against Your law—at least in appearance, since I had no power to do so in fact, the delight a prisoner might have in making some small gesture of liberty—getting a deceptive sense of omnipotence from doing something forbidden without immediate punishment. I was that slave, who fled from his Lord and pursued his Lord's shadow. O rottenness, O monstrousness of life and abyss of death! Could you find pleasure only in what was forbidden, and only because it was forbidden?

VII

What shall I render unto the Lord, that I can recall these things and yet not be afraid! *I shall love Thee, Lord, and shall give thanks to Thee and confess Thy name,* because Thou hast forgiven me such great sins and evil deeds. I know that it is only by Thy grace and mercy that Thou hast melted away the ice of my sins. And the evil I have not done, that also I know is by Thy grace: for what might I not have done, seeing that I loved evil solely because it was evil? I confess that Thou hast forgiven all alike—the sins I committed of my own motion, the sins I would have committed but for Thy grace.

Would any man, considering his own weakness, dare to attribute his chastity or his innocence to his own powers and so love Thee less—as if he did not need the same mercy as those who return to Thee after sin? If any man has heard Thy voice and followed it and done none of the things he finds me here recording and confessing, still he must not scorn me: for I am healed by the same doctor who preserved him from falling into sickness, or at least into such grievous sickness. But let him love Thee even more: seeing me rescued out of such sickness of sin, and himself saved from falling into such sickness of sin, by the one same Saviour.

VIII

What fruit therefore had I (in my vileness) *in those things of which I am now ashamed?* Especially in that piece of thieving, in which I loved nothing except the thievery—though that in itself was no *thing* and I only the more wretched for it. Now—as I think back on the state of my mind then—I am altogether certain that I would not have done it alone. Perhaps then what I really loved was the companionship of those with whom I did it. If so, can I still say that I loved nothing over and above the thievery? Surely I can; that companionship was nothing over and above, because it was nothing. What is the truth of it? Who shall show me, unless He that illumines my heart and brings light into its dark places? What is the thing that I am trying to get at in all this discussion? If I had liked the pears that I stole and wanted to enjoy eating them, I might have committed the offence alone, if that had been sufficient, to get me the pleasure I wanted; I should not have needed to inflame the itch of my desires by rubbing against accomplices. But since the pleasure I got was not in the pears, it must have been in the crime itself, and put there by the companionship of others sinning with me.

IX

What was my feeling in all this? Depraved, undoubtedly, and woe is me that I had it. But what exactly was it? *Who can understand sins?* We laughed together as if our hearts were tickled to be playing a trick upon the owners, who had no notion of what we were doing and would very strongly have objected. But what delight did I find in that, which I would not equally have found if I had done it alone? Because we are not much given to laughing when we are alone? Not much given, perhaps, but laughter does sometimes overcome a man when no one else is about, if something especially ridiculous is seen or heard or floats into the mind. Yet I would not have done this by myself: quite definitely I would not have done it by myself.

Here, then, O God, is the memory still vivid in my mind. I would not have committed that theft alone: my pleasure in it was not what I stole but that I stole: yet I would not have enjoyed doing it, I would not have done it, alone. O friendship unfriendly, unanalysable attraction for the mind, greediness to do damage for the mere sport and jest of it, desire for another's loss with no gain to oneself or vengeance to be satisfied! Someone cries, "Come on, let's do it!"—and we would be ashamed to be ashamed.

X

Who can unravel that complex twisted knottedness? It is unclean, I hate to think of it or look at it. I long for Thee, O Justice and Innocence, Joy and Beauty of the clear of sight, I long for Thee with unquenchable longing. There is sure repose in Thee and life untroubled. He that enters into Thee, enters into the joy of his Lord and shall not fear and shall be well in Him who is the Best. I went away from Thee, my God; in my youth I strayed too far from Thy sustaining power, and I became to myself a barren land.

Part II

Some Modern Views of Human Nature

6

Hobbes

Thomas Hobbes lived in the seventeenth century, in a time of turmoil and civic disintegration. The central event was the English Civil War, in which puritan-led armies attacked the forces of King Charles I. The puritans won, and the king was beheaded. Hobbes was a royalist sympathizer and fled to the continent. But after the puritans had been in power for some years, he returned to England. The social disintegration of the civil war provided Hobbes with a strong sense of the dangers that attend a collapse of law and order. Some of us can have this sense in relation to disintegration—in living memory—in places like the former Yugoslavia and in Rwanda.

Hobbes is best known for his conception of something that can prevent a collapse of law and order. This is the social contract. The social contract can be thought of as an agreement on morality and to respect the apparatus of law.

It would be tempting to imagine such an agreement among primitive human beings. But such images seem implausible. A more plausible view is that civilized societies develop so that it is *as if* their members had agreed to respect law and at least most of established morality. As we all know, this agreement is not 100 percent. What we can say is that a civilized society requires that the vast majority of people have a fairly strong (implicit) tendency to respect law and at least most of established morality.

It should be added that real-life social contracts can be unfair, favoring some groups over others. There is no clear indication that Hobbes would deny this. But it does look clear that Hobbes would hold that even a defective social contract is better than none at all. Perhaps we all would?

Leviathan

Chapter XIII

Of the Natural Condition of Mankind, As Concerning Their Felicity, and Misery

[1] Nature hath made men so equal in the faculties of body and mind as that, though there be found one man sometimes manifestly stronger in body or of quicker mind than another, yet when all is reckoned together the difference between man and man is not so considerable as that one man can thereupon claim to himself any benefit to which another may not pretend as well as he. For as to the strength of body, the weakest has strength enough to kill the strongest, either by secret machination, or by confederacy with others that are in the same danger with himself.

[2] And as to the faculties of the mind—setting aside the arts grounded upon words, and especially that skill of proceeding upon general and infallible rules called science (which very few have, and but in few things), as being not a native faculty (born with us), nor attained (as prudence) while we look after somewhat else—I find yet a greater equality amongst men than that of strength. For prudence is but experience, which equal time equally bestows on all men in those things they equally apply themselves unto. That which may perhaps make such equality incredible is but a vain conceit of one's own wisdom, which almost all men think they have in a greater degree than the vulgar, that is, than all men but themselves and a few others whom, by fame or for concurring with themselves, they approve. For such is the nature of men that howsoever they may acknowledge many others to be more witty, or more eloquent, or more learned, yet they will hardly believe there be many so wise as themselves. For they see their own wit at hand, and other men's at a distance. But this proveth rather that men are in that point equal, than unequal. For there is not ordinarily a greater sign of the equal distribution of anything than that every man is contented with his share.

[3] From this equality of ability ariseth equality of hope in the attaining of our ends. And therefore, if any two men desire the same thing, which nevertheless they cannot both enjoy, they become enemies; and in the way to their end, which is principally their own conservation,

and sometimes their delectation only, endeavour to destroy or subdue one another. And from hence it comes to pass that, where an invader hath no more to fear than another man's single power, if one plant, sow, build, or possess a convenient seat, others may probably be expected to come prepared with forces united, to dispossess and deprive him, not only of the fruit of his labour, but also of his life or liberty. And the invader again is in the like danger of another.

[4] And from this diffidence of one another, there is no way for any man to secure himself so reasonable as anticipation, that is, by force or wiles to master the persons of all men he can, so long till he see no other power great enough to endanger him. And this is no more than his own conservation requireth, and is generally allowed. Also, because there be some that taking pleasure in contemplating their own power in the acts of conquest, which they pursue farther than their security requires, if others (that otherwise would be glad to be at ease within modest bounds) should not by invasion increase their power, they would not be able, long time, by standing only on their defence, to subsist. And by consequence, such augmentation of dominion over men being necessary to a man's conservation, it ought to be allowed him.

[5] Again, men have no pleasure, but on the contrary a great deal of grief, in keeping company where there is no power able to over-awe them all. For every man looketh that his companion should value him at the same rate he sets upon himself, and upon all signs of contempt, or undervaluing, naturally endeavours, as far as he dares (which amongst them that have no common power to keep them in quiet, is far enough to make them destroy each other), to extort a greater value from his contemners, by damage, and from others, by the example.

[6] So that in the nature of man we find three principal causes of quarrel: first, competition; secondly, diffidence; thirdly, glory.

[7] The first maketh men invade for gain; the second, for safety; and the third, for reputation. The first use violence to make themselves masters of other men's persons, wives, children, and cattle; the second, to defend them; the third, for trifles, as a word, a smile, a different opinion, and any other sign of undervalue, either direct in their persons or by reflection in their kindred, their friends, their nation, their profession, or their name.

[8] Hereby it is manifest that during the time men live without a common power to keep them all in awe, they are in that condition which is called war, and such a war as is of every man against every man. For war consisteth not in battle only, or the act of fighting, but in a tract of time wherein the will to contend by battle is sufficiently

known. And therefore, the notion of *time* is to be considered in the nature of war, as it is in the nature of weather. For as the nature of foul weather lieth not in a shower or two of rain, but in an inclination thereto of many days together, so the nature of war consisteth not in actual fighting, but in the known disposition thereto during all the time there is no assurance to the contrary. All other time is PEACE.

[9] Whatsoever therefore is consequent to a time of war, where every man is enemy to every man, the same is consequent to the time wherein men live without other security than what their own strength and their own invention shall furnish them withal. In such condition there is no place for industry, because the fruit thereof is uncertain, and consequently, no culture of the earth, no navigation, nor use of the commodities that may be imported by sea, no commodious building, no instruments of moving and removing such things as require much force, no knowledge of the face of the earth, no account of time, no arts, no letters, no society, and which is worst of all, continual fear and danger of violent death, and the life of man, solitary, poor, nasty, brutish, and short.

[10] It may seem strange, to some man that has not well weighed these things, that nature should thus dissociate, and render men apt to invade and destroy one another. And he may, therefore, not trusting to this inference made from the passions, desire perhaps to have the same confirmed by experience. Let him therefore consider with himself—when taking a journey, he arms himself and seeks to go well accompanied; when going to sleep, he locks his doors; when even in his house, he locks his chests; and this when he knows there be laws, and public officers, armed, to revenge all injuries shall be done him—what opinion he has of his fellow subjects, when he rides armed; of his fellow citizens, when he locks his doors; and of his children and servants, when he locks his chests. Does he not there as much accuse mankind by his actions, as I do by my words? But neither of us accuse man's nature in it. The desires and other passions of man are in themselves no sin. No more are the actions that proceed from those passions, till they know a law that forbids them—which till laws be made they cannot know. Nor can any law be made, till they have agreed upon the person that shall make it.

[11] It may peradventure be thought, there was never such a time nor condition of war as this; and I believe it was never generally so, over all the world. But there are many places where they live so now. For the savage people in many places of *America* (except the government of small families, the concord whereof dependeth on natural lust) have no government at all, and live at this day in that brutish

manner as I said before. Howsoever, it may be perceived what manner of life there would be where there were no common power to fear, by the manner of life which men that have formerly lived under a peaceful government use to degenerate into, in a civil war.

[12] But though there had never been any time wherein particular men were in a condition of war one against another, yet in all times kings and persons of sovereign authority, because of their independency, are in continual jealousies and in the state and posture of gladiators, having their weapons pointing and their eyes fixed on one another, that is, their forts, garrisons, and guns upon the frontiers of their kingdoms, and continual spies upon their neighbours, which is a posture of war. But because they uphold thereby the industry of their subjects, there does not follow from it that misery which accompanies the liberty of particular men.

[13] To this war of every man against every man, this also is consequent: that nothing can be unjust. The notions of right and wrong, justice and injustice, have there no place. Where there is no common power, there is no law; where no law, no injustice. Force and fraud are in war the two cardinal virtues. Justice and injustice are none of the faculties neither of the body, nor mind. If they were, they might be in a man that were alone in the world, as well as his senses and passions. They are qualities that relate to men in society, not in solitude. It is consequent also to the same condition that there be no propriety, no dominion, no *mine* and *thine* distinct, but only that to be every man's that he can get, and for so long as he can keep it. And thus much for the ill condition which man by mere nature is actually placed in, though with a possibility to come out of it, consisting partly in the passions, partly in his reason.

[14] The passions that incline men to peace are fear of death, desire of such things as are necessary to commodious living, and a hope by their industry to obtain them. And reason suggesteth convenient articles of peace, upon which men may be drawn to agreement. These articles are they which otherwise are called the Laws of Nature, whereof I shall speak more particularly in the two following chapters.

Chapter XIV

Of the First and Second Natural Laws and of Contracts

[1] The Right of Nature, which writers commonly call *jus naturale,* is the liberty each man hath to use his own power, as he will himself, for the preservation of his own nature, that is to say, of his own life,

and consequently of doing anything which, in his own judgment and reason, he shall conceive to be the aptest means thereunto.

[2] By LIBERTY is understood, according to the proper signification of the word, the absence of external impediments, which impediments may oft take away part of a man's power to do what he would, but cannot hinder him from using the power left him, according as his judgment and reason shall dictate to him.

[3] A LAW OF NATURE (*lex naturalis*) is a precept or general rule, found out by reason, by which a man is forbidden to do that which is destructive of his life or taketh away the means of preserving the same, and to omit that by which he thinketh it may be best preserved. For though they that speak of this subject use to confound *jus* and *lex* (*right* and *law*), yet they ought to be distinguished, because RIGHT consisteth in liberty to do or to forbear, whereas LAW determineth and bindeth to one of them; so that law and right differ as much as obligation and liberty, which in one and the same matter are inconsistent.

[4] And because the condition of man (as hath been declared in the precedent chapter) is a condition of war of everyone against everyone (in which case everyone is governed by his own reason and there is nothing he can make use of that may not be a help unto him in preserving his life against his enemies), it followeth that in such a condition every man has a right to everything, even to one another's body. And therefore, as long as this natural right of every man to everything endureth, there can be no security to any man (how strong or wise soever he be) of living out the time which nature ordinarily alloweth men to live. And consequently it is a precept, or general rule, of reason *that every man ought to endeavour peace, as far as he has hope of obtaining it, and when he cannot obtain it, that he may seek and use all helps and advantages of war.* The first branch of which rule containeth the first and fundamental law of nature, which is *to seek peace, and follow it.* The second, the sum of the right of nature, which is *by all means we can, to defend ourselves.*

[5] From this fundamental law of nature, by which men are commanded to endeavour peace, is derived this second law: *that a man be willing, when others are so too, as far-forth as for peace and defence of himself he shall think it necessary, to lay down this right to all things, and be contented with so much liberty against other men, as he would allow other men against himself.* For as long as every man holdeth this right of doing anything he liketh, so long are all men in the condition of war. But if other men will not lay down their right as well as he, then there is no reason for anyone to divest himself of his; for that were to expose himself to prey (which no man is bound to), rather than to dispose himself

to peace. This is that law of the Gospel: "whatsoever you require that others should do to you, that do ye to them." And that law of all men: *quod tibi fieri non vis, alteri ne feceris.*

[6] To *lay down* a man's *right* to anything is to *divest* himself of the *liberty* of hindering another of the benefit of his own right to the same. For he that renounceth or passeth away his right giveth not to any other man a right which he had not before (because there is nothing to which every man had not right by nature), but only standeth out of his way, that he may enjoy his own original right without hindrance from him, not without hindrance from another. So that the effect which redoundeth to one man by another man's defect of right is but so much diminution of impediments to the use of his own right original.

[7] Right is laid aside either by simply renouncing it or by transferring it to another. By *simply* RENOUNCING, when he cares not to whom the benefit thereof redoundeth. By TRANSFERRING, when he intendeth the benefit thereof to some certain person or persons. And when a man hath in either manner abandoned or granted away his right, then is he said to be OBLIGED or BOUND not to hinder those to whom such right is granted or abandoned from the benefit of it; and [it is said] that he *ought,* and it is his DUTY, not to make void that voluntary act of his own, and that such hindrance is INJUSTICE, and INJURY, as being *sine jure* [without right], the right being before renounced or transferred. So that *injury* or *injustice,* in the controversies of the world, is somewhat like to that which in the disputations of scholars is called absurdity. For as it is there called an *absurdity* to contradict what one maintained in the beginning, so in the world it is called injustice and injury voluntarily to undo that which from the beginning he had voluntarily done.

The way by which a man either simply renounceth or transferreth his right is a declaration, or signification by some voluntary and sufficient sign or signs, that he doth so renounce or transfer, or hath so renounced or transferred the same, to him that accepteth it. And these signs are either words only, or actions only, or (as it happeneth most often) both words and actions. And the same are the BONDS by which men are bound and obliged, bonds that have their strength, not from their own nature (for nothing is more easily broken than a man's word) but from fear of some evil consequence upon the rupture.

[8] Whensoever a man transferreth his right or renounceth it, it is either in consideration of some right reciprocally transferred to himself or for some other good he hopeth for thereby. For it is a voluntary act, and of the voluntary acts of every man, the object is some *good to himself.* And therefore there be some rights which no man can be understood by any words or other signs to have abandoned

or transferred. As, first, a man cannot lay down the right of resisting them that assault him by force, to take away his life, because he cannot be understood to aim thereby at any good to himself. [Second], the same may be said of wounds, and chains, and imprisonment, both because there is no benefit consequent to such patience (as there is to the patience of suffering another to be wounded or imprisoned), as also because a man cannot tell, when he seeth men proceed against him by violence, whether they intend his death or not. [Third] and lastly, the motive and end for which this renouncing and transferring of right is introduced, is nothing else but the security of a man's person, in his life and in the means of so preserving life as not to be weary of it. And therefore if a man by words or other signs seem to despoil himself of the end for which those signs were intended, he is not to be understood as if he meant it, or that it was his will, but that he was ignorant of how such words and actions were to be interpreted.

[9] The mutual transferring of right is that which men call CONTRACT.

[10] There is difference between transferring of right to the thing and transferring (or tradition, that is, delivery) of the thing itself. For the thing may be delivered together with the translation of the right (as in buying and selling with ready money, or exchange of goods or lands); and it may be delivered some time after.

[11] Again, one of the contractors may deliver the thing contracted for on his part, and leave the other to perform his part at some determinate time after (and in the meantime be trusted); and then the contract on his part is called PACT, or COVENANT; or both parts may contract now, to perform hereafter, in which cases he that is to perform in time to come, being trusted, his performance is called *keeping of promise*, or *faith*, and the failing of performance (if it be voluntary) *violation of faith*.

[12] When the transferring of right is not mutual, but one of the parties transferreth in hope to gain thereby friendship or service from another (or from his friends), or in hope to gain the reputation of charity or magnanimity, or to deliver his mind from the pain of compassion, or in hope of reward in heaven, this is not contract, but GIFT, FREE-GIFT, GRACE, which words signify one and the same thing.

[13] Signs of contract are either *express* or *by inference*. Express are words spoken with understanding of what they signify; and such words are either of the time *present* or *past* (as, *I give, I grant, I have given, I have granted, I will that this be yours*), or of the future (as, *I will give, I will grant*), which words of the future are called PROMISE.

[14] Signs by inference are: sometimes the consequence of words, sometimes the consequence of silence; sometimes the consequence of actions, sometimes the consequence of forbearing an action; and

generally a sign by inference of any contract is whatsoever sufficiently argues the will of the contractor.

[15] Words alone, if they be of the time to come, and contain a bare promise, are an insufficient sign of a free-gift, and therefore not obligatory. For if they be of the time to come (as, *tomorrow I will give*), they are a sign I have not given yet, and consequently that my right is not transferred, but remaineth till I transfer it by some other act. But if the words be of the time present or past (as, *I have given, or do give to be delivered tomorrow*), then is my tomorrow's right given away today; and that by the virtue of the words, though there were no other argument of my will. And there is a great difference in the signification of these words: *volo hoc tuum esse cras* and *cras dabo* (that is, between *I will that this be thine tomorrow* and *I will give it thee tomorrow*); for the word *I will* in the former manner of speech signifies an act of the will present, but in the latter it signifies a promise of an act of the will to come; and therefore the former words, being of the present, transfer a future right; the latter, that be of the future, transfer nothing.

But if there be other signs of the will to transfer a right besides words, then though the gift be free, yet may the right be understood to pass by words of the future (as, if a man propound a prize to him that comes first to the end of a race, the gift is free, and though the words be of the future, yet the right passeth; for if he would not have his words so be understood, he should not have let them run).

[16] In contracts the right passeth, not only where the words are of the time present or past, but also where they are of the future, because all contract is mutual translation, or change of right; and therefore he that promiseth only (because he hath already received the benefit for which he promiseth) is to be understood as if he intended the right should pass; for unless he had been content to have his words so understood, the other would not have performed his part first. And for that cause, in buying and selling, and other acts of contract, a promise is equivalent to a covenant, and therefore obligatory.

[17] He that performeth first in the case of a contract is said to MERIT that which he is to receive by the performance of the other, and he hath it as *due*. Also when a prize is propounded to many, which is to be given to him only that winneth (or money is thrown amongst many, to be enjoyed by them that catch it), though this be a free-gift, yet so to win (or so to catch) is to *merit*, and to have it as DUE. For the right is transferred in the propounding of the prize (and in throwing down the money), though it be not determined to whom but by the event of the contention.

But there is between these two sorts of merit, this difference: that in contract I merit by virtue of my own power, and the contractor's need; but in this case of free-gift, I am enabled to merit only by the benignity of the giver; in contract I merit at the contractor's hand that he should depart with his right; in this case of gift, I merit not that the giver should part with his right, but that when he has parted with it, it should be mine rather than another's.

And this I think to be the meaning of that distinction of the Schools between *meritum congrui* and *meritum condigni*. For God Almighty having promised Paradise to those men (hoodwinked with carnal desires) that can walk through this world according to the precepts and limits prescribed by him, they say: he that shall so walk shall merit Paradise *ex congruo*. But because no man can demand a right to it, by his own righteousness or any other power in himself, but by the free grace of God only, they say: no man can merit Paradise *ex condigno*. This, I say, I think is the meaning of that distinction; but because disputers do not agree upon the signification of their own terms of art longer than it serves their turn, I will not affirm anything of their meaning. Only this I say: when a gift is given indefinitely, as a prize to be contended for, he that winneth meriteth, and may claim the prize as due.

[18] If a covenant be made wherein neither of the parties perform presently, but trust one another, in the condition of mere nature (which is a condition of war of every man against every man) upon any reasonable suspicion it is void; but if there be a common power set over them both, with right and force sufficient to compel performance, it is not void. For he that performeth first has no assurance the other will perform after, because the bonds of words are too weak to bridle men's ambition, avarice, anger, and other passions, without the fear of some coercive power; which in the condition of mere nature, where all men are equal and judges of the justness of their own fears, cannot possibly be supposed. And therefore, he which performeth first does but betray himself to his enemy, contrary to the right (he can never abandon) of defending his life and means of living.

[19] But in a civil estate, where there is a power set up to constrain those that would otherwise violate their faith, that fear is no more reasonable; and for that cause, he which by the covenant is to perform first is obliged so to do.

[20] The cause of fear which maketh such a covenant invalid must be always something arising after the covenant made (as some new fact or other sign of the will not to perform), else it cannot make the covenant void. For that which could not hinder a man from promising, ought not to be admitted as a hindrance of performing.

[21] He that transferreth any right transferreth the means of enjoying it, as far as lieth in his power. As he that selleth land is understood to transfer the herbage and whatsoever grows upon it; nor can he that sells a mill turn away the stream that drives it. And they that give to a man the right of government in sovereignty are understood to give him the right of levying money to maintain soldiers, and of appointing magistrates for the administration of justice.

[22] To make covenants with brute beasts is impossible because, not understanding our speech, they understand not, nor accept of, any translation of right, nor can translate any right to another; and without mutual acceptation, there is no covenant.

[23] To make covenant with God is impossible, but by mediation of such as God speaketh to (either by revelation supernatural or by His lieutenants that govern under him and in his name); for otherwise we know not whether our covenants be accepted or not. And therefore, they that vow anything contrary to any law of nature vow in vain, as being a thing unjust to pay such vow. And if it be a thing commanded by the law of nature, it is not the vow, but the law that binds them.

[24] The matter or subject of a covenant is always something that falleth under deliberation (for to covenant is an act of the will; that is to say an act, and the last act, of deliberation) and is therefore always understood to be something to come, and which is judged possible for him that covenanteth to perform.

[25] And therefore, to promise that which is known to be impossible is no covenant. But if that prove impossible afterwards which before was thought possible, the covenant is valid and bindeth, though not to the thing itself, yet to the value; or, if that also be impossible, to the unfeigned endeavour of performing as much as is possible (for to more no man can be obliged).

[26] Men are freed of their covenants two ways: by performing or by being forgiven. For performance is the natural end of obligation; and forgiveness, the restitution of liberty (as being a retransferring of that right in which the obligation consisted).

[27] Covenants entered into by fear, in the condition of mere nature, are obligatory. For example, if I covenant to pay a ransom, or service, for my life, to an enemy, I am bound by it. For it is a contract wherein one receiveth the benefit of life; the other is to receive money, or service, for it; and consequently, where no other law (as in the condition of mere nature) forbiddeth the performance, the covenant is valid. Therefore prisoners of war, if trusted with the payment of their ransom, are obliged to pay it; and if a weaker prince make a

disadvantageous peace with a stronger, for fear, he is bound to keep it, unless (as hath been said before [¶20]) there ariseth some new and just cause of fear, to renew the war. And even in commonwealths, if I be forced to redeem myself from a thief by promising him money, I am bound to pay it, till the civil law discharge me. For whatsoever I may lawfully do without obligation, the same I may lawfully covenant to do through fear; and what I lawfully covenant, I cannot lawfully break.

[28] A former covenant makes void a later. For a man that hath passed away his right to one man today, hath it not to pass tomorrow to another; and therefore the later promise passeth no right, but is null.

[29] A covenant not to defend myself from force by force is always void. For (as I have showed before) no man can transfer or lay down his right to save himself from death, wounds, and imprisonment (the avoiding whereof is the only end of laying down any right), and therefore the promise of not resisting force in no covenant transferreth any right, nor is obliging. For though a man may covenant thus *unless I do so, or so, kill me,* he cannot covenant thus *unless I do so, or so, I will not resist you, when you come to kill me.* For man by nature chooseth the lesser evil, which is danger of death in resisting, rather than the greater, which is certain and present death in not resisting. And this is granted to be true by all men, in that they lead criminals to execution and prison with armed men, notwithstanding that such criminals have consented to the law by which they are condemned.

[30] A covenant to accuse oneself, without assurance of pardon, is likewise invalid. For in the condition of nature, where every man is judge, there is no place for accusation; and in the civil state the accusation is followed with punishment, which being force, a man is not obliged not to resist. The same is also true of the accusation of those by whose condemnation a man falls into misery (as, of a father, wife, or benefactor). For the testimony of such an accuser, if it be not willingly given, is presumed to be corrupted by nature, and therefore not to be received; and where a man's testimony is not to be credited, he is not bound to give it. Also accusations upon torture are not to be reputed as testimonies. For torture is to be used but as means of conjecture and light in the further examination and search of truth; and what is in that case confessed tendeth to the ease of him that is tortured, not to the informing of the torturers, and therefore ought not to have the credit of a sufficient testimony; for whether he deliver himself by true or false accusation, he does it by the right of preserving his own life.

[31] The force of words being (as I have formerly noted) too weak to hold men to the performance of their covenants, there are in man's nature but two imaginable helps to strengthen it. And those are either a fear of the consequence of breaking their word, or a glory or pride in appearing not to need to break it. This latter is a generosity too rarely found to be presumed on, especially in the pursuers of wealth, command, or sensual pleasure (which are the greatest part of mankind).

The passion to be reckoned upon is fear, whereof there be two very general objects: one, the power of spirits invisible; the other, the power of those men they shall therein offend. Of these two, though the former be the greater power, yet the fear of the latter is commonly the greater fear. The fear of the former is in every man his own religion, which hath place in the nature of man before civil society. The latter hath not so, at least not place enough to keep men to their promises, because in the condition of mere nature the inequality of power is not discerned but by the event of battle.

So that before the time of civil society, or in the interruption thereof by war, there is nothing can strengthen a covenant of peace agreed on, against the temptations of avarice, ambition, lust, or other strong desire, but the fear of that invisible power which they every one worship as God and fear as a revenger of their perfidy. All therefore that can be done between two men not subject to civil power is to put one another to swear by the God he feareth; which *swearing*, or OATH, is a *form of speech, added to a promise, by which he that promiseth signifieth that unless he perform, he renounceth the mercy of his God, or calleth to him for vengeance on himself.* Such was the heathen form *Let* Jupiter *kill me else, as I kill this beast.* So is our form *I shall do thus, and thus, so help me God.* And this, with the rites and ceremonies which everyone useth in his own religion, that the fear of breaking faith might be the greater.

[32] By this it appears that an oath taken according to any other form or rite than his that sweareth is in vain, and no oath, and that there is no swearing by anything which the swearer thinks not God. For though men have sometimes used to swear by their kings, for fear or flattery, yet they would have it thereby understood they attributed to them divine honour. And that swearing unnecessarily by God is but profaning of his name, and swearing by other things, as men do in common discourse, is not swearing, but an impious custom, gotten by too much vehemence of talking.

[33] It appears also that the oath adds nothing to the obligation. For a covenant, if lawful, binds in the sight of God without the oath as much as with it; if unlawful, bindeth not at all, though it be confirmed with an oath.

Chapter XV

Of Other Laws of Nature

[1] From that law of nature by which we are obliged to transfer to another such rights as, being retained, hinder the peace of mankind, there followeth a third, which is this *that men perform their covenants made,* without which covenants are in vain, and but empty words, and the right of all men to all things remaining, we are still in the condition of war.

[2] And in this law of nature consisteth the fountain and original of JUSTICE. For where no covenant hath preceded, there hath no right been transferred, and every man has right to everything; and consequently, no action can be unjust. But when a covenant is made, then to break it is *unjust;* and the definition of INJUSTICE is no other than *the not performance of covenant.* And whatsoever is not unjust, is *just.*

[3] But because covenants of mutual trust where there is a fear of not performance on either part (as hath been said in the former chapter [xiv, 18–20]) are invalid, though the original of justice be the making of covenants, yet injustice actually there can be none till the cause of such fear be taken away, which, while men are in the natural condition of war, cannot be done. Therefore, before the names of just and unjust can have place, there must be some coercive power to compel men equally to the performance of their covenants, by the terror of some punishment greater than the benefit they expect by the breach of their covenant, and to make good that propriety which by mutual contract men acquire, in recompense of the universal right they abandon; and such power there is none before the erection of a commonwealth. And this is also to be gathered out of the ordinary definition of justice in the Schools; for they say that *justice is the constant will of giving to every man his own.* And therefore where there is no *own,* that is, no propriety, there is no injustice; and where there is no coercive power erected, that is, where there is no commonwealth, there is no propriety, all men having right to all things; therefore where there is no commonwealth, there nothing is unjust. So that the nature of justice consisteth in keeping of valid covenants; but the validity of covenants begins not but with the constitution of a civil power sufficient to compel men to keep them; and then it is also that propriety begins.

[4] The fool hath said in his heart: "there is no such thing as justice"; and sometimes also with his tongue, seriously alleging that: "every man's conservation and contentment being committed to his own care, there could be no reason why every man might not do what he

thought conduced thereunto, and therefore also to make or not make, keep or not keep, covenants was not against reason, when it conduced to one's benefit." He does not therein deny that there be covenants, and that they are sometimes broken, sometimes kept, and that such breach of them may be called injustice, and the observance of them justice; but he questioneth whether injustice, taking away the fear of God (for the same fool hath said in his heart there is no God), may not sometimes stand with that reason which dictateth to every man his own good; and particularly then, when it conduceth to such a benefit as shall put a man in a condition to neglect, not only the dispraise and revilings, but also the power of other men.

"The kingdom of God is gotten by violence; but what if it could be gotten by unjust violence? were it against reason so to get it, when it is impossible to receive hurt by it? and if it be not against reason, it is not against justice; or else justice is not to be approved for good."

From such reasoning as this, successful wickedness hath obtained the name of virtue, and some that in all other things have disallowed the violation of faith, yet have allowed it when it is for the getting of a kingdom. And the heathen that believed that *Saturn* was deposed by his son *Jupiter* believed nevertheless the same *Jupiter* to be the avenger of injustice, somewhat like to a piece of law in *Coke's* Commentaries on *Littleton,* where he says: if the right heir of the crown be attainted of treason, yet the crown shall descend to him, and *eo instante* [immediately] the attainder be void; from which instances a man will be very prone to infer that "when the heir apparent of a kingdom shall kill him that is in possession, though his father, you may call it injustice, or by what other name you will, yet it can never be against reason, seeing all the voluntary actions of men tend to the benefit of themselves, and those actions are most reasonable that conduce most to their ends." This specious reasoning is nevertheless false.

[5] For the question is not of promises mutual where there is no security of performance on either side (as when there is no civil power erected over the parties promising), for such promises are no covenants, but either where one of the parties has performed already, or where there is a power to make him perform, there is the question whether it be against reason, that is, against the benefit of the other to perform or not. And I say it is not against reason. For the manifestation whereof we are to consider: first, that when a man doth a thing which, notwithstanding anything can be foreseen and reckoned on, tendeth to his own destruction (howsoever some accident which he could not expect, arriving, may turn it to his benefit), yet such events do not make it reasonably or wisely done. Secondly, that in a condition of

war wherein every man to every man (for want of a common power to keep them all in awe) is an enemy, there is no man can hope by his own strength or wit to defend himself from destruction without the help of confederates (where everyone expects the same defence by the confederation that anyone else does); and therefore, he which declares he thinks it reason to deceive those that help him can in reason expect no other means of safety than what can be had from his own single power. He, therefore, that breaketh his covenant, and consequently declareth that he thinks he may with reason do so, cannot be received into any society that unite themselves for peace and defence but by the error of them that receive him; nor when he is received, be retained in it without seeing the danger of their error; which errors a man cannot reasonably reckon upon as the means of his security; and therefore, if he be left or cast out of society, he perisheth; and if he live in society, it is by the errors of other men, which he could not foresee nor reckon upon; and consequently [he has acted] against the reason of his preservation, and so as all men that contribute not to his destruction forbear him only out of ignorance of what is good for themselves.

[6] As for the instance of gaining the secure and perpetual felicity of heaven by any way, it is frivolous, there being but one way imaginable, and that is not breaking, but keeping of covenant.

[7] And for the other instance of attaining sovereignty by rebellion, it is manifest that, though the event follow, yet because it cannot reasonably be expected (but rather the contrary), and because (by gaining it so) others are taught to gain the same in like manner, the attempt thereof is against reason. Justice, therefore, that is to say, keeping of covenant, is a rule of reason by which we are forbidden to do anything destructive to our life, and consequently a law of nature.

[8] There be some that proceed further, and will not have the law of nature to be those rules which conduce to the preservation of man's life on earth, but to the attaining of an eternal felicity after death, to which they think the breach of covenant may conduce, and consequently be just and reasonable (such are they that think it a work of merit to kill, or depose, or rebel against the sovereign power constituted over them by their own consent.) But because there is no natural knowledge of man's estate after death, much less of the reward that is then to be given to breach of faith, but only a belief grounded upon other men's saying that they know it supernaturally, or that they know those that knew them that knew others that knew it supernaturally, breach of faith cannot be called a precept of reason or nature.

[9] Others, that allow for a law of nature the keeping of faith, do nevertheless make exception of certain persons (as heretics and such as use not to perform their covenant to others); and this also is against reason. For if any fault of a man be sufficient to discharge our covenant made, the same ought in reason to have been sufficient to have hindered the making of it.

[10] The names of just and unjust, when they are attributed to men, signify one thing; and when they are attributed to actions, another. When they are attributed to men, they signify conformity or inconformity of manners to reason. But when they are attributed to actions, they signify the conformity or inconformity to reason, not of manners or manner of life, but of particular actions. A just man, therefore, is he that taketh all the care he can that his actions may be all just; and an unjust man is he that neglecteth it. And such men are more often in our language styled by the names of righteous and unrighteous, than just and unjust, though the meaning be the same. Therefore a righteous man does not lose that title by one or a few unjust actions that proceed from sudden passion or mistake of things or persons; nor does an unrighteous man lose his character for such actions as he does or forbears to do for fear, because his will is not framed by the justice, but by the apparent benefit of what he is to do. That which gives to human actions the relish of justice is a certain nobleness or gallantness of courage (rarely found) by which a man scorns to be beholden for the contentment of his life to fraud or breach of promise. This justice of the manners is that which is meant where justice is called a virtue, and injustice a vice.

[11] But the justice of actions denominates men, not just, but *guiltless;* and the injustice of the same (which is also called injury) gives them but the name of *guilty.*

[12] Again, the injustice of manners is the disposition or aptitude to do injury, and is injustice before it proceed to act and without supposing any individual person injured. But the injustice of an action (that is to say injury) supposeth an individual person injured, namely, him to whom the covenant was made; and therefore, many times the injury is received by one man, when the damage redoundeth to another. As when the master commandeth his servant to give money to a stranger; if it be not done, the injury is done to the master, whom he had before covenanted to obey, but the damage redoundeth to the stranger, to whom he had no obligation, and therefore could not injure him. And so also in commonwealths, private men may remit to one another their debts, but not robberies or other violences whereby they are endamaged; because the detaining of debt is an injury to

themselves, but robbery and violence are injuries to the person of the commonwealth.

[13] Whatsoever is done to a man conformable to his own will, signified to the doer, is no injury to him. For if he that doeth it hath not passed away his original right to do what he please by some antecedent covenant, there is no breach of covenant, and therefore no injury done him. And if he have, then his will [i.e., that of the person acted on] to have it done being signified, is a release of that covenant; and so again there is no injury done him.

[14] Justice of actions is by writers divided into *commutative* and *distributive;* and the former they say consisteth in proportion arithmetical; the latter, in proportion geometrical. Commutative, therefore, they place in the equality of value of the things contracted for; and distributive, in the distribution of equal benefit to men of equal merit (as if it were injustice to sell dearer than we buy, or to give more to a man than he merits). The value of all things contracted for is measured by the appetite of the contractors; and therefore the just value is that which they be contented to give. And merit (besides that which is by covenant, where the performance on one part meriteth the performance of the other part, and falls under justice commutative, not distributive) is not due by justice, but is rewarded of grace only.

And therefore this distinction, in the sense wherein it useth to be expounded, is not right. To speak properly, commutative justice is the justice of a contractor, that is, a performance of covenant (in buying and selling, hiring and letting to hire, lending and borrowing, exchanging, bartering, and other acts of contract). [15] And distributive justice [is] the justice of an arbitrator, that is to say, the act of defining what is just. Wherein (being trusted by them that make him arbitrator) if he perform his trust, he is said to distribute to every man his own; and this is indeed just distribution, and may be called (though improperly) distributive justice (but more properly, equity, which also is a law of nature, as shall be shown in due place [¶24]).

[16] As justice dependeth on antecedent covenant, so does GRATITUDE depend on antecedent grace, that is to say, antecedent free-gift; and is the fourth law of nature, which may be conceived in this form *that a man which receiveth benefit from another of mere grace endeavour that he which giveth it have no reasonable cause to repent him of his good will.* For no man giveth but with intention of good to himself, because gift is voluntary, and of all voluntary acts the object is to every man his own good; of which, if men see they shall be frustrated, there will be no beginning of benevolence or trust; nor, consequently, of mutual help,

nor of reconciliation of one man to another; and therefore they are to remain still in the condition of war, which is contrary to the first and fundamental law of nature, which commandeth men to *seek peace.* The breach of this law is called *ingratitude,* and hath the same relation to grace that injustice hath to obligation by covenant.

[17] A fifth law of nature is COMPLAISANCE, that is to say, *that every man strive to accommodate himself to the rest.* For the understanding whereof we may consider that there is, in men's aptness to society, a diversity of nature rising from their diversity of affections, not unlike to that we see in stones brought together for building of an edifice. For as that stone which (by the asperity and irregularity of figure) takes more room from others than itself fills, and (for the hardness) cannot be easily made plain, and thereby hindereth the building, is by the builders cast away as unprofitable and troublesome, so also a man that (by asperity of nature) will strive to retain those things which to himself are superfluous and to others necessary, and (for the stubbornness of his passions) cannot be corrected, is to be left or cast out of society as cumbersome thereunto. For seeing every man, not only by right, but also by necessity of nature, is supposed to endeavour all he can to obtain that which is necessary for his conservation, he that shall oppose himself against it for things superfluous is guilty of the war that thereupon is to follow; and, therefore, doth that which is contrary to the fundamental law of nature, which commandeth *to seek peace.* The observers of this law may be called SOCIABLE (the Latins call them *commodi*); the contrary, *stubborn, insociable, forward, intractable.*

[18] A sixth law of nature is this *that upon caution of the future time, a man ought to pardon the offences past of them that, repenting, desire it.* For PARDON is nothing but granting of peace, which (though granted to them that persevere in their hostility be not peace but fear, yet) not granted to them that give caution of the future time is sign of an aversion to peace; and therefore contrary to the law of nature.

[19] A seventh is *that in revenges* (that is, retribution of evil for evil) *men look not at the greatness of the evil past, but the greatness of the good to follow.* Whereby we are forbidden to inflict punishment with any other design than for correction of the offender, or direction of others. For this law is consequent to the next before it, that commandeth pardon upon security of the future time. Besides, revenge without respect to the example and profit to come is a triumph, or glorying, in the hurt of another, tending to no end (for the end is always somewhat to come); and glorying to no end is vain-glory, and contrary to reason; and to hurt without reason tendeth to the introduction of war, which is against the law of nature, and is commonly styled by the name of *cruelty.*

[20] And because all signs of hatred or contempt provoke to fight, insomuch as most men choose rather to hazard their life than not to be revenged, we may in the eighth place, for a law of nature, set down this precept *that no man by deed, word, countenance, or gesture, declare hatred or contempt of another.* The breach of which law is commonly called *contumely.*

[21] The question 'who is the better man?' has no place in the condition of mere nature, where (as has been shewn before) all men are equal. The inequality that now is, has been introduced by the laws civil. I know that *Aristotle* (in the first book of his Politics [ch. iii–vii], for a foundation of his doctrine) maketh men by nature, some more worthy to command (meaning the wiser sort, such as he thought himself to be for his philosophy), others to serve (meaning those that had strong bodies, but were not philosophers as he), as if master and servant were not introduced by consent of men, but by difference of wit; which is not only against reason, but also against experience. For there are very few so foolish that had not rather govern themselves than be governed by others; nor when the wise in their own conceit contend by force with them who distrust their own wisdom, do they always, or often, or almost at any time, get the victory. If nature therefore have made men equal, that equality is to be acknowledged; or if nature have made men unequal, yet because men that think themselves equal will not enter into conditions of peace but upon equal terms, such equality must be admitted. And therefore for the ninth law of nature, I put this *that every man acknowledge other for his equal by nature.* The breach of this precept is *pride.*

[22] On this law dependeth another: *that at the entrance into conditions of peace, no man require to reserve to himself any right which he is not content should be reserved to every one of the rest.* As it is necessary, for all men that seek peace, to lay down certain rights of nature (that is to say, not to have liberty to do all they list), so is it necessary, for man's life to retain some (as, right to govern their own bodies, [right to] enjoy air, water, motion, ways to go from place to place, and all things else without which a man cannot live, or not live well). If in this case, at the making of peace, men require for themselves that which they would not have to be granted to others, they do contrary to the precedent law, that commandeth the acknowledgment of natural equality, and therefore also against the law of nature. The observers of this law are those we call *modest,* and the breakers *arrogant* men. The Greeks call the violation of this law *pleonexia,* that is, a desire of more than their share.

[23] Also *if a man be trusted to judge between man and man,* it is a precept of the law of nature that *he deal equally between them.* For without

that, the controversies of men cannot be determined but by war. He, therefore, that is partial in judgment doth what in him lies to deter men from the use of judges and arbitrators; and consequently (against the fundamental law of nature), is the cause of war.

[24] The observance of this law (from the equal distribution to each man of that which in reason belongeth to him) is called EQUITY, and (as I have said before) distributive justice; the violation [is called] *acception of persons* (*prosopolepsia*).

[25] And from this followeth another law: *that such things as cannot be divided be enjoyed in common, if it can be; and if the quantity of the thing permit, without stint; otherwise proportionably to the number of them that have right*. For otherwise the distribution is unequal, and contrary to equity.

[26] But some things there be that can neither be divided nor enjoyed in common. Then the law of nature which prescribeth equity requireth *that the entire right (or else, making the use alternate, the first possession) be determined by lot*. For equal distribution is of the law of nature, and other means of equal distribution cannot be imagined.

[27] Of *lots* there be two sorts: *arbitrary* and *natural*. Arbitrary is that which is agreed on by the competitors; natural is either *primogeniture* (which the Greek calls *kleronomia*, which signifies, *given by lot*) or *first seizure*.

[28] And therefore those things which cannot be enjoyed in common, nor divided, ought to be adjudged to the first possessor; and in some cases to the first-born, as acquired by lot.

[29] It is also a law of nature *that all men that mediate peace be allowed safe conduct*. For the law that commandeth peace, as the *end*, commandeth intercession, as the *means*; and to intercession the means is safe conduct.

[30] And because (though men be never so willing to observe these laws) there may nevertheless arise questions concerning a man's action (first, whether it were done or not done; secondly, if done, whether against the law or not against the law; the former whereof is called a question *of fact*; the latter a question *of right*), therefore unless the parties to the question covenant mutually to stand to the sentence of another, they are as far from peace as ever. This other to whose sentence they submit, is called an ARBITRATOR. And therefore it is of the law of nature *that they that are at controversy, submit their right to the judgment of an arbitrator*.

[31] And seeing every man is presumed to do all things in order to his own benefit, *no man is a fit arbitrator in his own cause*; and if he were never so fit, yet (equity allowing to each party equal benefit) if

one be admitted to be judge, the other is to be admitted also; and so the controversy, that is, the cause of war, remains, against the law of nature.

[32] For the same reason no man in any cause ought to be received for arbitrator, to whom greater profit, or honour, or pleasure apparently ariseth out of the victory of one party, than of the other; for he hath taken (though an unavoidable bribe, yet) a bribe; and no man can be obliged to trust him. And thus also the controversy, and the condition of war remaineth, contrary to the law of nature.

[33] And in a controversy of *fact* the judge (being to give no more credit to one [litigant] than to the other, if there be no other arguments) must give credit to a third [a non-litigant witness], or to a third and fourth; or more; for else the question is undecided, and left to force, contrary to the law of nature.

[34] These are the laws of nature dictating peace for a means of the conservation of men in multitudes; and which only concern the doctrine of civil society. There be other things tending to the destruction of particular men (as drunkenness and all other parts of intemperance), which may therefore also be reckoned amongst those things which the law of nature hath forbidden; but are not necessary to be mentioned, nor are pertinent enough to this place.

[35] And though this may seem too subtle a deduction of the laws of nature to be taken notice of by all men (whereof the most part are too busy in getting food, and the rest too negligent, to understand), yet to leave all men inexcusable they have been contracted into one easy sum, intelligible even to the meanest capacity, and that is *Do not that to another, which thou wouldst not have done to thyself;* which sheweth him that he has no more to do in learning the laws of nature but (when, weighing the actions of other men with his own, they seem too heavy) to put them into the other part of the balance, and his own into their place, that his own passions and self-love may add nothing to the weight; and then there is none of these laws of nature that will not appear unto him very reasonable.

[36] The laws of nature oblige *in foro interno,* that is to say, they bind to a desire they should take place; but *in foro externo,* that is, to the putting them in act, not always. For he that should be modest and tractable, and perform all he promises, in such time and place where no man else should do so, should but make himself a prey to others, and procure his own certain ruin, contrary to the ground of all laws of nature, which tend to nature's preservation. And again, he that having sufficient security that others shall observe the same laws towards him, observes them not himself,

seeketh not peace, but war, and consequently the destruction of his nature by violence.

[37] And whatsoever laws bind *in foro interno* may be broken, not only by a fact contrary to the law, but also by a fact according to it, in case a man think it contrary. For though his action in this case be according to the law, yet his purpose was against the law, which, where the obligation is *in foro interno,* is a breach.

[38] The laws of nature are immutable and eternal; for injustice, ingratitude, arrogance, pride, iniquity, acception of persons, and the rest, can never be made lawful. For it can never be that war shall preserve life, and peace destroy it.

[39] The same laws, because they oblige only to a desire and endeavour (I mean an unfeigned and constant endeavour) are easy to be observed. For in that they require nothing but endeavour, he that endeavoureth their performance fulfilleth them; and he that fulfilleth the law is just.

[40] And the science of them [the laws of nature] is the true and only moral philosophy. For moral philosophy is nothing else but the science of what is *good* and *evil* in the conversation and society of mankind. *Good* and *evil* are names that signify our appetites and aversions, which in different tempers, customs, and doctrines of men are different; and divers men differ not only in their judgment on the senses (of what is pleasant and unpleasant to the taste, smell, hearing, touch, and sight), but also of what is conformable or disagreeable to reason in the actions of common life. Nay, the same man in divers times differs from himself, and one time praiseth (that is, calleth good) what another time he dispraiseth (and calleth evil); from whence arise disputes, controversies, and at last war. And therefore so long as man is in the condition of mere nature (which is a condition of war) as private appetite is the measure of good and evil; and consequently, all men agree on this, that peace is good; and therefore also the way or means of peace (which, as I have shewed before, are *justice, gratitude, modesty, equity, mercy,* and the rest of the laws of nature) are good (that is to say, *moral virtues*), and their contrary vices, evil.

Now the science of virtue and vice is moral philosophy; and therefore the true doctrine of the laws of nature is the true moral philosophy. But the writers of moral philosophy, though they acknowledge the same virtues and vices, yet not seeing wherein consisted their goodness, nor that they come to be praised as the means of peaceable, sociable, and comfortable living, place them in a mediocrity of passions (as if not the cause, but the degree of daring, made fortitude; or not the cause, but the quantity of a gift, made liberality).

[41] These dictates of reason men use to call by the name of laws, but improperly; for they are but conclusions or theorems concerning what conduceth to the conservation and defence of themselves, whereas law, properly, is the word of him that by right hath command over others. But yet if we consider the same theorems, as delivered in the word of God, that by right commandeth all things, then are they properly called laws.

7

Butler and Hume: Inherent Tendencies toward Altruism

Joseph Butler as a protestant bishop was a deeply committed Christian. He lived in the early eighteenth century. David Hume, in the next generation, was a "free thinker"—definitely not a committed Christian. There is evidence that Hume was denied academic appointments because of his irreligious views. Nevertheless Hume and Butler shared some philosophical beliefs, and Hume actually wrote an admiring letter to Butler.

They shared a sense of the psychological root of morality. This was the benevolent inclination that we already have noted the Chinese philosopher Mencius held was a feature of normal human nature. In relation to this, Butler is almost unique among philosophers. Philosophers notoriously tend to argue with one another, and even the most distinguished philosophical work is likely to draw objections. To the best of my knowledge, Butler's thesis about benevolent inclination (in normal human natures) is hardly ever attacked.

As Hume saw it, Butler was right, and his rightness was the key to understanding the phenomenon of morality. The sympathy that goes along with benevolent inclination allows us to identify with someone who is harmed or mistreated. This contributes to a sense that such things should not be permitted, which is translated into the formation of moral rules.

Benevolent inclination and sympathy not only accounted for the development of morality but also helped account for the fuller development of the social contract. As Hume pointed out, even primitive people have families that they may care about. This lends itself to a general readiness to care about other people. This in turn can contribute to a fuller sense of a social contract.

Sermon I

Upon Human Nature

For as we have many members in one body, and all members have not the same office: so we, being many, are one body in Christ, and every one members one of another (Romans 12:4–5).

[1] The epistles of the New Testament have all of them a particular reference to the condition and usages of the Christian world at the time they were written. Therefore, as they cannot be thoroughly understood unless that condition and those usages are known and attended to, so further, though they be known, yet if they be discontinued or changed, exhortations, precepts, and illustrations of things, which refer to such circumstances now ceased or altered, cannot at this time be urged in that manner and with that force which they were to the primitive Christians. Thus the text now before us, in its first intent and design, relates to the decent management of those extraordinary gifts which were then in the church,[1] but which are now totally ceased. And even as the allusion, that "we are one body in Christ," though what the apostle here intends is equally true of Christians in all circumstances—and the consideration of it is plainly still an additional motive, over and above moral considerations, to the discharge of the several duties and offices of a Christian—yet it is manifest this allusion must have appeared with much greater force to those who, by the many difficulties they went through for the sake of their religion, were led to keep always in view the relation they stood in to their Saviour, who had undergone the same; to those who, from the idolatries of all around them and their ill treatment, were taught to consider themselves as not of the world in which they lived, but as a distinct society of themselves, with laws and ends, and principles of life and action, quite contrary to those which the world professed themselves at that time influenced by. Hence the relation of a Christian was by them considered as nearer than that of affinity and blood; and they almost literally esteemed themselves as members one of another.

From Joseph Butler, *Five Sermons*, ed. Stephen L. Darwall (Indianapolis: Hackett Publishing Co., 1983). Reprinted by permission of the publisher.

1. 1 Corinthians 12.

[2] It cannot indeed possibly be denied that our being God's creatures, and virtue being the natural law we are born under, and the whole constitution of man being plainly adapted to it, are prior obligations to piety and to virtue than the consideration that God sent his Son into the world to save it, and the motives which arise from the peculiar relation of Christians, as members one of another under Christ our Head. However, though all this be allowed, as it expressly is by the inspired writers, yet it is manifest that Christians at the time of the revelation, and immediately after, could not but insist mostly upon considerations of this latter kind.

[3] These observations show the original particular reference of the text; and the peculiar force with which the thing intended by the allusion in it, must have been felt by the primitive Christian world. They likewise afford a reason for treating it at this time in a more general way.

[4] The relation which the several parts or members of the natural body have to each other and to the whole body is here compared to the relation which each particular person in society has to other particular persons and to the whole society; and the latter is intended to be illustrated by the former. And if there be a likeness between these two relations, the consequence is obvious: that the latter shows us [we were intended] to do good to others, as the former shows us that [the several members of the natural body were intended to be instruments of good to each other and to the whole body]. But as there is scarce any ground for a comparison between society and the mere material body, this without the mind being a dead unactive thing, much less can the comparison be carried to any length. And since the apostle speaks of the several members as having distinct offices, which implies the mind, it cannot be thought an unallowable liberty, instead of the *body* and *its members,* to substitute the *whole nature of man* and *all the variety of internal principles which belong to it*. And then the comparison will be between the nature of man as respecting self and tending to private good, his own preservation and happiness, and the nature of man as having respect to society and tending to promote public good, the happiness of that society. These ends do indeed perfectly coincide; and to aim at public and private good are so far from being inconsistent that they mutually promote each other; yet in the following discourse they must be considered as entirely distinct, otherwise the nature of man as tending to one, or as tending to the other, cannot be compared. There can no comparison be made without considering the things compared as distinct and different.

[5] From this review and comparison of the nature of man as respecting self as respecting society, it will plainly appear that there are as real and the same kind of indications in human nature that we were made for society and to do good to our fellow creatures, as that we were intended to take care of our own life and health and private good; and that the same objections lie against one of these assertions as against the other.

For,

[6] First, there is a natural principle of *benevolence*[2] in man, which is in some degree to *society* what *self-love* is to the *individual*. And if

2. Suppose a man of learning to be writing a grave book upon *human nature*, and to show in several parts of it that he had an insight into the subject he was considering; amongst other things, the following one would require to be accounted for: the appearance of benevolence or goodwill in men towards each other in the instances of natural relation, and in others (Hobbes, *Of Human Nature*, c. ix. §7). Cautious of being deceived with outward show, he retires within himself to see exactly what that is in the mind of man from whence this appearance proceeds; and, upon deep reflection, asserts the principle in the mind to be only the love of power, and delight in the exercise of it. Would not everybody think here was a mistake of one word for another; that the philosopher was contemplating and accounting for some other human actions, some other behavior of man to man? And could anyone be thoroughly satisfied that what is commonly called benevolence or goodwill was really the affection meant, but only by being made to understand that this learned person had a general hypothesis to which the appearance of goodwill could no otherwise be reconciled? That what has this appearance is often nothing but ambition; that delight in superiority often (suppose always) mixes itself with benevolence, only makes it more specious to call it ambition than hunger, of the two: but in reality that passion does no more account for the whole appearances of goodwill than this appetite does. Is there not often the appearance of one man's wishing that good to another which he knows himself unable to procure him; and rejoicing in it, though bestowed by a third person? And can love of power anyway possibly come in to account for this desire or delight? Is there not often the appearance of men's distinguishing between two or more persons, preferring one before another, to do good to, in cases where love of power cannot in the least account for the distinction and preference? For this principle can no otherwise distinguish between objects than as it is a greater instance and exertion of power to do good to one rather than to another. Again, suppose goodwill in the mind of man to be nothing but delight in the exercise of power; men might indeed be restrained by distant and accidental considerations; but these restraints being removed, they would have a disposition to, and delight in, mischief as an exercise and proof of power: and this disposition and delight would arise from or be the same principle in the mind, as a disposition to, and delight in, charity. Thus cruelty, as distinct from envy and resentment, would

there be in mankind any disposition to friendship; if there be any such thing as compassion, for compassion is momentary love; if there be any such things as the paternal of filial affections; if there be any affection in human nature the object and end of which is the good of another—this is itself benevolence or the love of another. Be it even so short, be it in ever so low a degree, or ever so unhappily confined, it proves the assertion and points out what we were designed for, as really as though it were in a higher degree and more extensive. I must however remind you that though benevolence and self-love are different, though the former tends most directly to public good, and the latter to private, yet they are so perfectly coincident that the greatest satisfactions to ourselves depend upon our having benevolence

---

be exactly the same in the mind of man as goodwill—that one tends to the happiness, the other to the misery of our fellow creatures, is, it seems, merely an accidental circumstance, which the mind has not the least regard to. These are the absurdities which even men of capacity run into when they have occasion to belie their nature, and will perversely disclaim that image of God which was originally stamped upon it, the traces of which, however faint, are plainly discernible upon the mind of man.

If any person can in earnest doubt whether there be such a thing as goodwill in one man toward another (for the question is not concerning either the degree or extensiveness of it, but concerning the affection itself), let it be observed that whether man be thus or otherwise constituted, what is the inward frame in this particular, is a mere question of fact or natural history, not provable immediately by reason. It is therefore to be judged of and determined in the same way other facts or matters of natural history are: by appealing to the external senses or inward perceptions respectively, as the matter under consideration is cognizable by one or the other; by arguing from acknowledged facts and actions; for a great number of actions in the same kind, in different circumstances, and respecting different objects, will prove, to a certainty, what principles they do not, and, to the greatest probability, what principles they do proceed from; and, lastly, by the testimony of mankind. Now, that there is some degree of benevolence amongst men may be as strongly and plainly proved in all these ways, as it could possibly be proved, supposing there was this affection in our nature. And should anyone think fit to assert that resentment in the mind of man was of absolutely nothing but reasonable concern for our own safety, the falsity of this, and what is the real nature of that passion, could be shown in no other ways than those in which it may be shown, that there is such a thing in some degree as real goodwill in man toward man. It is sufficient that the seeds of it be implanted in our nature by God. There is, it is owned, much left for us to do upon our own heart and temper; to cultivate, to improve, to call it forth, to exercise it in a steady, uniform manner. This is our work; this is virtue and religion.

in a due degree, and that self-love is one chief security of our right behavior toward society. It may be added that their mutual coinciding, so that we can scarce promote one without the other, is equally a proof that we were made for both.

[7] Secondly, this will further appear, from observing that the *several passions and affections*, which are distinct[3] both from benevolence and self-love, do in general contribute and lead us to *public* good as really as to *private*. It might be thought too minute and particular, and would carry us too great a length, to distinguish between and compare together the several passions or appetites distinct from benevolence, whose primary use and intention is the security and good of society; and the passions distinct from self-love, whose primary intention

3. Everybody makes a distinction between self-love and the several particular passions, appetites, and affections; and yet they are often confounded again. That they are totally different, will be seen by any one who will distinguish between the passions and appetites themselves, and endeavoring after the means of their gratification. Consider the appetite of hunger, and the desire of esteem; these being the occasion both of pleasure and pain, the coolest self-love, as well as the appetites and passions themselves, may put us upon making use of the proper methods of obtaining that pleasure, and avoiding that pain; but the feelings themselves, the pain of hunger and shame, and the delight from esteem, are no more self-love than they are anything in the world. Though a man hated himself, he would as much feel the pain of hunger as he would that of the gout; and it is plainly supposable there may be creatures with self-love in them to the highest degree, who may be quite insensible and indifferent (as men in some cases are) to the contempt and esteem of those upon whom their happiness does not in some further respects depend. And as self-love and the several particular passions and appetites are in themselves totally different, so that some actions proceed from one, and some from the other, will be manifest to any who will observe the two following very supposable cases. One man rushes upon certain ruin for the gratification of a present desire; nobody will call the principle of this action self-love. Suppose another man to go through some laborious work upon promise of a great reward, without any distinct knowledge what the reward will be; this course of action cannot be ascribed to any particular passion. The former of these actions is plainly to be imputed to some particular passion or affection, the latter as plainly to the general affection or principle of self-love. That there are some particular pursuits or actions concerning which we cannot determine how far they are owing to one, and how far to the other, proceeds from this that the two principles are frequently mixed together, and run up into each other. This distinction is further explained in the eleventh sermon.

and design is the security and good of the individual.[4] It is enough to the present argument that desire of esteem from others, contempt and esteem of them, love of society as distinct from affection to the good of it, indignation against successful vice—that these are public affections or passions, have an immediate respect to others, naturally lead us to regulate our behavior in such a manner as will be of service to our fellow creatures. If any or all of these may be considered likewise as private affections, as tending to private good, this does not hinder them from being public affections, too, or destroy the good influence of them upon society, and their tendency to public good. It may be added that as persons without any conviction from reason of the desirableness of life would yet of course preserve it merely from the appetite of hunger, so by acting merely from regard (suppose) to reputation, without any consideration of the good of others, men often contribute to public good. In both these instances they are plainly instruments in the hands of another, in the hands of Providence, to carry on ends, the preservation of the individual and good of society, which they themselves have not in their view or intention. The sum is, men have various appetites, passions, and particular affections, quite distinct both from self-love and from benevolence—all of these have a tendency to promote both public and private good, and may be considered as respecting others and ourselves equally and in common; but some of them seem most immediately to respect others, or tend to public good, others of them most immediately to respect self, or tend to private good; as the former are not benevolence, so the latter are not self-love; neither sort are instances of our love either to ourselves or others, but only instances of our Maker's care and love both of the individual and the species, and proofs that He intended we should be instruments of good to each other, as well as that we should be so to ourselves.

4. If any desire to see this distinction and comparison made in a particular instance, the appetite and passion now mentioned may serve for one. Hunger is to be considered as a private appetite; because the end for which it was given us is the preservation of the individual. Desire of esteem is a public passion; because the end for which it was given us is to regulate our behavior toward society. The respect which this has to private good is as remote as the respect that has to public good: and the appetite is no more self-love than the passion is benevolence. The object and end of the former is merely food; the object and end of the latter is merely esteem; but the latter can no more be gratified without contributing to the good of society, than the former can be gratified without contributing to the preservation of the individual.

[8] Thirdly, there is a principle of reflection in men by which they distinguish between, approve and disapprove their own actions. We are plainly constituted such sort of creatures as to reflect upon our own nature. The mind can take a view of what passes within itself, its propensions, aversions, passions, affections, as respecting such objects and in such degrees, and of the several actions consequent thereupon. In this survey it approves of one, disapproves of another, and toward a third is affected in neither of these ways, but is quite indifferent. This principle in man by which he approves or disapproves his heart, temper, and actions, is conscience [for this is the strict sense of the word, though sometimes it is used so as to take in more]. And that this faculty tends to restrain men from doing mischief to each other, and leads them to do good, is too manifest to need being insisted upon. Thus, a parent has the affection of love to his children; this leads him to take care of, to educate, to make due provision for them; the natural affection leads to this, but the reflection that it is his proper business, what belongs to him, that it is right and commendable so to do—this added to the affection becomes a much more settled principle and carries him on through more labor and difficulties for the sake of his children than he would undergo from that affection alone, if he thought it, and the course of action it led to, either indifferent or criminal. This indeed is impossible, to do that which is good and not to approve of it; for which reason they are frequently not considered as distinct, though they really are, for men often approve of the actions of others which they will not imitate, and likewise do that which they approve not. It cannot possibly be denied that there is this principle of reflection or conscience in human nature. Suppose a man to relieve an innocent person in distress, suppose the same man afterwards, in the fury of anger, to do the greatest mischief to a person who had given no just cause of offense; to aggravate the injury, add the circumstances of former friendship and obligation from the injured person, let the man who is supposed to have done these two different actions coolly reflect upon them afterwards, without regard to their consequences to himself; to assert that any common man would be affected in the same way toward these different actions, that he would make no distinction between them, but approve or disapprove them equally, is too glaring a falsity to need being confuted. There is therefore this principle of reflection or conscience in mankind. It is needless to compare the respect it has to private good with the respect it has to public, since it plainly tends as much to the latter as to the former, and is commonly thought to tend chiefly to the latter. This faculty is now mentioned merely as another part in the inward frame of man, pointing out to us

in some degree what we are intended for, and as what will naturally and of course have some influence. The particular place assigned to it by nature, what authority it has, and how great influence it ought to have, shall be hereafter considered.

[9] From this comparison of benevolence and self-love, of our public and private affections, of the courses of life they lead to, and of the principle of reflection or conscience as respecting each of them, it is as manifest that we were made for society and to promote the happiness of it, as that we were intended to take care of our own life and health and private good.

[10] And from this whole review must be given a different draught of human nature from what we are often presented with. Mankind are by nature so closely united, there is such a correspondence between the inward sensations of one man and those of another that disgrace is as much avoided as bodily pain, and to be the object of esteem and love as much desired as any external goods; and in many particular cases, persons are carried on to do good to others, as the end their affection tends to and rests in, and manifest that they find real satisfaction and enjoyment in this course of behavior. There is such a natural principle of attraction in man toward man that having trod the same tract of land, having breathed in the same climate, barely having been born in the same artificial district or division, becomes the occasion of contracting acquaintances and familiarities many years after; for anything may serve the purpose. Thus relations merely nominal are sought and invented, not by governors, but by the lowest of the people; which are found sufficient to hold mankind together in little fraternities and copartnerships—weak ties indeed, and what may afford fund enough for ridicule if they are absurdly considered as the real principles of that union; but they are in truth merely the occasions, as anything may be of anything, upon which our nature carries us on according to its own previous bent and bias; which occasions therefore would be nothing at all were there not this prior disposition and bias of nature. Men are so much one body that in a peculiar manner they feel for each other; shame, sudden danger, resentment, honor, prosperity, distress; one or another, or all of these, from the social nature in general, from benevolence, upon the occasion of natural relation, acquaintance, protection, dependence—each of these being distinct cements of society. And therefore to have no restraint from, no regard to, others in our behavior is the speculative absurdity of considering ourselves as single and independent, as having nothing in our nature which has respect to our fellow creatures, reduced to action and practice. And this is the same absurdity as to suppose a

hand or any part to have no natural respect to any other or to the whole body.

[11] But allowing all this, it may be asked, "Has not man dispositions and principles within, which lead him to do evil to others as well as to do good? Whence come the many miseries else, which men are the authors and instruments of to each other?" These questions, so far as they relate to the foregoing discourse, may be answered by asking, Has not man also dispositions and principles within, which lead him to do evil to himself as well as good? Whence come the many miseries else, sickness, pain, and death, which men are the instruments and authors of to themselves?

[12] It may be thought more easy to answer one of these questions than the other, but the answer to both is really the same—that mankind have ungoverned passions which they will gratify at any rate, as well to the injury of others as in contradiction to known private interest, but that as there is no such thing as self-hatred, so neither is there any such thing as ill-will in one man toward another, emulation and resentment being away, whereas there is plainly benevolence or good-will; there is no such thing as love of injustice, oppression, treachery, ingratitude, but only eager desires after such and such external goods, which, according to a very ancient observation, the most abandoned would choose to obtain by innocent means if they were as easy and as effectual to their end that even emulation and resentment, by any one who will consider what these passions really are in nature,[5] will be found nothing to the purpose of this objection; and that the principles and passions in the mind of man, which are distinct both from self-love and benevolence, primarily and most directly lead to right behavior with regard to others as well as himself, and only secondarily and accidentally to what is evil. Thus, though men, to avoid the shame of one villainy, are sometimes guilty of a greater, yet it is easy to see that

5. Emulation is merely the desire and hope of equality with, or superiority over, others with whom we compare ourselves. There does not appear to be any other grief in the natural passion, but only that want which is implied in desire. However, this may be so strong as to be the occasion of great grief. To desire the attainment of this equality or superiority by the particular means of others being brought down to our own level, or below it, is, I think, the distinct notion of envy. From whence it is easy to see that the real end, which the natural passion, emulation, and which the unlawful one, envy, aims at, is exactly the same—namely, that equality or superiority and consequently that to do mischief is not the end of envy, but merely the means it makes use of to attain its end. As to resentment, see the eighth sermon.

the original tendency of shame is to prevent the doing of shameful actions; and its leading men to conceal such actions when done is only in consequence of their being done, that is, of the passion's not having answered its first end.

[13] If it be said that there are persons in the world who are in great measure without the natural affections toward their fellow creatures, there are likewise instances of persons without the common natural affections to themselves; but the nature of man is not to be judged of by either of these, but by what appears in the common world, in the bulk of mankind.

[14] I am afraid it would be thought very strange if to confirm the truth of this account of human nature and make out the justness of the foregoing comparison, it should be added that, from what appears, men in fact as much and as often contradict that *part* of their nature which respects *self* and which leads them to their *own private* good and happiness, as they contradict that *part* of it which respects *society* and tends to *public* good; that there are as few persons who attain the greatest satisfaction and enjoyment which they might attain in the present world, as who do the greatest good to others which they might do—nay, that there are as few who can be said really and in earnest to aim at one as at the other. Take a survey of mankind: the world in general, the good and bad, almost without exception, equally are agreed that were religion out of the case, the happiness of the present life would consist in a manner wholly in riches, honors, sensual gratifications, insomuch that one scarce hears a reflection made upon prudence, life, conduct, but upon this supposition. Yet on the contrary, that persons in the greatest affluence of fortune are no happier than such as have only a competency; that the cares and disappointments of ambition for the most part far exceed the satisfactions of it; as also the miserable intervals of intemperance and excess, and the many untimely deaths occasioned by a dissolute course of life—these things are all seen, acknowledged, by every one acknowledged, but are thought no objections against, though they expressly contradict this universal principle that the happiness of the present life consists in one or other of them. Whence is all this absurdity and contradiction? Is not the middle way obvious? Can anything be more manifest than that the happiness of life consists in these possessed and enjoyed only to a certain degree, that to pursue them beyond this degree is always attended with more inconvenience than advantage to a man's self, and often with extreme misery and unhappiness? Whence then, I say, is all this absurdity and contradiction? Is it really the result of consideration in mankind how they may become most easy to themselves, most free

from care, and enjoy the chief happiness attainable in this world? Or is it not manifestly owing either to this that they have not cool and reasonable concern enough for themselves to consider wherein their chief happiness in the present life consists, or else, if they do consider it, that they will not act conformably to what is the result of that consideration; that is, reasonable concern for themselves, or cool self-love, is prevailed over by passion and appetite. So that, from what appears, there is no ground to assert [that those principles in the nature of man which most directly lead to promote the good of our fellow creatures are more generally or in a greater degree violated than those which most directly lead us to promote our own private good and happiness.]

[15] The sum of the whole is plainly this. The nature of man considered in his single capacity, and with respect only to the present world, is adapted and leads him to attain the greatest happiness he can for himself in the present world. The nature of man considered in his public or social capacity leads him to a right behavior in society, to that course of life which we call virtue. Men follow or obey their nature in both these capacities and respects to a certain degree, but not entirely; their actions do not come up to the whole of what their nature leads them to in either of these capacities or respects; and they often violate their nature in both. That is, as they neglect the duties they owe to their fellow creatures, to which their nature leads them, and an injurious, to which their nature is abhorrent, so there is a manifest negligence in men of their real happiness or interest in the present world when that interest is inconsistent with a present gratification, for the sake of which they negligently, nay, even knowingly, are the authors and instruments of their own misery and ruin. Thus they are as often unjust to themselves as to others, and for the most part are equally so to both by the same actions.

A Treatise of Human Nature

Book II: Of the Passions

Part I: Of Pride and Humility

Section VII. Of Vice and Virtue

[1] Taking these limitations along with us, let us proceed to examine the causes of pride and humility; and see, whether in every case we can

From David Hume, *Moral Philosophy*, ed. Geoffrey Sayre-McCord (Indianapolis: Hackett Publishing Co., 2006). Reprinted by permission of the publisher.

discover the double relations, by which they operate on the passions. If we find that all these causes are related to self, and produce a pleasure or uneasiness separate from the passion, there will remain no farther scruple with regard to the present system. We shall principally endeavour to prove the latter point; the former being in a manner self-evident.

[2] To begin with VICE and VIRTUE, which are the most obvious causes of these passions; 'twou'd be entirely foreign to my present purpose to enter upon the controversy, which of late years has so much excited the curiosity of the publick, *whether these moral distinctions be founded on natural and original principles, or arise from interest and education.* The examination of this I reserve for the following book; and in the mean time shall endeavour to show, that my system maintains its ground upon either of these hypotheses; which will be a strong proof of its solidity.

[3] For granting that morality had no foundation in nature, it must still be allow'd, that vice and virtue, either from self-interest or the prejudices of education, produce in us a real pain and pleasure; and this we may observe to be strenuously asserted by the defenders of that hypothesis. Every passion, habit, or turn of character (say they) which has a tendency to our advantage or prejudice, gives a delight or uneasiness; and 'tis from thence the approbation or disapprobation arises. We easily gain from the liberality of others, but are always in danger of losing by their avarice: Courage defends us, but cowardice lays us open to every attack: Justice is the support of society, but injustice, unless check'd, wou'd quickly prove its ruin: Humility exalts; but pride mortifies us. For these reasons the former qualities are esteem'd virtues, and the latter regarded as vices. Now since 'tis granted there is a delight or uneasiness still attending merit or demerit of every kind, this is all that is requisite for my purpose. [4] But I go farther, and observe, that this moral hypothesis and my present system not only agree together, but also that, allowing the former to be just, 'tis an absolute and invincible proof of the latter. For if all morality be founded on the pain or pleasure, which arises from the prospect of any loss or advantage, that may result from our own characters, or from those of others, all the effects of morality must be deriv'd from the same pain or pleasure, and among the rest, the passions of pride and humility. The very essence of virtue, according to this hypothesis, is to produce pleasure, and that of vice to give pain. The virtue and vice must be part of our character in order to excite pride or humility. What farther proof can we desire for the double relation of impressions and ideas?

[5] The same unquestionable argument may be deriv'd from the opinion of those, who maintain that morality is something real,

essential, and founded on nature. The most probable hypothesis, which has been advanc'd to explain the distinction betwixt vice and virtue, and the origin of moral rights and obligations, is, that from a primary constitution of nature certain characters and passions, by the very view and contemplation, produce a pain, and others in like manner excite a pleasure. The uneasiness and satisfaction are not only inseparable from vice and virtue, but constitute their very nature and essence. To approve of a character is to feel an original delight upon its appearance. To disapprove of it is to be sensible of an uneasiness. The pain and pleasure, therefore, being the primary causes of vice and virtue, must also be the causes of all their effects, and consequently of pride and humility, which are the unavoidable attendants of that distinction.

[6] But supposing this hypothesis of moral philosophy shou'd be allow'd to be false, 'tis still evident, that pain and pleasure, if not the causes of vice and virtue, are at least inseparable from them. A generous and noble character affords a satisfaction even in the survey; and when presented to us, tho' only in a poem or fable, never fails to charm and delight us. On the other hand cruelty and treachery displease from their very nature; nor is it possible ever to reconcile us to these qualities, either in ourselves or others. Thus one hypothesis of morality is an undeniable proof of the foregoing system, and the other at worst agrees with it.

[7] But pride and humility arise not from these qualities alone of the mind, which, according to the vulgar systems of ethicks, have been comprehended as parts of moral duty, but from any other that has a connexion with pleasure and uneasiness. Nothing flatters our vanity more than the talent of pleasing by our wit, good humour, or any other accomplishment; and nothing gives us a more sensible mortification than a disappointment in any attempt of that nature. No one has ever been able to tell what *wit* is, and to shew why such a system of thought must be receiv'd under that denomination, and such another rejected. 'Tis only by taste we can decide concerning it, nor are we possest of any other standard, upon which we can form a judgment of this kind. Now what is this *taste*, from which true and false wit in a manner receive their being, and without which no thought can have a title to either of these denominations? 'Tis plainly nothing but a sensation of pleasure from true wit, and of uneasiness from false, without our being able to tell the reasons of that pleasure or uneasiness. The power of bestowing these opposite sensations is, therefore, the very essence of true and false wit; and consequently the cause of that pride or humility, which arises from them.

[8] There may, perhaps, be some, who being accustom'd to the style of the schools and pulpit, and having never consider'd human nature in any other light, than that in which *they* place it, may here be surpriz'd to hear me talk of virtue as exciting pride, which they look upon as a vice; and of vice as producing humility, which they have been taught to consider as a virtue. But not to dispute about words, I observe, that by *pride* I understand that agreeable impression, which arises in the mind, when the view either of our virtue, beauty, riches or power makes us satisfy'd with ourselves: And that by *humility* I mean the opposite impression. 'Tis evident the former impression is not always vicious, nor the latter virtuous. The most rigid morality allows us to receive a pleasure from reflecting on a generous action; and 'tis by none esteem'd a virtue to feel any fruitless remorses upon the thoughts of past villainy and baseness. Let us, therefore, examine these impressions, consider'd in themselves; and enquire into their causes, whether plac'd on the mind or body, without troubling ourselves at present with that merit or blame, which may attend them.

Book III: Of Morals

Part I: Of Virtue and Vice in General

Section I. Moral Distinctions Not Deriv'd from Reason

[1] There is an inconvenience which attends all abstruse reasoning, that it may silence, without convincing an antagonist, and requires the same intense study to make us sensible of its force, that was at first requisite for its invention. When we leave our closet, and engage in the common affairs of life, its conclusions seem to vanish, like the phantoms of the night on the appearance of the morning; and 'tis difficult for us to retain even that conviction, which we had attain'd with difficulty. This is still more conspicuous in a long chain of reasoning, where we must preserve to the end the evidence of the first propositions, and where we often lose sight of all the most receiv'd maxims, either of philosophy or common life. I am not, however, without hopes, that the present system of philosophy will acquire new force as it advances; and that our reasonings concerning *morals* will corroborate whatever has been said concerning the *understanding* and the *passions*. Morality is a subject that interests us above all others: We fancy the peace of society to be at stake in every decision concerning it; and 'tis evident, that this concern must make our speculations appear more real and solid, than where the subject is, in a great measure, indifferent to us. What affects us, we conclude can never be a chimera; and as

our passion is engag'd on the one side or the other, we naturally think that the question lies within human comprehension; which, in other cases of this nature, we are apt to entertain some doubt of. Without this advantage I never shou'd have ventur'd upon a third volume of such abstruse philosophy, in an age, wherein the greatest part of men seem agreed to convert reading into an amusement, and to reject every thing that requires any considerable degree of attention to be comprehended.

[2] It has been observ'd, that nothing is ever present to the mind but its perceptions; and that all the actions of seeing, hearing, judging, loving, hating, and thinking, fall under this denomination. The mind can never exert itself in any action, which we may not comprehend under the term of *perception;* and consequently that term is no less applicable to those judgments, by which we distinguish moral good and evil, than to every other operation of the mind. To approve of one character, to condemn another, are only so many different perceptions.

[3] Now as perceptions resolve themselves into two kinds, viz. *impressions* and *ideas,* this distinction gives rise to a question, with which we shall open up our present enquiry concerning morals, *Whether 'tis by means of our* ideas *or* impressions *we distinguish betwixt vice and virtue, and pronounce an action blameable or praise-worthy?* This will immediately cut off all loose discourses and declamations, and reduce us to something precise and exact on the present subject.

[4] Those who affirm that virtue is nothing but a conformity to reason; that there are eternal fitnesses and unfitnesses of things, which are the same to every rational being that considers them; that the immutable measures of right and wrong impose an obligation, not only on human creatures, but also on the Deity himself: All these systems concur in the opinion, that morality, like truth, is discern'd merely by ideas, and by their juxtaposition and comparison. In order, therefore, to judge of these systems, we need only consider, whether it be possible, from reason alone, to distinguish betwixt moral good and evil, or whether there must concur some other principles to enable us to make that distinction.

[5] If morality had naturally no influence on human passions and actions, 'twere in vain to take such pains to inculcate it; and nothing wou'd be more fruitless than that multitude of rules and precepts, with which all moralists abound. Philosophy is commonly divided into *speculative* and *practical;* and as morality is always comprehended under the latter division, 'tis suppos'd to influence our passions and actions, and to go beyond the calm and indolent judgments of

the understanding. And this is confirm'd by common experience, which informs us, that men are often govern'd by their duties, and are deter'd from some actions by the opinion of injustice, and impell'd to others by that of obligation.

[6] Since morals, therefore, have an influence on the actions and affections, it follows, that they cannot be deriv'd from reason; and that because reason alone, as we have already prov'd, can never have any such influence. Morals excite passions, and produce or prevent actions. Reason of itself is utterly impotent in this particular. The rules of morality, therefore, are not conclusions of our reason.

[7] No one, I believe, will deny the justness of this inference; nor is there any other means of evading it, than by denying that principle, on which it is founded. As long as it is allow'd, that reason has no influence on our passions and actions, 'tis in vain to pretend, that morality is discover'd only by a deduction of reason. An active principle can never be founded on an inactive; and if reason be inactive in itself, it must remain so in all its shapes and appearances, whether it exerts itself in natural or moral subjects, whether it considers the powers of external bodies, or the actions of rational beings.

[8] It would be tedious to repeat all the arguments, by which I have prov'd,[6] that reason is perfectly inert, and can never either prevent or produce any action or affection. 'Twill be easy to recollect what has been said upon that subject. I shall only recall on this occasion one of these arguments, which I shall endeavour to render still more conclusive, and more applicable to the present subject.

[9] Reason is the discovery of truth or falshood. Truth or falshood consists in an agreement or disagreement either to the *real* relations of ideas, or to *real* existence and matter of fact. Whatever, therefore, is not susceptible of this agreement or disagreement, is incapable of being true or false, and can never be an object of our reason. Now 'tis evident our passions, volitions, and actions, are not susceptible of any such agreement or disagreement; being original facts and realities, compleat in themselves, and implying no reference to other passions, volitions, and actions. 'Tis impossible, therefore, they can be pronounc'd either true or false, and be either contrary or conformable to reason.

[10] This argument is of double advantage to our present purpose. For it proves *directly*, that actions do not derive their merit from a conformity to reason, nor their blame from a contrariety to it; and it

6. Book II. Part III. Sect. 3.

proves the same truth more *indirectly*, by shewing us, that as reason can never immediately prevent or produce any action by contradicting or approving of it, it cannot be the source of the distinction betwixt moral good and evil, which are found to have that influence. Actions may be laudable or blameable; but they cannot be reasonable or unreasonable: Laudable or blameable, therefore, are not the same with reasonable or unreasonable. The merit and demerit of actions frequently contradict, and sometimes controul our natural propensities. But reason has no such influence. Moral distinctions, therefore, are not the offspring of reason. Reason is wholly inactive, and can never be the source of so active a principle as conscience, or a sense of morals.

[11] But perhaps it may be said, that tho' no will or action can be immediately contradictory to reason, yet we may find such a contradiction in some of the attendants of the action, that is, in its causes or effects. The action may cause a judgment, or may be *obliquely* caus'd by one, when the judgment concurs with a passion; and by an abusive way of speaking, which philosophy will scarce allow of, the same contrariety may, upon that account, be ascrib'd to the action. How far this truth or falsehood may be the source of morals, 'twill now be proper to consider.

[12] It has been observ'd, that reason, in a strict and philosophical sense, can have an influence on our conduct only after two ways: Either when it excites a passion by informing us of the existence of something which is a proper object of it; or when it discovers the connexion of causes and effects, so as to afford us means of exerting any passion. These are the only kinds of judgment, which can accompany our actions, or can be said to produce them in any manner; and it must be allow'd, that these judgments may often be false and erroneous. A person may be affected with passion, by supposing a pain or pleasure to lie in an object, which has no tendency to produce either of these sensations, or which produces the contrary to what is imagin'd. A person may also take false measures for the attaining his end, and may retard, by his foolish conduct, instead of forwarding the execution of any project. These false judgments may be thought to affect the passions and actions, which are connected with them, and may be said to render them unreasonable, in a figurative and improper way of speaking. But tho' this be acknowledg'd, 'tis easy to observe, that these errors are so far from being the source of all immorality, that they are commonly very innocent, and draw no manner of guilt upon the person who is so unfortunate as to fall into them. They extend not beyond a mistake of *fact*, which moralists have not generally suppos'd criminal, as being perfectly involuntary. I am more to be lamented

than blam'd, if I am mistaken with regard to the influence of objects in producing pain or pleasure, or if I know not the proper means of satisfying my desires. No one can ever regard such errors as a defect in my moral character. A fruit, for instance, that is really disagreeable, appears to me at a distance, and thro' mistake, I fancy it to be pleasant and delicious. Here is one error. I choose certain means of reaching this fruit, which are not proper for my end. Here is a second error; nor is there any third one, which can ever possibly enter into our reasonings concerning actions. I ask, therefore, if a man, in this situation, and guilty of these two errors, is to be regarded as vicious and criminal, however unavoidable they might have been? Or if it be possible to imagine, that such errors are the sources of all immorality?

[13] And here it may be proper to observe, that if moral distinctions be deriv'd from the truth or falsehood of those judgments, they must take place wherever we form the judgments; nor will there be any difference, whether the question be concerning an apple or a kingdom, or whether the error be avoidable or unavoidable. For as the very essence of morality is suppos'd to consist in an agreement or disagreement to reason, the other circumstances are entirely arbitrary, and can never either bestow on any action the character of virtuous or vicious, or deprive it of that character. To which we may add, that this agreement or disagreement, not admitting of degrees, all virtues and vices wou'd of course be equal. [14] Shou'd it be pretended, that tho' a mistake of *fact* be not criminal, yet a mistake of *right* often is; and that this may be the source of immorality: I wou'd answer, that 'tis impossible such a mistake can ever be the original source of immorality, since it supposes a real right and wrong; that is, a real distinction in morals, independent of these judgments. A mistake, therefore, of right may become a species of immorality; but 'tis only a secondary one, and is founded on some other, antecedent to it.

[15] As to those judgments which are the *effects* of our actions, and which, when false, give occasion to pronounce the actions contrary to truth and reason; we may observe, that our actions never cause any judgment, either true or false, in ourselves, and that 'tis only on others they have such an influence. 'Tis certain, that an action, on many occasions, may give rise to false conclusions in others; and that a person, who thro' a window sees any lewd behaviour of mine with my neighbour's wife, may be so simple as to imagine she is certainly my own. In this respect my action resembles somewhat a lye or falshood; only with this difference, which is material, that I perform not the action with any intention of giving rise to a false judgment in another, but merely to satisfy my lust and passion. It causes, however, a mistake

and false judgment by accident; and the falsehood of its effects may be ascrib'd, by some odd figurative way of speaking, to the action itself. But still I can see no pretext of reason for asserting, that the tendency to cause such an error is the first spring or original source of all immorality.[7]

7. One might think it were entirely superfluous to prove this, if a late author, who has had the good fortune to obtain some reputation, had not seriously affirmed, that such a falshood is the foundation of all guilt and moral deformity. That we may discover the fallacy of his hypothesis, we need only consider, that a false conclusion is drawn from an action, only by means of an obscurity of natural principles, which makes a cause be secretly interrupted in its operation, by contrary causes, and renders the connexion betwixt two objects uncertain and variable. Now, as a like uncertainty and variety of causes take place, even in natural objects, and produce a like error in our judgment, if that tendency to produce error were the very essence of vice and immorality, it shou'd follow, that even inanimate objects might be vicious and immoral.

'Tis in vain to urge, that inanimate objects act without liberty and choice. For as liberty and choice are not necessary to make an action produce in us an erroneous conclusion, they can be, in no respect, essential to morality; and I do not readily perceive, upon this system, how they can ever come to be regarded by it. If the tendency to cause error be the origin of immorality, that tendency and immorality wou'd in every case be inseparable.

Add to this, that if I had used the precaution of shutting the windows, while I indulg'd myself in those liberties with my neighbour's wife, I should have been guilty of no immorality; and that because my action, being perfectly conceal'd, wou'd have had no tendency to produce any false conclusion.

For the same reason, a thief, who steals in by a ladder at a window, and takes all imaginable care to cause no disturbance, is in no respect criminal. For either he will not be perceiv'd, or if he be, 'tis impossible he can produce any error, nor will any one, from these circumstances, take him to be other than what he really is.

'Tis well known, that those who are squint-sighted, do very readily cause mistakes in others, and that we imagine they salute or are talking to one person, while they address themselves to another. Are they therefore, upon that account, immoral?

Besides, we may easily observe, that in all those arguments there is an evident reasoning in a circle. A person who takes possession of *another's* goods, and uses them as his *own,* in a manner declares them to be his own; and this falshood is the source of the immorality of injustice. But is property, or right, or obligation, intelligible, without an antecedent morality?

A man that is ungrateful to his benefactor, in a manner affirms, that he never received any favours from him. But in what manner? Is it because 'tis his duty to be grateful? But this supposes, that there is some antecedent rule of duty and morals. Is it because human nature is generally grateful, and

[16] Thus upon the whole, 'tis impossible, that the distinction betwixt moral good and evil, can be made by reason; since that distinction has an influence upon our actions, of which reason alone is incapable. Reason and judgment may, indeed, be the mediate cause of an action, by prompting, or by directing a passion: But it is not pretended that a judgment of this kind, either in its truth or falshood, is attended with virtue or vice. And as to the judgments, which are caus'd by our actions, they can still less bestow those moral qualities on the actions, which are their causes.

[17] But to be more particular, and to shew, that those eternal immutable fitnesses and unfitnesses of things cannot be defended by sound philosophy, we may weigh the following considerations.

[18] If the thought and understanding were alone capable of fixing the boundaries of right and wrong, the character of virtuous and vicious either must lie in some relations of objects, or must be a matter of fact, which is discover'd by our reasoning. This consequence is evident. As the operations of human understanding divide themselves into two kinds, the comparing of ideas, and the inferring of matter of fact; were virtue discover'd by the understanding; it must be an object of one of these operations; nor is there any third operation of the understanding, which can discover it. There has been an opinion very industriously propagated by certain philosophers, that morality is susceptible of demonstration; and tho' no one has ever been able to advance a single step in those demonstrations; yet 'tis taken for granted that this science may be brought to an equal certainty with geometry or algebra. Upon this supposition, vice and virtue must con-

---

makes us conclude, that a man who does any harm never received any favour from the person he harm'd? But human nature is not so generally grateful, as to justify such a conclusion. Or if it were, is an exception to a general rule in every case criminal, for no other reason than because it is an exception?

But what may suffice entirely to destroy this whimsical system is, that it leaves us under the same difficulty to give a reason why truth is virtuous and falshood vicious, as to account for the merit or turpitude of any other action. I shall allow, if you please, that all immorality is derived from this supposed falshood in action, provided you can give me any plausible reason, why such a falshood is immoral. If you consider rightly of the matter, you will find yourself in the same difficulty as at the beginning.

This last argument is very conclusive; because, if there be not an evident merit or turpitude annex'd to this species of truth or falshood, it can never have any influence upon our actions. For, who ever thought off or bearing any action, because others might possibly draw false conclusions from it? Or, who ever perform'd any, that he might give rise to true conclusions?

sist in some relations; since 'tis allow'd on all hands, that no matter of fact is capable of being demonstrated. Let us, therefore, begin with examining this hypothesis, and endeavour, if possible, to fix those moral qualities, which have been so long the objects of our fruitless researches. Point out distinctly the relations, which constitute morality or obligation, that we may know wherein they consist, and after what manner we must judge of them.

[19] If you assert, that vice and virtue consist in relations susceptible of certainty and demonstration, you must confine yourself to those *four* relations which alone admit of that degree of evidence; and in that case you run into absurdities, from which you will never be able to extricate yourself. For as you make the very essence of morality to lie in the relations, and as there is no one of these relations but what is applicable, not only to an irrational but also to an inanimate object; it follows, that even such objects must be susceptible of merit or demerit. *Resemblance, contrariety, degrees in quality,* and *proportions in quantity and number;* all these relations belong as properly to matter as to our actions, passions, and volitions. 'Tis unquestionable, therefore, that morality lies not in any of these relations, nor the sense of it in their discovery.[8]

[20] Shou'd it be asserted, that the sense of morality consists in the discovery of some relation, distinct from these, and that our enumeration was not compleat, when we comprehended all demonstrable relations under four general heads: To this I know not what to reply, till some one be so good as to point out to me this new relation. 'Tis impossible to refute a system, which has never yet been explain'd. In

8. As a proof, how confus'd our way of thinking on this subject commonly is, we may observe, that those who assert, that morality is demonstrable, do not say, that morality lies in the relations, and that the relations are distinguishable by reason. They only say, that reason can discover such an action, in such relations, to be virtuous, and such another vicious. It seems they thought it sufficient, if they cou'd bring the word, Relation, into the proposition, without troubling themselves whether it was to the purpose or not. But here, I think, is plain argument. Demonstrative reason discovers only relations. But that reason, according to this hypothesis, discovers also vice and virtue. These moral qualities, therefore, must be relations. When we blame any action, in any situation, the whole complicated object, of action and situation, must form certain relations, wherein the essence of vice consists. This hypothesis is not otherwise intelligible. For what does reason discover, when it pronounces any action vicious? Does it discover a relation or a matter of fact? These questions are decisive, and must not be eluded.

such a manner of fighting in the dark, a man loses his blows in the air, and often places them where the enemy is not present.

[21] I must, therefore, on this occasion, rest contented with requiring the two following conditions of any one that wou'd undertake to clear up this system. *First,* As moral good and evil belong only to the actions of the mind, and are deriv'd from our situation with regard to external objects, the relations, from which these moral distinctions arise, must lie only betwixt internal actions, and external objects, and must not be applicable either to internal actions, compar'd among themselves, or to external objects, when plac'd in opposition to other external objects. For as morality is suppos'd to attend certain relations, if these relations cou'd belong to internal actions consider'd singly, it wou'd follow, that we might be guilty of crimes in ourselves, and independent of our situation, with respect to the universe: And in like manner, if these moral relations cou'd be apply'd to external objects, it wou'd follow, that even inanimate beings wou'd be susceptible of moral beauty and deformity. Now it seems difficult to imagine, that any relation can be discover'd betwixt our passions, volitions and actions, compar'd to external objects, which relation might not belong either to these passions and volitions, or to these external objects, compar'd among *themselves.*

[22] But it will be still more difficult to fulfil the *second* condition, requisite to justify this system. According to the principles of those who maintain an abstract rational difference betwixt moral good and evil, and a natural fitness and unfitness of things, 'tis not only suppos'd, that these relations, being eternal and immutable, are the same, when consider'd by every rational creature, but their *effects* are also suppos'd to be necessarily the same; and 'tis concluded they have no less, or rather a greater, influence in directing the will of the deity, than in governing the rational and virtuous of our own species. These two particulars are evidently distinct. 'Tis one thing to know virtue, and another to conform the will to it. In order, therefore, to prove that the measures of right and wrong are eternal laws, *obligatory* on every rational mind, 'tis not sufficient to shew the relations upon which they are founded: We must also point out the connexion betwixt the relation and the will; and must prove that this connexion is so necessary, that in every well-dispos'd mind, it must take place and have its influence; tho' the difference betwixt these minds be in other respects immense and infinite. Now besides what I have already prov'd, that even in human nature no relation can ever alone produce any action; besides this, I say, it has been shewn, in treating of the understanding, that there is no connexion of cause and effect, such as

this is suppos'd to be, which is discoverable otherwise than by experience, and of which we can pretend to have any security by the simple consideration of the objects. All beings in the universe, consider'd in themselves, appear entirely loose and independent of each other. 'Tis only by experience we learn their influence and connexion; and this influence we ought never to extend beyond experience.

[23] Thus it will be impossible to fulfil the *first* condition required to the system of eternal rational measures of right and wrong; because it is impossible to shew those relations, upon which such a distinction may be founded: And 'tis as impossible to fulfil the *second* condition; because we cannot prove *a priori*, that these relations, if they really existed and were perceiv'd, wou'd be universally forcible and obligatory.

[24] But to make these general reflections more clear and convincing, we may illustrate them by some particular instances, wherein this character of moral good or evil is the most universally acknowledg'd. Of all crimes that human creatures are capable of committing, the most horrid and unnatural is ingratitude, especially when it is committed against parents, and appears in the more flagrant instances of wounds and death. This is acknowledg'd by all mankind, philosophers as well as the people; the question only arises among philosophers, whether the guilt or moral deformity of this action be discover'd by demonstrative reasoning, or be felt by an internal sense, and by means of some sentiment, which the reflecting on such an action naturally occasions. This question will soon be decided against the former opinion, if we can shew the same relations in other objects, without the notion of any guilt or iniquity attending them. Reason or science is nothing but the comparing of ideas, and the discovery of their relations; and if the same relations have different characters, it must evidently follow, that those characters are not discover'd merely by reason. To put the affair, therefore, to this trial, let us chuse any inanimate object, such as an oak or elm; and let us suppose, that by the dropping of its seed, it produces a sapling below it, which springing up by degrees, at last overtops and destroys the parent tree: I ask, if in this instance there be wanting any relation, which is discoverable in parricide or ingratitude? Is not the one tree the cause of the other's existence; and the latter the cause of the destruction of the former, in the same manner as when a child murders his parent? 'Tis not sufficient to reply, that a choice or will is wanting. For in the case of parricide, a will does not give rise to any *different* relations, but is only the cause from which the action is deriv'd; and consequently produces the *same* relations, that in the oak or elm arise from some other principles. 'Tis a

will or choice, that determines a man to kill his parent; and they are the laws of matter and motion, that determine a sapling to destroy the oak, from which it sprung. Here then the same relations have different causes; but still the relations are the same: And as their discovery is not in both cases attended with a notion of immorality, it follows, that that notion does not arise from such a discovery.

[25] But to chuse an instance, still more resembling; I wou'd fain ask any one, why incest in the human species is criminal, and why the very same action, and the same relations in animals have not the smallest moral turpitude and deformity? If it be answer'd, that this action is innocent in animals, because they have not reason sufficient to discover its turpitude; but that man, being endow'd with that faculty, which *ought* to restrain him to his duty, the same action instantly becomes criminal to him; shou'd this be said, I wou'd reply, that this is evidently arguing in a circle. For before reason can perceive this turpitude, the turpitude must exist; and consequently is independent of the decisions of our reason, and is their object more properly than their effect. According to this system, then, every animal, that has sense, and appetite, and will; that is, every animal must be susceptible of all the same virtues and vices, for which we ascribe praise and blame to human creatures. All the difference is, that our superior reason may serve to discover the vice or virtue, and by that means may augment the blame or praise: But still this discovery supposes a separate being in these moral distinctions, and a being, which depends only on the will and appetite, and which, both in thought and reality, may be distinguish'd from the reason. Animals are susceptible of the same relations, with respect to each other, as the human species, and therefore wou'd also be susceptible of the same morality, if the essence of morality consisted in these relations. Their want of a sufficient degree of reason may hinder them from perceiving the duties and obligations of morality, but can never hinder these duties from existing; since they must antecedently exist, in order to their being perceiv'd. Reason must find them, and can never produce them. This argument deserves to be weigh'd, as being, in my opinion, entirely decisive.

[26] Nor does this reasoning only prove, that morality consists not in any relations, that are the objects of science; but if examin'd, will prove with equal certainty, that it consists not in any *matter of fact*, which can be discover'd by the understanding. This is the *second* part of our argument; and if it can be made evident, we may conclude, that morality is not an object of reason. But can there be any difficulty in proving, that vice and virtue are not matters of fact,

whose existence we can infer by reason? Take any action allow'd to be vicious: Wilful murder, for instance. Examine it in all lights, and see if you can find that matter of fact, or real existence, which you call *vice.* In which-ever way you take it, you find only certain passions, motives, volitions, and thoughts. There is no other matter of fact in the case. The vice entirely escapes you, as long as you consider the object. You never can find it, till you turn your reflection into your own breast, and find a sentiment of disapprobation, which arises in you, towards this action. Here is a matter of fact; but 'tis the object of feeling, not of reason. It lies in yourself, not in the object. So that when you pronounce any action or character to be vicious, you mean nothing, but that from the constitution of your nature you have a feeling or sentiment of blame from the contemplation of it. Vice and virtue, therefore, may be compar'd to sounds, colours, heat and cold, which, according to modern philosophy, are not qualities in objects, but perceptions in the mind: And this discovery in morals, like that other in physics, is to be regarded as a considerable advancement of the speculative sciences; tho', like that too, it has little or no influence on practice. Nothing can be more real, or concern us more, than our own sentiments of pleasure and uneasiness; and if these be favourable to virtue, and unfavourable to vice, no more can be requisite to the regulation of our conduct and behaviour.

[27] I cannot forbear adding to these reasonings an observation, which may, perhaps, be found of some importance. In every system of morality, which I have hitherto met with, I have always remark'd, that the author proceeds for some time in the ordinary way of reasoning, and establishes the being of a God, or makes observations concerning human affairs; when of a sudden I am surpriz'd to find, that instead of the usual copulations of propositions, *is,* and *is not,* I meet with no proposition that is not connected with an *ought,* or an *ought not.* This change is imperceptible; but is, however, of the last consequence. For as this *ought,* or *ought not,* expresses some new relation or affirmation, 'tis necessary that it shou'd be observ'd and explain'd; and at the same time that a reason shou'd be given, for what seems altogether inconceivable, how this new relation can be a deduction from others, which are entirely different from it. But as authors do not commonly use this precaution, I shall presume to recommend it to the readers; and am persuaded, that this small attention wou'd subvert all the vulgar systems of morality, and let us see, that the distinction of vice and virtue is not founded merely on the relations of objects, nor is perceiv'd by reason.

Section II. Moral Distinctions Deriv'd from a Moral Sense

[1] Thus the course of the argument leads us to conclude, that since vice and virtue are not discoverable merely by reason, or the comparison of ideas, it must be by means of some impression or sentiment they occasion, that we are able to mark the difference betwixt them. Our decisions concerning moral rectitude and depravity are evidently perceptions; and as all perceptions are either impressions or ideas, the exclusion of the one is a convincing argument for the other. Morality, therefore, is more properly felt than judg'd of; tho' this feeling or sentiment is commonly so soft and gentle, that we are apt to confound it with an idea, according to our common custom of taking all things for the same, which have any near resemblance to each other.

[2] The next question is, of what nature are these impressions, and after what manner do they operate upon us? Here we cannot remain long in suspense, but must pronounce the impression arising from virtue, to be agreeable, and that proceeding from vice to be uneasy. Every moment's experience must convince us of this. There is no spectacle so fair and beautiful as a noble and generous action; nor any which gives us more abhorrence than one that is cruel and treacherous. No enjoyment equals the satisfaction we receive from the company of those we love and esteem; as the greatest of all punishments is to be oblig'd to pass our lives with those we hate or contemn. A very play or romance may afford us instances of this pleasure, which virtue conveys to us; and pain, which arises from vice.

[3] Now since the distinguishing impressions, by which moral good or evil is known, are nothing but *particular* pains or pleasures; it follows, that in all enquiries concerning these moral distinctions, it will be sufficient to shew the principles, which make us feel a satisfaction or uneasiness from the survey of any character, in order to satisfy us why the character is laudable or blameable. An action, or sentiment, or character is virtuous or vicious; why? because its view causes a pleasure or uneasiness of a particular kind. In giving a reason, therefore, for the pleasure or uneasiness, we sufficiently explain the vice or virtue. To have the sense of virtue, is nothing but to *feel* a satisfaction of a particular kind from the contemplation of a character. The very *feeling* constitutes our praise or admiration. We go no farther; nor do we enquire into the cause of the satisfaction. We do not infer a character to be virtuous, because it pleases: But in feeling that it pleases after such a particular manner, we in effect feel that it is virtuous. The case is the same as in our judgments concerning all kinds of beauty, and

tastes, and sensations. Our approbation is imply'd in the immediate pleasure they convey to us.

[4] I have objected to the system, which establishes eternal rational measures of right and wrong, that 'tis impossible to shew, in the actions of reasonable creatures, any relations, which are not found in external objects; and therefore, if morality always attended these relations, 'twere possible for inanimate matter to become virtuous or vicious. Now it may, in like manner, be objected to the present system, that if virtue and vice be determin'd by pleasure and pain, these qualities must, in every case, arise from the sensations; and consequently any object, whether animate or inanimate, rational or irrational, might become morally good or evil, provided it can excite a satisfaction or uneasiness. But tho' this objection seems to be the very same, it has by no means the same force, in the one case as in the other. For, *first*, 'tis evident, that under the term *pleasure*, we comprehend sensations, which are very different from each other, and which have only such a distant resemblance, as is requisite to make them be express'd by the same abstract term. A good composition of music and a bottle of good wine equally produce pleasure; and, what is more, their goodness is determin'd merely by the pleasure. But shall we say upon that account, that the wine is harmonious, or the music of a good flavour? In like manner an inanimate object, and the character or sentiments of any person may, both of them, give satisfaction; but as the satisfaction is different, this keeps our sentiments concerning them from being confounded, and makes us ascribe virtue to the one, and not to the other. Nor is every sentiment of pleasure or pain, which arises from characters and actions, of that *peculiar* kind, which makes us praise or condemn. The good qualities of an enemy are hurtful to us; but may still command our esteem and respect. 'Tis only when a character is consider'd in general, without reference to our particular interest, that it causes such a feeling or sentiment, as denominates it morally good or evil. 'Tis true, those sentiments, from interest and morals, are apt to be confounded, and naturally run into one another. It seldom happens, that we do not think an enemy vicious, and can distinguish betwixt his opposition to our interest and real villainy or baseness. But this hinders not, but that the sentiments are, in themselves, distinct; and a man of temper and judgment may preserve himself from these illusions. In like manner, tho' 'tis certain a musical voice is nothing but one that naturally gives a *particular* kind of pleasure; yet 'tis difficult for a man to be sensible, that the voice of an enemy is agreeable, or to allow it to be musical. But a person of a fine ear, who has the command of himself, can separate these feelings, and give praise to what deserves it.

[5] *Secondly,* We may call to remembrance the preceding system of the passions, in order to remark a still more considerable difference among our pains and pleasures. Pride and humility, love and hatred are excited, when there is any thing presented to us, that both bears a relation to the object of the passion, and produces a separate sensation related to the sensation of the passion. Now virtue and vice are attended with these circumstances. They must necessarily be plac'd either in ourselves or others, and excite either pleasure or uneasiness; and therefore must give rise to one of these four passions; which clearly distinguishes them from the pleasure and pain arising from inanimate objects, that often bear no relation to us: And this is, perhaps, the most considerable effect that virtue and vice have upon the human mind.

[6] It may now be ask'd *in general,* concerning this pain or pleasure, that distinguishes moral good and evil, *From what principles is it deriv'd, and whence does it arise in the human mind?* To this I reply, *first,* that 'tis absurd to imagine, that in every particular instance, these sentiments are produc'd by an *original* quality and *primary* constitution. For as the number of our duties is, in a manner, infinite, 'tis impossible that our original instincts shou'd extend to each of them, and from our very first infancy impress on the human mind all that multitude of precepts, which are contain'd in the compleatest system of ethics. Such a method of proceeding is not conformable to the usual maxims, by which nature is conducted, where a few principles produce all that variety we observe in the universe, and every thing is carry'd on in the easiest and most simple manner. 'Tis necessary, therefore, to abridge these primary impulses, and find some more general principles, upon which all our notions of morals are founded.

[7] But in the *second* place, shou'd it be ask'd, whether we ought to search for these principles in *nature,* or whether we must look for them in some other origin? I wou'd reply, that our answer to this question depends upon the definition of the word, Nature, than which there is none more ambiguous and equivocal. If *nature* be oppos'd to miracles, not only the distinction betwixt vice and virtue is natural, but also every event, which has ever happen'd in the world, *excepting those miracles, on which our religion is founded.* In saying, then, that the sentiments of vice and virtue are natural in this sense, we make no very extraordinary discovery.

[8] But *nature* may also be opposed to rare and unusual; and in this sense of the word, which is the common one, there may often arise disputes concerning what is natural or unnatural; and one may in general affirm, that we are not possess'd of any very precise standard, by which these disputes can be decided. Frequent and rare depend

upon the number of examples we have observ'd; and as this number may gradually encrease or diminish, 'twill be impossible to fix any exact boundaries betwixt them. We may only affirm on this head, that if ever there was any thing, which cou'd be call'd natural in this sense, the sentiments of morality certainly may; since there never was any nation of the world, nor any single person in any nation, who was utterly depriv'd of them, and who never, in any instance, showed the least approbation or dislike of manners. These sentiments are so rooted in our constitution and temper, that without entirely confounding the human mind by disease or madness, 'tis impossible to extirpate and destroy them.

[9] But *nature* may also be opposed to artifice, as well as to what is rare and unusual; and in this sense it may be disputed, whether the notions of virtue be natural or not. We readily forget, that the designs, and projects, and views of men are principles as necessary in their operation as heat and cold, moist and dry: But taking them to be free and entirely our own, 'tis usual for us to set them in opposition to the other principles of nature. Shou'd it, therefore, be demanded, whether the sense of virtue be natural or artificial, I am of opinion, that 'tis impossible for me at present to give any precise answer to this question. Perhaps it will appear afterwards, that our sense of some virtues is artificial, and that of others natural. The discussion of this question will be more proper, when we enter upon an exact detail of each particular vice and virtue.[9]

[10] Mean while it may not be amiss to observe from these definitions of *natural* and *unnatural*, that nothing can be more unphilosophical than those systems, which assert, that virtue is the same with what is natural, and vice with what is unnatural. For in the first sense of the word, Nature, as opposed to miracles, both vice and virtue are equally natural; and in the second sense, as oppos'd to what is unusual, perhaps virtue will be found to be the most unnatural. At least it must be own'd, that heroic virtue, being as unusual, is as little natural as the most brutal barbarity. As to the third sense of the word, 'tis certain, that both vice and virtue are equally artificial, and out of nature. For however it may be disputed, whether the notion of a merit or demerit in certain actions be natural or artificial, 'tis evident, that the actions themselves are artificial, and are perform'd with a certain design and intention; otherwise they cou'd never be rank'd under any of these

9. In the following discourse *natural* is also opposed sometimes to *civil*, sometimes to *moral*. The opposition will always discover the sense, in which it is taken.

denominations. 'Tis impossible, therefore, that the character of natural and unnatural can ever, in any sense, mark the boundaries of vice and virtue.

[11] Thus we are still brought back to our first position, that virtue is distinguished by the pleasure, and vice by the pain, that any action, sentiment or character, gives us by the mere view and contemplation. This decision is very commodious; because it reduces us to this simple question, *Why any action or sentiment, upon the general view or survey, gives a certain satisfaction or uneasiness,* in order to shew the origin of its moral rectitude or depravity, without looking for any incomprehensible relations and qualities, which never did exist in nature, nor even in our imagination, by any clear and distinct conception. I flatter myself I have executed a great part of my present design by a state of the question, which appears to me so free from ambiguity and obscurity.

8

Kant: The Need for Reason to Dominate

Many philosophy teachers and students, asked to name three or four great philosophers, would include Kant on the list. There is an odd contrast between Kant's philosophical greatness and his very quiet and static academic life in the town of Konigsberg in the northeastern part of Germany. We only slightly know Kant the person.

There are two interesting stories that do point to different aspects of his personality. One concerns his emphasis on keeping promises, including the promise to be somewhere at a certain time. Kant often went to meet his friend Green, to ride along in Green's carriage. Green was obsessive about time. On one occasion Kant was a bit late, and Green became cross and set out in a huff without him. Someone asked Kant about this, and Kant said that of course Green was justified and that he (Kant) had been in the wrong.

The other story reports Kant's presence at a dinner party given by officers of the Russian army, which at the moment was occupying Konigsberg. Kant is described as having been lively and charming. Despite his quiet life, he was clearly cosmopolitan.

Kant's major philosophical achievements are both in ethics and in relation to our knowledge of the world. They reflect rigorous thought but also (in relation to our knowledge of the world) exhibit an imaginative turn in thought.

A short version of reason in ethics (according to Kant) is this. If we are about to do X, we can ask whether it would be okay from our point of view if it were a universal law that everyone did X. This would include of course doing X to us. You should not allow yourself to lie or steal unless you would not mind other people lying to you or stealing from you. In short, one form of Kant's "categorical imperative" is that nothing is acceptable if it would not be acceptable as a universal law.

Another version of the categorical imperative, which has attracted growing interest in recent decades, is the general requirement of respect for persons: treating people as having inherent value rather than regarding some of them as useful objects for oneself. In taking persons as having an inherent right to be treated with respect, Kant was in accord with some other eighteenth-century philosophers, including Rousseau and had a bust of Rousseau in his study.

Kant's primary insight in relation to our knowledge of the world is this. One might think that we simply can, as it were, read reality off from what we experience. But, Kant insists, in experiencing the world we employ interpretative categories and assumptions. We know some things "a priori" (in advance). An example of such an assumption is that every event has a cause. The philosopher W. H. Walsh has given an example of the inherent plausibility of this. Suppose that you are riding in a car and the car suddenly stops. You ask what made it stop, and the reply is that nothing made it stop: it just did. Another Walsh example that also is revealing is this. Your cuff links have disappeared. Where did they go? you wonder; but you are told, "They just vanished into thin air."

There are certain familiar structures of human thought that involve such things as cause and effect or, with qualifications, conservation of matter. (The qualifications concern cases in which matter is converted into energy.) What we experience includes these structures.

Aliens from outer space might have experience that involves different structures, something that might make communication difficult. This imaginable difference connects Kant's philosophy with the general topic of human nature. Kant clearly (like Aristotle before him) believed that one feature of human nature is that it normally includes rationality. But beyond this, Kant holds that human nature includes the fact that there are structures of thought (involving such things as cause and effect and, with qualifications, conservation of matter) that we normally project into our experiences.

If we want to know exactly what the reality is that there is to experience, apart from these familiar structures that we project, Kant's answer is this: God experiences the world as it really is (in itself). This is called the "noumenal world." What we experience is the phenomenal world, the human-structured world as available to us humans.

Grounding for the Metaphysics of Morals

First Section

Transition from the Ordinary Rational Knowledge of Morality to the Philosophical

There is no possibility of thinking of anything at all in the world, or even out of it, which can be regarded as good without qualification,

From Immanuel Kant, *Grounding for the Metaphysics of Morals*, trans. James W. Ellington (Indianapolis: Hackett Publishing Co., 1981). Reprinted by permission of the publisher.

except a *good will.* Intelligence, wit, judgment, and whatever talents of the mind one might want to name are doubtless in many respects good and desirable, as are such qualities of temperament as courage, resolution, perseverance. But they can also become extremely bad and harmful if the will, which is to make use of these gifts of nature and which in its special constitution is called character, is not good. The same holds with gifts of fortune; power, riches, honor, even health, and that complete well-being and contentment with one's condition which is called happiness make for pride and often hereby even arrogance, unless there is a good will to correct their influence on the mind and herewith also to rectify the whole principle of action and make it universally conformable to its end. The sight of a being who is not graced by any touch of a pure and good will but who yet enjoys an uninterrupted prosperity can never delight a rational and impartial spectator. Thus a good will seems to constitute the indispensable condition of being even worthy of happiness.

Some qualities are even conducive to this good will itself and can facilitate its work. Nevertheless, they have no intrinsic unconditional [394] worth; but they always presuppose, rather, a good will, which restricts the high esteem in which they are otherwise rightly held, and does not permit them to be regarded as absolutely good. Moderation in emotions and passions, self-control, and calm deliberation are not only good in many respects but even seem to constitute part of the intrinsic worth of a person. But they are far from being rightly called good without qualification (however unconditionally they were commended by the ancients). For without the principles of a good will, they can become extremely bad; the coolness of a villain makes him not only much more dangerous but also immediately more abominable in our eyes than he would have been regarded by us without it.

A good will is good not because of what it effects or accomplishes, nor because of its fitness to attain some proposed end; it is good only through its willing, i.e., it is good in itself. When it is considered in itself, then it is to be esteemed very much higher than anything which it might ever bring about merely in order to favor some inclination, or even the sum total of all inclinations. Even if, by some especially unfortunate fate or by the niggardly provision of stepmotherly nature, this will should be wholly lacking in the power to accomplish its purpose; if with the greatest effort it should yet achieve nothing, and only the good will should remain (not, to be sure, as a mere wish but as the summoning of all the means in our power), yet would it, like a jewel, still shine by its own light as something which has its full value in itself. Its usefulness or fruitlessness can neither augment nor diminish this value. Its usefulness would be, as it were, only the setting to enable us to handle it in ordinary dealings or to attract to it the attention of those who are not yet experts, but not to recommend it to real experts or to determine its value.

But there is something so strange in this idea of the absolute value of a mere will, in which no account is taken of any useful results, that in spite of all the agreement received even from ordinary reason, yet there must arise the suspicion that such an idea may perhaps have as its hidden basis merely some high-flown fancy, and that we may have misunderstood the purpose of nature in assigning to reason the governing of our will. [395] Therefore, this idea will be examined from this point of view.

In the natural constitution of an organized being, i.e., one suitably adapted to the purpose of life, let there be taken as a principle that in such a being no organ is to be found for any end unless it be the most fit and the best adapted for that end. Now if that being's preservation, welfare, or in a word its happiness, were the real end of nature in the case of a being having reason and will, then nature would have hit upon a very poor arrangement in having the reason of the creature carry out this purpose. For all the actions which such a creature has to perform with this purpose in view, and the whole rule of his conduct would have been prescribed much more exactly by instinct; and the purpose in question could have been attained much more certainly by instinct than it ever can be by reason. And if in addition reason had been imparted to this favored creature, then it would have had to serve him only to contemplate the happy constitution of his nature, to admire that nature, to rejoice in it, and to feel grateful to the cause that bestowed it; but reason would not have served him to subject his faculty of desire to its weak and delusive guidance nor would it have served him to meddle incompetently with the purpose of nature. In a word, nature would have taken care that reason did not strike out into a practical use nor presume, with its weak insight, to think out for itself a plan for happiness and the means for attaining it. Nature would have taken upon herself not only the choice of ends but also that of the means, and would with wise foresight have entrusted both to instinct alone.

And, in fact, we find that the more a cultivated reason devotes itself to the aim of enjoying life and happiness, the further does man get away from true contentment. Because of this there arises in many persons, if only they are candid enough to admit it, a certain degree of misology, i.e., hatred of reason. This is especially so in the case of those who are the most experienced in the use of reason, because after calculating all the advantages they derive, I say not from the invention of all the arts of common luxury, but even from the sciences (which in the end seem to them to be also a luxury of the understanding), they yet find that they have in fact only brought more trouble on their heads than they have gained in happiness. [396] Therefore, they come to envy, rather than despise, the more common run of men who are closer to the guidance of mere natural instinct and who do not allow their reason much influence on their conduct. And we must admit that the judgment of those who would temper, or even reduce below zero, the boastful eulogies on behalf of the advantages which reason is supposed to provide as regards the happiness and contentment of life is by no means morose or ungrateful to the goodness with which the world is governed. There lies at the root of such judgments, rather, the idea that existence has another and much more worthy purpose, for which, and not for happiness, reason is quite properly intended, and which must, therefore, be regarded as the supreme condition to which the private purpose of men must, for the most part, defer.

Reason, however, is not competent enough to guide the will safely as regards its objects and the satisfaction of all our needs (which it in part even multiplies); to this end would an implanted natural instinct have led much more certainly. But inasmuch as reason has been imparted to us as a practical faculty, i.e., as one which is to have influence on the will, its true function must be to produce a will which is not merely good as a means to some further end, but is good in itself. To produce a will good in itself reason was absolutely necessary, inasmuch as nature in distributing her capacities has everywhere gone to work in a purposive manner. While such a will may not indeed be the sole and complete good, it must, nevertheless, be the highest good and the condition of all the rest, even of the desire for happiness. In this case there is nothing inconsistent with the wisdom of nature that the cultivation of reason, which is requisite for the first and unconditioned purpose, may in many ways restrict, at least in this life, the attainment of the second purpose, viz., happiness, which is always conditioned. Indeed happiness can even be reduced to less than nothing, without nature's failing thereby in her purpose; for reason recognizes as its highest practical function the establishment of a good will, whereby in the attainment of this end reason is capable only of its own kind of satisfaction, viz., that of fulfilling a purpose which is in turn determined only by reason, even though such fulfillment were often to interfere with the purposes of inclination.

The concept of a will estimable in itself and good without regard to any [397] further end must now be developed. This concept already dwells in the natural sound understanding and needs not so much to be taught as merely to be elucidated. It always holds first place in estimating the total worth of our actions and constitutes the condition of all the rest. Therefore, we shall take up the concept of *duty,* which includes that of a good will, though with certain subjective restrictions and hindrances, which far from hiding a good will or rendering it unrecognizable, rather bring it out by contrast and make it shine forth more brightly.

I here omit all actions already recognized as contrary to duty, even though they may be useful for this or that end; for in the case of these the question does not arise at all as to whether they might be done from duty, since they even conflict with duty. I also set aside those actions which are really in accordance with duty, yet to which men have no immediate inclination, but perform them because they are impelled thereto by some other inclination. For in this [second] case to decide whether the action which is in accord with duty has been done from duty or from some selfish purpose is easy. This difference is far more difficult to note in the [third] case where the action accords with duty and the subject has in addition an immediate inclination to do the action. For example, that a dealer should not overcharge an inexperienced purchaser certainly accords with duty; and where there is much commerce, the prudent merchant does not overcharge but keeps to a fixed price for everyone in general, so that a child may buy from him just as well as everyone else may. Thus customers are honestly served, but this is not nearly enough for making us believe that the merchant has acted this way from duty and from principles of honesty; his own advantage required him to do it. He cannot, however, be assumed to have in addition [as in the third case] an immediate inclination toward his buyers, causing him, as it were, out of love to give no one as far as price is concerned any advantage over another. Hence the action was done neither from duty nor from immediate inclination, but merely for a selfish purpose.

On the other hand, to preserve one's life is a duty; and, furthermore, everyone has also an immediate inclination to do so. But on this account [398] the often anxious care taken by most men for it has no intrinsic worth, and the maxim of their action has no moral content. They preserve their lives, to be sure, in accordance with duty, but not from duty. On the other hand, if adversity and hopeless sorrow have completely taken away the taste for life, if an unfortunate man, strong in soul and more indignant at his fate than despondent or dejected, wishes for death and yet preserves his life without loving it—not from inclination or fear, but from duty—then his maxim indeed has a moral content.

To be beneficent where one can is a duty; and besides this, there are many persons who are so sympathetically constituted that, without any further motive of vanity or self-interest, they find an inner pleasure in spreading joy around them and can rejoice in the satisfaction of others as their own work. But I maintain that in such a case an action of this kind, however dutiful and amiable it may be, has nevertheless no true moral worth. It is on a level with such actions as arise from other inclinations, e.g., the inclination for honor, which if fortunately directed to what is in fact beneficial and accords with duty and is thus honorable, deserves praise and encouragement, but not esteem; for its maxim lacks the moral content of an action done not from inclination but from duty. Suppose then the mind of this friend of mankind to be clouded over with his own sorrow so that all sympathy with the lot of others is extinguished, and suppose him still to have the power to benefit others in distress, even though he is not touched by their trouble because he is sufficiently absorbed with his own; and now suppose that, even though no inclination moves him any longer, he nevertheless tears himself from this deadly insensibility and performs the action without any inclination at all, but solely from duty—then for the first time his action has genuine moral worth. Further still, if nature has put little sympathy in this or that man's heart, if (while being an honest man in other respects) he is by temperament cold and indifferent to the sufferings of others, perhaps because as regards his own sufferings he is endowed with the special gift of patience and fortitude and expects or even requires that others should have the same; if such a man (who would truly not be nature's worst product) had not been exactly fashioned by her to be a philanthropist, would he not yet find in himself a source from which he might give himself a worth far higher than any that a good-natured temperament might have? By all means, because just here [399] does the worth of the character come out; this worth is moral and incomparably the highest of all, viz., that he is beneficent, not from inclination, but from duty.

To secure one's own happiness is a duty (at least indirectly); for discontent with one's condition under many pressing cares and amid unsatisfied wants might easily become a great temptation to transgress one's duties. But here also do men of themselves already have, irrespective of duty, the strongest and deepest inclination toward happiness, because just in this idea are all inclinations combined into a sum total. But the precept of happiness is often so constituted as greatly to interfere with some inclinations, and yet men cannot form any definite and certain concept of the sum of satisfaction of all inclinations that is called happiness. Hence there is no wonder that a single inclination which is determinate both as to what it promises and as to the time within which it can be satisfied may outweigh a fluctuating idea; and there is no wonder that a man, e.g., a gouty patient, can choose to enjoy what he likes and to suffer what he may, since by his calculation he has here at least not sacrificed the enjoyment of the present moment to some possibly groundless expectations of the good fortune that is supposed to be found in health. But even in this case, if the universal inclination to happiness did not determine his will and if health, at least for him, did not figure as so necessary an element in his calculations; there still remains here, as in all other cases, a law, viz., that he should promote his happiness not from inclination but from duty, and thereby for the first time does his conduct have real moral worth.

Undoubtedly in this way also are to be understood those passages of Scripture which command us to love our neighbor and even our enemy. For love as an inclination cannot be commanded; but beneficence from duty, when no inclination impels us and even when a natural and unconquerable aversion opposes such beneficence, is practical, and not pathological, love. Such love resides in the will and not in the propensities of feeling, in principles of action and not in tender sympathy; and only this practical love can be commanded.

The second proposition is this: An action done from duty has its moral worth, not in the purpose that is to be attained by it, but in the maxim according to which the action is determined. The moral worth depends, therefore, not on the realization of the object of the action, but merely on [400] the principle of volition according to which, without regard to any objects of the faculty of desire, the action has been done. From what has gone before it is clear that the purposes which we may have in our actions, as well as their effects regarded as ends and incentives of the will, cannot give to actions any unconditioned and moral worth. Where, then, can this worth lie if it is not to be found in the will's relation to the expected effect? Nowhere but in the principle of the will, with no regard to the ends that can be brought about through such action. For the will stands, as it were, at a crossroads between its a priori principle, which is formal, and its a posteriori incentive, which is material; and since it must be determined by something, it must be determined by the formal principle of volition, if the action is done from duty—and in that case every material principle is taken away from it.

The third proposition, which follows from the other two, can be expressed thus: Duty is the necessity of an action done out of respect for the law. I can indeed have an inclination for an object as the effect of my proposed action; but I can never have respect for such an object, just because it is merely an effect and is not an activity of the will. Similarly, I can have no respect for inclination as such, whether my own or that of another. I can at most, if my own inclination, approve it; and, if that of another, even love it, i.e., consider it to be favorable to my own advantage. An object of respect can only be what is connected with my will solely as ground and never as effect—something that does not serve my inclination but, rather, outweighs it, or at least excludes it from consideration when some choice is made—in other words, only the law itself can be an object of respect and hence can be a command. Now an action done from duty must altogether exclude the influence of inclination and therewith every object of the will. Hence there is nothing left which can determine the will except objectively the law and subjectively pure respect for this practical law, i.e., the will can be subjectively determined by the maxim[1] that I should follow such a law even if all my inclinations are thereby thwarted.

[401] Thus the moral worth of an action does not lie in the effect expected from it nor in any principle of action that needs to borrow its motive from this expected effect. For all these effects (agreeableness of one's condition and even the furtherance of other people's happiness) could have been brought about also through other causes and would not have required the will of a rational being, in which the highest and unconditioned good can alone be found. Therefore, the pre-eminent good which is called moral can consist in nothing but the representation of the law in itself, and such a representation can admittedly be found only in a rational being insofar as this representation, and not some expected effect, is the determining ground of the will. This good is already present in the person who acts according to this representation, and such good need not be awaited merely from the effect.[2]

1. A maxim is the subjective principle of volition. The objective principle (i.e., one which would serve all rational beings also subjectively as a practical principle if reason had full control over the faculty of desire) is the practical law.

2. There might be brought against me here an objection that I take refuge behind the word "respect" in an obscure feeling, instead of giving a clear answer to the question by means of a concept of reason. But even though respect is a feeling, it is not one received through any outside influence but is, rather, one that is self-produced by means of a rational concept; hence it is specifically different from all feelings of the first kind, which can all be reduced to inclination or fear. What I recognize immediately as a law for me, I recognize with respect; this means merely the consciousness of the subordination of my will to a law without the mediation of other influences upon my sense. The immediate determination of the will by the law, and the consciousness thereof, is called respect, which

[402] But what sort of law can that be the thought of which must determine the will without reference to any expected effect, so that the will can be called absolutely good without qualification? Since I have deprived the will of every impulse that might arise for it from obeying any particular law, there is nothing left to serve the will as principle except the universal conformity of its actions to law as such, i.e., I should never act except in such a way that I can also will that my maxim should become a universal law. Here mere conformity to law as such (without having as its basis any law determining particular actions) serves the will as principle and must so serve it if duty is not to be a vain delusion and a chimerical concept. The ordinary reason of mankind in its practical judgments agrees completely with this, and always has in view the aforementioned principle.

For example, take this question. When I am in distress, may I make a promise with the intention of not keeping it? I readily distinguish here the two meanings which the question may have; whether making a false promise conforms with prudence or with duty. Doubtless the former can often be the case. Indeed I clearly see that escape from some present difficulty by means of such a promise is not enough. In addition I must carefully consider whether from this lie there may later arise far greater inconvenience for me than from what I now try to escape. Furthermore, the consequences of my false promise are not easy to forsee, even with all my supposed cunning; loss of confidence in me might prove to be far more disadvantageous than the misfortune which I now try to avoid. The more prudent way might be to act according to a universal maxim and to make it a habit not to promise anything without intending to keep it. But that such a maxim

---

is hence regarded as the effect of the law upon the subject and not as the cause of the law. Respect is properly the representation of a worth that thwarts my self-love. Hence respect is something that is regarded as an object of neither inclination nor fear, although it has at the same time something analogous to both. The object of respect is, therefore, nothing but the law—indeed that very law which we impose on ourselves and yet recognize as necessary in itself. As law, we are subject to it without consulting self-love; as imposed on us by ourselves, it is a consequence of our will. In the former aspect, it is analogous to fear; in the latter, to inclination. All respect for a person is properly only respect for the law (of honesty, etc.) of which the person provides an example. Since we regard the development of our talents as a duty, we think of a man of talent as being also a kind of example of the law (the law of becoming like him by practice), and that is what constitutes our respect for him. All so-called moral interest consists solely in respect for the law.

is, nevertheless, always based on nothing but a fear of consequences becomes clear to me at once. To be truthful from duty is, however, quite different from being truthful from fear of disadvantageous consequences; in the first case the concept of the action itself contains a law for me, while in the second I must first look around elsewhere to see what are the results for me that might be connected with the action. For to deviate from the principle of duty is quite certainly bad; but to [403] abandon my maxim of prudence can often be very advantageous for me, though to abide by it is certainly safer. The most direct and infallible way, however, to answer the question as to whether a lying promise accords with duty is to ask myself whether I would really be content if my maxim (of extricating myself from difficulty by means of a false promise) were to hold as a universal law for myself as well as for others, and could I really say to myself that everyone may promise falsely when he finds himself in a difficulty from which he can find no other way to extricate himself. Then I immediately become aware that I can indeed will the lie but cannot at all will a universal law to lie. For by such a law there would really be no promises at all, since in vain would my willing future actions be professed to other people who would not believe what I professed, or if they over-hastily did believe, then they would pay me back in like coin. Therefore, my maxim would necessarily destroy itself just as soon as it was made a universal law.

Therefore, I need no far-reaching acuteness to discern what I have to do in order that my will may be morally good. Inexperienced in the course of the world and incapable of being prepared for all its contingencies, I only ask myself whether I can also will that my maxim should become a universal law. If not, then the maxim must be rejected, not because of any disadvantage accruing to me or even to others, but because it cannot be fitting as a principle in a possible legislation of universal law, and reason exacts from me immediate respect for such legislation. Indeed I have as yet no insight into the grounds of such respect (which the philosopher may investigate). But I at least understand that respect is an estimation of a worth that far outweighs any worth of what is recommended by inclination, and that the necessity of acting from pure respect for the practical law is what constitutes duty, to which every other motive must give way because duty is the condition of a will good in itself, whose worth is above all else.

Thus within the moral cognition of ordinary human reason we have arrived at its principle. To be sure, such reason does not think of this principle abstractly in its universal form, but does always have it actually in view and does use it as the standard of judgment. It would here be easy to [404] show how ordinary reason, with this compass in hand, is well able to distinguish, in every case that occurs, what is good or evil, in accord with duty or contrary to duty, if we do not in the least try to teach reason anything new but only make it attend, as Socrates did, to its own principle—and thereby do we show that neither science nor philosophy is needed in order to know what one must do to be honest and good, and even wise and virtuous. Indeed we might even have conjectured beforehand that cognizance of what every man is obligated to do, and hence also to know, would be available to every man, even the most ordinary. Yet we cannot but observe with admiration how great an advantage the power of practical judgment has over the theoretical in ordinary human understanding. In the theoretical, when ordinary reason ventures to depart from the laws of experience and the perceptions of sense, it falls into sheer inconceivabilities and self-contradictions, or at least into a chaos of uncertainty, obscurity, and instability. In the practical, however, the power of judgment first begins to show itself to advantage when ordinary understanding excludes all sensuous incentives from practical laws. Such understanding then becomes even subtle, whether in quibbling with its own conscience or with other claims regarding what is to be called right, or whether in wanting to determine correctly for its own instruction the worth of various actions. And the most extraordinary thing is that ordinary understanding in this practical case may have just as good a hope of hitting the mark as that which any philosopher may promise himself. Indeed it is almost more certain in this than even a philosopher is, because he can have no principle other than what ordinary understanding has, but he may easily confuse his judgment by a multitude of foreign and irrelevant considerations and thereby cause it to swerve from the right way. Would it not, therefore, be wiser in moral matters to abide by the ordinary rational judgment or at most to bring in philosophy merely for the purpose of rendering the system of morals more complete and intelligible and of presenting its rules in a way that is more convenient for use (especially in disputation), but not for the purpose of leading ordinary human understanding away from its happy simplicity in practical matters and of bringing it by means of philosophy into a new path of inquiry and instruction?

[405] Innocence is indeed a glorious thing; but, unfortunately, it does not keep very well and is easily led astray. Consequently, even wisdom—which consists more in doing and not doing than in knowing—needs science, not in order to learn from it, but in order that wisdom's precepts may gain acceptance and permanence. Man

feels within himself a powerful counterweight to all the commands of duty, which are presented to him by reason as being so pre-eminently worthy of respect; this counterweight consists of his needs and inclinations, whose total satisfaction is summed up under the name of happiness. Now reason irremissibly commands its precepts, without thereby promising the inclinations anything; hence it disregards and neglects these impetuous and at the same time so seemingly plausible claims (which do not allow themselves to be suppressed by any command). Hereby arises a natural dialectic, i.e., a propensity to quibble with these strict laws of duty, to cast doubt upon their validity, or at least upon their purity and strictness, and to make them, where possible, more compatible with our wishes and inclinations. Thereby are such laws corrupted in their very foundations and their whole dignity is destroyed—something which even ordinary practical reason cannot in the end call good.

Thus is ordinary human reason forced to go outside its sphere and take a step into the field of practical philosophy, not by any need for speculation (which never befalls such reason so long as it is content to be mere sound reason) but on practical grounds themselves. There it tries to obtain information and clear instruction regarding the source of its own principle and the correct determination of this principle in its opposition to maxims based on need and inclination, so that reason may escape from the perplexity of opposite claims and may avoid the risk of losing all genuine moral principles through the ambiguity into which it easily falls. Thus when ordinary practical reason cultivates itself, there imperceptibly arises in it a dialectic which compels it to seek help in philosophy. The same thing happens in reason's theoretical use; in this case, just as in the other, peace will be found only in a thorough critical examination of our reason.

Second Section

Transition from Popular Moral Philosophy to a Metaphysics of Morals

[406] If we have so far drawn our concept of duty from the ordinary use of our practical reason, one is by no means to infer that we have treated it as a concept of experience. On the contrary, when we pay attention to our experience of the way human beings act, we meet frequent and—as we ourselves admit—justified complaints that there cannot be cited a single certain example of the disposition to act from pure duty; and we meet complaints that although much may be done

that is in accordance with what duty commands, yet there are always doubts as to whether what occurs has really been done from duty and so has moral worth. Hence there have always been philosophers who have absolutely denied the reality of this disposition in human actions and have ascribed everything to a more or less refined self-love. Yet in so doing they have not cast doubt upon the rightness of the concept of morality. Rather, they have spoken with sincere regret as to the frailty and impurity of human nature, which they think is noble enough to take as its precept an idea so worthy of respect but yet is too weak to follow this idea: reason, which should legislate for human nature, is used only to look after the interest of inclinations, whether singly or, at best, in their greatest possible harmony with one another.

In fact there is absolutely no possibility by means of experience to make [407] out with complete certainty a single case in which the maxim of an action that may in other respects conform to duty has rested solely on moral grounds and on the representation of one's duty. It is indeed sometimes the case that after the keenest self-examination we can find nothing except the moral ground of duty that could have been strong enough to move us to this or that good action and to such great sacrifice. But there cannot with certainty be at all inferred from this that some secret impulse of self-love, merely appearing as the idea of duty, was not the actual determining cause of the will. We like to flatter ourselves with the false claim to a more noble motive; but in fact we can never, even by the strictest examination, completely plumb the depths of the secret incentives of our actions. For when moral value is being considered, the concern is not with the actions, which are seen, but rather with their inner principles, which are not seen.

Moreover, one cannot better serve the wishes of those who ridicule all morality as being a mere phantom of human imagination getting above itself because of self-conceit than by conceding to them that the concepts of duty must be drawn solely from experience (just as from indolence one willingly persuades himself that such is the case as regards all other concepts as well). For by so conceding, one prepares for them a sure triumph. I am willing to admit out of love for humanity that most of our actions are in accordance with duty; but if we look more closely at our planning and striving, we everywhere come upon the dear self, which is always turning up, and upon which the intent of our actions is based rather than upon the strict command of duty (which would often require self-denial). One need not be exactly an enemy of virtue, but only a cool observer who does not take the liveliest wish for the good to be straight off its realization, in order to become doubtful at times whether any true virtue is actually to be found in the world. Such is especially the case when years increase and one's power of judgment is made shrewder by experience and keener in observation. Because of these things nothing can protect us from a complete falling away from our ideas of duty and preserve in the soul a well-grounded respect for duty's law except the clear conviction that, even if [408] there never have been actions springing from such pure sources, the question at issue here is not whether this or that has happened but that reason of itself and independently of all experience commands what ought to happen. Consequently, reason unrelentingly commands actions of which the world has perhaps hitherto never provided an example and whose feasibility might well be doubted by one who bases everything upon experience; for instance, even though there might never yet have been a sincere friend, still pure sincerity in friendship is nonetheless required of every man, because this duty, prior to all experience, is contained as duty in general in the idea of a reason that determines the will by means of a priori grounds.

There may be noted further that unless we want to deny to the concept of morality all truth and all reference to a possible object, we cannot but admit that the moral law is of such widespread significance that it must hold not merely for men but for all rational beings generally, and that it must be valid not merely under contingent conditions and with exceptions but must be absolutely necessary. Clearly, therefore, no experience can give occasion for inferring even the possibility of such apodeictic laws. For with what right could we bring into unlimited respect as a universal precept for every rational nature what is perhaps valid only under the contingent conditions of humanity? And how could laws for the determination of our will be regarded as laws for the determination of a rational being in general and of ourselves only insofar as we are rational beings, if these laws were merely empirical and did not have their source completely a priori in pure, but practical, reason?

Moreover, worse service cannot be rendered morality than that an attempt be made to derive it from examples. For every example of morality presented to me must itself first be judged according to principles of morality in order to see whether it is fit to serve as an original example, i.e., as a model. But in no way can it authoritatively furnish the concept of morality. Even the Holy One of the gospel must first be compared with our ideal of moral perfection before he is recognized as such. Even he says of himself, "Why do you call me (whom you see) good? None is good (the archetype of the good) except God only (whom you do not see)." But [409] whence have we the concept of God as the highest good? Solely from the idea of moral perfection, which reason frames a priori and connects inseparably with the concept of a free will. Imitation has no place at all in moral matters. And examples serve only for encouragement, i.e., they put beyond doubt the feasibility of what the law commands and they make visible what the practical rule expresses more generally. But examples can never justify us in setting aside their true original, which lies in reason, and letting ourselves be guided by them.

If there is then no genuine supreme principle of morality that must rest merely on pure reason, independently of all experience, I think it is unnecessary even to ask whether it is a good thing to exhibit these concepts generally (*in abstracto*), which, along with the principles that belong to them, hold a priori, so far as the knowledge involved is to be distinguished from ordinary knowledge and is to be called philosophical. But in our times it may well be necessary to do so. For if one were to take a vote as to whether pure rational knowledge separated from everything empirical, i.e., metaphysics of morals, or whether popular practical philosophy is to be preferred, one can easily guess which side would be preponderant.

This descent to popular thought is certainly very commendable once the ascent to the principles of pure reason has occurred and has been satisfactorily accomplished. That would mean that the doctrine of morals has first been grounded on metaphysics and that subsequently acceptance for morals has been won by giving it a popular character after it has been firmly established. But it is quite absurd to try for popularity in the first inquiry, upon which depends the total correctness of the principles. Not only can such a procedure never lay claim to the very rare merit of a true philosophical popularity, inasmuch as there is really no art involved at all in being generally intelligible if one thereby renounces all basic insight, but such a procedure turns out a disgusting mishmash of patchwork observations and half-reasoned principles in which shallowpates revel because all this is something quite useful for the chitchat of everyday life. Persons of insight, on the other hand, feel confused by all this and turn their eyes away with a dissatisfaction which they nevertheless cannot cure. Yet philosophers, who quite see through the delusion, get little hearing when [410] they summon people for a time from this pretended popularity in order that they may be rightfully popular only after they have attained definite insight.

One need only look at the attempts to deal with morality in the way favored by popular taste. What he will find in an amazing mixture is at one time the particular constitution of human nature (but along with this also the idea of a rational nature in general), at another time perfection, at another happiness; here moral feeling, and there the fear of God; something of this, and also something of that. But the thought never occurs to ask whether the principles of morality are to be sought at all in the knowledge of human nature (which can be had only from experience). Nor does the thought occur that if these principles are not to be sought here but to be found, rather, completely a priori and free from everything empirical in pure rational concepts only, and are to be found nowhere else even to the slightest extent—then there had better be adopted the plan of undertaking this investigation as a separate inquiry, i.e., as pure practical philosophy or (if one may use a name so much decried) as a metaphysics[3] of morals. It is better to bring this investigation to full completeness entirely by itself and to bid the public, which demands popularity, to await the outcome of this undertaking.

But such a completely isolated metaphysics of morals, not mixed with any anthropology, theology, physics, or hyperphysics, and still less with occult qualities (which might be called hypophysical), is not only an indispensable substratum of all theoretical and precisely defined knowledge of duties, but is at the same time a desideratum of the highest importance for the actual fulfillment of their precepts. For the pure thought of duty and of the moral law generally, unmixed with any extraneous addition of empirical inducements, has by the way of reason alone (which first becomes aware hereby that it can of itself be practical) an influence on [411] the human heart so much more powerful than all other incentives[4] which may be derived from

3. Pure philosophy of morals (metaphysics) may be distinguished from the applied (viz., applied to human nature) just as pure mathematics is distinguished from applied mathematics and pure logic from applied logic. By this designation one is also immediately reminded that moral principles are not grounded on the peculiarities of human nature but must subsist a priori of themselves, and that from such principles practical rules must be derivable for every rational nature, and accordingly for human nature.

4. I have a letter from the late excellent Sulzer [Johann Georg Sulzer (1720–1779), an important Berlin savant, who translated Hume's *Inquiry Concerning the Principles of Morals* into German in 1755] in which he asks me why it is that moral instruction accomplishes so little, even though it contains so much that is convincing to reason. My answer was delayed so that I might make it complete. But it is just that the teachers themselves have not purified their concepts: since they try to do too well by looking everywhere for motives for being morally good, they spoil the medicine by trying to make it

the empirical field that reason in the consciousness of its dignity despises such incentives and is able gradually to become their master. On the other hand, a mixed moral philosophy, compounded both of incentives drawn from feelings and inclinations and at the same time of rational concepts, must make the mind waver between motives that cannot be brought under any principle and that can only by accident lead to the good but often can also lead to the bad.

It is clear from the foregoing that all moral concepts have their seat and origin completely a priori in reason, and indeed in the most ordinary human reason just as much as in the most highly speculative. They cannot be abstracted from any empirical, and hence merely contingent, cognition. In this purity of their origin lies their very worthiness to serve us as supreme practical principles; and to the extent that something empirical is added to them, just so much is taken away from their genuine influence and from the absolute worth of the corresponding actions. Moreover, it is not only a requirement of the greatest necessity from a theoretical point of view, when it is a question of speculation, but also of the greatest practical importance, to draw these concepts and laws from pure reason, to present them pure and unmixed, and indeed to determine the extent of this entire practical and pure rational cognition, i.e., to determine the whole faculty of pure practical reason. The principles should not be made [412] to depend on the particular nature of human reason, as speculative philosophy may permit and even sometimes finds necessary; but, rather, the principles should be derived from the universal concept of a rational being in general, since moral laws should hold for every rational being as such. In this way all morals, which require anthropology in order to be applied to humans, must be entirely expounded at first independently of anthropology as pure philosophy, i.e., as metaphysics (which can easily be done in such distinct kinds of knowledge). One knows quite well that unless one is in possession of such a metaphysics, then the attempt is futile, I shall not say to determine exactly for speculative judgment the moral element of duty in all that accords

---

really strong. For the most ordinary observation shows that when a righteous act is represented as being done with a steadfast soul and sundered from all view to any advantage in this or another world, and even under the greatest temptations of need or allurement, it far surpasses and eclipses any similar action that was in the least affected by any extraneous incentive; it elevates the soul and inspires the wish to be able to act in this way. Even moderately young children feel this impression, and duties should never be represented to them in any other way.

with duty, but that the attempt is impossible, even in ordinary and practical usage, especially in that of moral instruction, to ground morals on their genuine principles and thereby to produce pure moral dispositions and engraft them on men's minds for the promotion of the highest good in the world.

In this study we must advance by natural stages not merely from ordinary moral judgment (which is here ever so worthy of respect) to philosophical judgment, as has already been done, but also from popular philosophy, which goes no further than it can get by groping about with the help of examples, to metaphysics (which does not permit itself to be held back any longer by what is empirical, and which, inasmuch as it must survey the whole extent of rational knowledge of this kind, goes right up to ideas, where examples themselves fail us). In order to make such an advance, we must follow and clearly present the practical faculty of reason from its universal rules of determination to the point where the concept of duty springs from it.

Everything in nature works according to laws. Only a rational being has the power to act according to his conception of laws, i.e., according to principles, and thereby has he a will. Since the derivation of actions from laws requires reason, the will is nothing but practical reason. If reason infallibly determines the will, then in the case of such a being actions which are recognized to be objectively necessary are also subjectively necessary, i.e., the will is a faculty of choosing only that which reason, independently of inclination, recognizes as being practically necessary, i.e., as good. But if reason of itself does not sufficiently determine the will, and if the [413] will submits also to subjective conditions (certain incentives) which do not always agree with objective conditions; in a word, if the will does not in itself completely accord with reason (as is actually the case with men), then actions which are recognized as objectively necessary are subjectively contingent, and the determination of such a will according to objective laws is necessitation. That is to say that the relation of objective laws to a will not thoroughly good is represented as the determination of the will of a rational being by principles of reason which the will does not necessarily follow because of its own nature.

The representation of an objective principle insofar as it necessitates the will is called a command (of reason), and the formula of the command is called an imperative.

All imperatives are expressed by an *ought* and thereby indicate the relation of an objective law of reason to a will that is not necessarily determined by this law because of its subjective constitution (the relation of necessitation). Imperatives say that something would be good to do or to refrain from doing, but they say it to a will that does not always therefore do something simply because it has been represented to the will as something good to do. That is practically good which determines the will by means of representations of reason and hence not by subjective causes, but objectively, i.e., on grounds valid for every rational being as such. It is distinguished from the pleasant as that which influences the will only by means of sensation from merely subjective causes, which hold only for this or that person's senses but do not hold as a principle of reason valid for everyone.[5]

[414] A perfectly good will would thus be quite as much subject to objective laws (of the good), but could not be conceived as thereby necessitated to act in conformity with law, inasmuch as it can of itself, according to its subjective constitution, be determined only by the representation of the good. Therefore no imperatives hold for the divine will, and in general for a holy will; the *ought* is here out of place, because the *would* is already of itself necessarily in agreement with the law. Consequently, imperatives are only formulas for expressing the relation of objective laws of willing in general to the subjective imperfection of the will of this or that rational being, e.g., the human will.

Now all imperatives command either hypothetically or categorically. The former represent the practical necessity of a possible action as a means for attaining something else that one wants (or may possibly want). The categorical imperative would be one which represented an action as objectively necessary in itself, without reference to another end.

5. The dependence of the faculty of desire on sensations is called inclination, which accordingly always indicates a need. The dependence of a contingently determinable will on principles of reason, however, is called interest. Therefore an interest is found only in a dependent will which is not of itself always in accord with reason; in the divine will no interest can be thought. But even the human will can take an interest in something without thereby acting from interest. The former signifies practical interest in the action, while the latter signifies pathological interest in the object of the action. The former indicates only dependence of the will on principles of reason by itself, while the latter indicates the will's dependence on principles of reason for the sake of inclination, i.e., reason merely gives the practical rule for meeting the need of inclination. In the former case the action interests me, while in the latter case what interests me is the object of the action (so far as this object is pleasant for me). In the First Section we have seen that in the case of an action done from duty regard must be given not to the interest in the object, but only to interest in the action itself and in its rational principle (viz., the law).

Every practical law represents a possible action as good and hence as necessary for a subject who is practically determinable by reason; therefore all imperatives are formulas for determining an action which is necessary according to the principle of a will that is good in some way. Now if the action would be good merely as a means to something else, so is the imperative hypothetical. But if the action is represented as good in itself, and hence as necessary in a will which of itself conforms to reason as the principle of the will, then the imperative is categorical.

An imperative thus says what action possible by me would be good, and it presents the practical rule in relation to a will which does not forthwith perform an action simply because it is good, partly because the subject does not always know that the action is good and partly because (even if he does know it is good) his maxims might yet be opposed to the objective principles of practical reason.

A hypothetical imperative thus says only that an action is good for some purpose, either possible or actual. In the first case it is a problematic practical [415] principle; in the second case an assertoric one. A categorical imperative, which declares an action to be of itself objectively necessary without reference to any purpose, i.e., without any other end, holds as an apodeictic practical principle.

Whatever is possible only through the powers of some rational being can be thought of as a possible purpose of some will. Consequently, there are in fact infinitely many principles of action insofar as they are represented as necessary for attaining a possible purpose achievable by them. All sciences have a practical part consisting of problems saying that some end is possible for us and of imperatives telling us how it can be attained. These can, therefore, be called in general imperatives of skill. Here there is no question at all whether the end is reasonable and good, but there is only a question as to what must be done to attain it. The prescriptions needed by a doctor in order to make his patient thoroughly healthy and by a poisoner in order to make sure of killing his victim are of equal value so far as each serves to bring about its purpose perfectly. Since there cannot be known in early youth what ends may be presented to us in the course of life, parents especially seek to have their children learn many different kinds of things, and they provide for skill in the use of means to all sorts of arbitrary ends, among which they cannot determine whether any one of them could in the future become an actual purpose for their ward, though there is always the possibility that he might adopt it. Their concern is so great that they commonly neglect to form and correct their children's judgment regarding the worth of things which might be chosen as ends.

There is, however, one end that can be presupposed as actual for all rational beings (so far as they are dependent beings to whom imperatives apply); and thus there is one purpose which they not merely can have but which can certainly be assumed to be such that they all do have by a natural necessity, and this is happiness. A hypothetical imperative which represents the practical necessity of an action as means for the promotion of happiness is assertoric. It may be expounded not simply as necessary to [416] an uncertain, merely possible purpose, but as necessary to a purpose which can be presupposed a priori and with certainty as being present in everyone because it belongs to his essence. Now skill in the choice of means to one's own greatest well-being can be called prudence[6] in the narrowest sense. And thus the imperative that refers to the choice of means to one's own happiness, i.e., the precept of prudence, still remains hypothetical; the action is commanded not absolutely but only as a means to a further purpose.

Finally, there is one imperative which immediately commands a certain conduct without having as its condition any other purpose to be attained by it. This imperative is categorical. It is not concerned with the matter of the action and its intended result, but rather with the form of the action and the principle from which it follows; what is essentially good in the action consists in the mental disposition, let the consequences be what they may. This imperative may be called that of morality.

Willing according to these three kinds of principles is also clearly distinguished by dissimilarity in the necessitation of the will. To make this dissimilarity clear I think that they are most suitably named in their order when they are said to be either *rules of skill, counsels of prudence,* or *commands* (*laws*) *of morality.* For law alone involves the concept of a necessity that is unconditioned and indeed objective and hence universally valid, and commands are laws which must be obeyed, i.e., must be followed even in opposition to inclination. Counsel does indeed involve necessity, but involves such necessity as

6. The word "prudence" is used in a double sense: firstly, it can mean worldly wisdom, and, secondly, private wisdom. The former is the skill of someone in influencing others so as to use them for his own purposes. The latter is the sagacity to combine all these purposes for his own lasting advantage. The value of the former is properly reduced to the latter, and it might better be said of one who is prudent in the former sense but not in the latter that he is clever and cunning, but on the whole imprudent.

is valid only under a subjectively contingent condition, viz., whether this or that man counts this or that as belonging to his happiness. On the other hand, the categorical imperative is limited by no condition, and can quite properly be called a command since it is absolutely, though practically, necessary. The first kind of imperatives might [417] also be called technical (belonging to art), the second kind pragmatic[7] (belonging to welfare), the third kind moral (belonging to free conduct as such, i.e., to morals).

The question now arises: how are all of these imperatives possible? This question does not seek to know how the fulfillment of the action commanded by the imperative can be conceived, but merely how the necessitation of the will expressed by the imperative in setting a task can be conceived. How an imperative of skill is possible requires no special discussion. Whoever wills the end, wills (so far as reason has decisive influence on his actions) also the means that are indispensably necessary to his actions and that lie in his power. This proposition, as far as willing is concerned, is analytic. For in willing an object as my effect there is already thought the causality of myself as an acting cause, i.e., the use of means. The imperative derives the concept of actions necessary to this end from the concept of willing this end. (Synthetic propositions are indeed required for determining the means to a proposed end; but such propositions are concerned not with the ground, i.e., the act of the will, but only with the way to realize the object of the will.) Mathematics teaches by nothing but synthetic propositions that in order to bisect a line according to a sure principle I must from each of its extremities draw arcs such that they intersect. But when I know that the proposed result can come about only by means of such an action, then the proposition (if I fully will the effect, then I also will the action required for it) is analytic. For it is one and the same thing to conceive of something as an effect that is possible in a certain way through me and to conceive of myself as acting in the same way with regard to the aforesaid effect.

If it were only as easy to give a determinate concept of happiness, then the imperatives of prudence would exactly correspond to those of skill and would be likewise analytic. For there could be said in this

7. It seems to me that the proper meaning of the word "pragmatic" could be defined most accurately in this way. For those sanctions are called pragmatic which properly flow not from the law of states as necessary enactments but from provision for the general welfare. A history is pragmatically written when it teaches prudence, i.e., instructs the world how it can provide for its interests better than, or at least as well as, has been done in former times.

case just as [418] in the former that whoever wills the end also wills (necessarily according to reason) the sole means thereto which are in his power. But, unfortunately, the concept of happiness is such an indeterminate one that even though everyone wishes to attain happiness, yet he can never say definitely and consistently what it is that he really wishes and wills. The reason for this is that all the elements belonging to the concept of happiness are unexceptionally empirical, i.e., they must be borrowed from experience, while for the idea of happiness there is required an absolute whole, a maximum of well-being in my present and in every future condition. Now it is impossible for the most insightful and at the same time most powerful, but nonetheless finite, being to frame here a determinate concept of what it is that he really wills. Does he want riches? How much anxiety, envy, and intrigue might he not thereby bring down upon his own head! Or knowledge and insight? Perhaps these might only give him an eye that much sharper for revealing that much more dreadfully evils which are at present hidden but are yet unavoidable, or such an eye might burden him with still further needs for the desires which already concern him enough. Or long life? Who guarantees that it would not be a long misery? Or health at least? How often has infirmity of the body kept one from excesses into which perfect health would have allowed him to fall, and so on? In brief, he is not able on any principle to determine with complete certainty what will make him truly happy, because to do so would require omniscience. Therefore, one cannot act according to determinate principles in order to be happy, but only according to empirical counsels, e.g., of diet, frugality, politeness, reserve, etc., which are shown by experience to contribute on the average the most to well-being. There follows from this that imperatives of prudence, strictly speaking, cannot command at all, i.e., present actions objectively as practically necessary. They are to be taken as counsels (*consilia*) rather than as commands (*praecepta*) of reason. The problem of determining certainly and universally what action will promote the happiness of a rational being is completely insoluble. Therefore, regarding such action no imperative that in the strictest sense could command what is to be done to make one happy is possible, inasmuch as happiness is not an ideal of [419] reason but of imagination. Such an ideal rests merely on empirical grounds; in vain can there be expected that such grounds should determine an action whereby the totality of an infinite series of consequences could be attained. This imperative of prudence would, nevertheless, be an analytic practical proposition if one assumes that the means to happiness could with certainty be assigned; for it differs from the imperative of skill only in that for it the end is given while for the latter the end is merely possible. Since both, however, command only the means to what is assumed to be willed as an end, the imperative commanding him who wills the end to will likewise the means thereto is in both cases analytic. Hence there is also no difficulty regarding the possibility of an imperative of prudence.

On the other hand, the question as to how the imperative of morality is possible is undoubtedly the only one requiring a solution. For it is not at all hypothetical; and hence the objective necessity which it presents cannot be based on any presupposition, as was the case with the hypothetical imperatives. Only there must never here be forgotten that no example can show, i.e., empirically, whether there is any such imperative at all. Rather, care must be taken lest all imperatives which are seemingly categorical may nevertheless be covertly hypothetical. For instance, when it is said that you should not make a false promise, the assumption is that the necessity of this avoidance is no mere advice for escaping some other evil, so that it might be said that you should not make a false promise lest you ruin your credit when the falsity comes to light. But when it is asserted that an action of this kind must be regarded as bad in itself, then the imperative of prohibition is therefore categorical. Nevertheless, it cannot with certainty be shown by means of an example that the will is here determined solely by the law without any other incentive, even though such may seem to be the case. For it is always possible that secretly there is fear of disgrace and perhaps also obscure dread of other dangers; such fear and dread may have influenced the will. Who can prove by experience that a cause is not present? Experience only shows that a cause is not perceived. But in such a case the so-called moral imperative, which as such appears to be categorical and unconditioned, would actually be only a pragmatic precept which makes us pay attention to our own advantage and merely teaches us to take such advantage into consideration.

We shall, therefore, have to investigate the possibility of a categorical imperative entirely a priori, inasmuch as we do not here have the advantage of having its reality given in experience and consequently of thus being [420] obligated merely to explain its possibility rather than to establish it. In the meantime so much can be seen for now: the categorical imperative alone purports to be a practical law, while all the others may be called principles of the will but not laws. The reason for this is that whatever is necessary merely in order to attain some arbitrary purpose can be regarded as in itself contingent, and the precept can always be ignored once the purpose is abandoned. Contrariwise, an unconditioned command does not leave the will free to choose the opposite at its own liking. Consequently, only such a command carries with it that necessity which is demanded from a law.

Second, in the case of this categorical imperative, or law of morality, the reason for the difficulty (of discerning its possibility) is quite serious. The categorical imperative is an a priori synthetic practical proposition;[8] and since discerning the possibility of propositions of this sort involves so much difficulty in theoretic knowledge, there may readily be gathered that there will be no less difficulty in practical knowledge.

In solving this problem, we want first to inquire whether perhaps the mere concept of a categorical imperative may not also supply us with the formula containing the proposition that can alone be a categorical imperative. For even when we know the purport of such an absolute command, the question as to how it is possible will still require a special and difficult effort, which we postpone to the last section.

If I think of a hypothetical imperative in general, I do not know beforehand what it will contain until its condition is given. But if I think of a categorical imperative, I know immediately what it contains. For since, besides the law, the imperative contains only the necessity that the [421] maxim[9] should accord with this law, while the law contains no condition to restrict it, there remains nothing but the universality of a law as such with which the maxim of the action should conform. This conformity alone is properly what is represented as necessary by the imperative.

Hence there is only one categorical imperative and it is this: Act only according to that maxim whereby you can at the same time will that it should become a universal law.

8. I connect a priori, and therefore necessarily, the act with the will without presupposing any condition taken from some inclination (though I make such a connection only objectively, i.e., under the idea of a reason having full power over all subjective motives). Hence this is a practical proposition which does not analytically derive the willing of an action from some other willing already presupposed (for we possess no such perfect will) but which connects the willing of an action immediately with the concept of the will of a rational being as something which is not contained in this concept.

9. A maxim is the subjective principle of acting and must be distinguished from the objective principle, viz., the practical law. A maxim contains the practical rule which reason determines in accordance with the conditions of the subject (often his ignorance or his inclinations) and is thus the principle according to which the subject does act. But the law is the objective principle valid for every rational being, and it is the principle according to which he ought to act, i.e., an imperative.

Now if all imperatives of duty can be derived from this one imperative as their principle, then there can at least be shown what is understood by the concept of duty and what it means, even though there is left undecided whether what is called duty may not be an empty concept.

The universality of law according to which effects are produced constitutes what is properly called nature in the most general sense (as to form), i.e., the existence of things as far as determined by universal laws. Accordingly, the universal imperative of duty may be expressed thus: Act as if the maxim of your action were to become through your will a universal law of nature.

We shall now enumerate some duties, following the usual division of them into duties to ourselves and to others and into perfect and imperfect duties.[10]

1. A man reduced to despair by a series of misfortunes feels sick of life [422] but is still so far in possession of his reason that he can ask himself whether taking his own life would not be contrary to his duty to himself. Now he asks whether the maxim of his action could become a universal law of nature. But his maxim is this: from self-love I make as my principle to shorten my life when its continued duration threatens more evil than it promises satisfaction. There only remains the question as to whether this principle of self-love can become a universal law of nature. One sees at once a contradiction in a system of nature whose law would destroy life by means of the very same feeling that acts so as to stimulate the furtherance of life, and hence there could be no existence as a system of nature. Therefore, such a maxim cannot possibly hold as a universal law of nature and is, consequently, wholly opposed to the supreme principle of all duty.

2. Another man in need finds himself forced to borrow money. He knows well that he won't be able to repay it, but he sees also that he will not get any loan unless he firmly promises to repay it within a

10. There should be noted here that I reserve the division of duties for a future *Metaphysics of Morals* [in Part II of the *Metaphysics of Morals*, entitled *The Metaphysical Principles of Virtue*, Ak. 417–474]. The division presented here stands as merely an arbitrary one (in order to arrange my examples). For the rest, I understand here by a perfect duty one which permits no exception in the interest of inclination. Accordingly, I have perfect duties which are external [to others], while other ones are internal [to oneself]. This classification runs contrary to the accepted usage of the schools, but I do not intend to justify it here, since there is no difference for my purpose whether this classification is accepted or not.

fixed time. He wants to make such a promise, but he still has conscience enough to ask himself whether it is not permissible and is contrary to duty to get out of difficulty in this way. Suppose, however, that he decides to do so. The maxim of his action would then be expressed as follows: when I believe myself to be in need of money, I will borrow money and promise to pay it back, although I know that I can never do so. Now this principle of self-love or personal advantage may perhaps be quite compatible with one's entire future welfare, but the question is now whether it is right. I then transform the requirement of self-love into a universal law and put the question thus: how would things stand if my maxim were to become a universal law? He then sees at once that such a maxim could never hold as a universal law of nature and be consistent with itself, but must necessarily be self-contradictory. For the universality of a law which says that anyone believing himself to be in difficulty could promise whatever he pleases with the intention of not keeping it would make promising itself and the end to be attained thereby quite impossible, inasmuch as no one would believe what was promised him but would merely laugh at all such utterances as being vain pretenses.

3. A third finds in himself a talent whose cultivation could make him a man useful in many respects. But he finds himself in comfortable circumstances [423] and prefers to indulge in pleasure rather than to bother himself about broadening and improving his fortunate natural aptitudes. But he asks himself further whether his maxim of neglecting his natural gifts, besides agreeing of itself with his propensity to indulgence, might agree also with what is called duty. He then sees that a system of nature could indeed always subsist according to such a universal law, even though every man (like South Sea Islanders) should let his talents rust and resolve to devote his life entirely to idleness, indulgence, propagation, and, in a word, to enjoyment. But he cannot possibly will that this should become a universal law of nature or be implanted in us as such a law by a natural instinct. For as a rational being he necessarily wills that all his faculties should be developed, inasmuch as they are given him for all sorts of possible purposes.

4. A fourth man finds things going well for himself but sees others (whom he could help) struggling with great hardships; and he thinks: what does it matter to me? Let everybody be as happy as Heaven wills or as he can make himself; I shall take nothing from him nor even envy him; but I have no desire to contribute anything to his well-being or to his assistance when in need. If such a way of thinking were to become a universal law of nature, the human race admittedly could

very well subsist and doubtless could subsist even better than when everyone prates about sympathy and benevolence and even on occasion exerts himself to practice them but, on the other hand, also cheats when he can, betrays the rights of man, or otherwise violates them. But even though it is possible that a universal law of nature could subsist in accordance with that maxim, still it is impossible to will that such a principle should hold everywhere as a law of nature. For a will which resolved in this way would contradict itself, inasmuch as cases might often arise in which one would have need of the love and sympathy of others and in which he would deprive himself, by such a law of nature springing from his own will, of all hope of the aid he wants for himself.

These are some of the many actual duties, or at least what are taken to [424] be such, whose derivation from the single principle cited above is clear. We must be able to will that a maxim of our action become a universal law; this is the canon for morally estimating any of our actions. Some actions are so constituted that their maxims cannot without contradiction even be thought as a universal law of nature, much less be willed as what should become one. In the case of others this internal impossibility is indeed not found, but there is still no possibility of willing that their maxim should be raised to the universality of a law of nature, because such a will would contradict itself. There is no difficulty in seeing that the former kind of action conflicts with strict or narrow [perfect] (irremissible) duty, while the second kind conflicts only with broad [imperfect] (meritorious) duty. By means of these examples there has thus been fully set forth how all duties depend as regards the kind of obligation (not the object of their action) upon the one principle.

If we now attend to ourselves in any transgression of a duty, we find that we actually do not will that our maxim should become a universal law—because this is impossible for us—but rather that the opposite of this maxim should remain a law universally. We only take the liberty of making an exception to thc law for ourselves (or just for this one time) to the advantage of our inclination. Consequently, if we weighed up everything from one and the same standpoint, namely, that of reason, we would find a contradiction in our own will, viz., that a certain principle be objectively necessary as a universal law and yet subjectively not hold universally but should admit of exceptions. But since we at one moment regard our action from the standpoint of a will wholly in accord with reason and then at another moment regard the very same action from the standpoint of a will affected by inclination, there is really no contradiction here. Rather, there is an opposition (*antagonismus*) of inclination to the precept of reason, whereby the universality (*universalitas*) of the principle is changed into a mere generality (*generalitas*) so that the practical principle of reason may meet the maxim halfway. Although this procedure cannot be justified in our own impartial judgment, yet it does show that we actually acknowledge the validity of the categorical imperative and (with all respect for it) merely allow ourselves a few exceptions which, as they seem to us, are unimportant and forced upon us.

We have thus at least shown that if duty is a concept which is to have [425] significance and real legislative authority for our actions, then such duty can be expressed only in categorical imperatives but not at all in hypothetical ones. We have also—and this is already a great deal—exhibited clearly and definitely for every application what is the content of the categorical imperative, which must contain the principle of all duty (if there is such a thing at all). But we have not yet advanced far enough to prove a priori that there actually is an imperative of this kind, that there is a practical law which of itself commands absolutely and without any incentives, and that following this law is duty.

In order to attain this proof there is the utmost importance in being warned that we must not take it into our mind to derive the reality of this principle from the special characteristics of human nature. For duty has to be a practical, unconditioned necessity of action; hence it must hold for all rational beings (to whom alone an imperative is at all applicable) and for this reason only can it also be a law for all human wills. On the other hand, whatever is derived from the special natural condition of humanity, from certain feelings and propensities, or even, if such were possible, from some special tendency peculiar to human reason and not holding necessarily for the will of every rational being—all of this can indeed yield a maxim valid for us, but not a law. This is to say that such can yield a subjective principle according to which we might act if we happen to have the propensity and inclination, but cannot yield an objective principle according to which we would be directed to act even though our every propensity, inclination, and natural tendency were opposed to it. In fact, the sublimity and inner worth of the command are so much the more evident in a duty, the fewer subjective causes there are for it and the more they oppose it; such causes do not in the least weaken the necessitation exerted by the law or take away anything from its validity.

Here philosophy is seen in fact to be put in a precarious position, which should be firm even though there is neither in Heaven nor on earth anything upon which it depends or is based. Here philosophy must show its purity as author of its laws, and not as the herald of such laws as are whispered to it by an implanted sense or by who knows what tutelary nature. Such laws may be better than nothing at all, but they can never [426] give us principles dictated by reason. These principles must have an origin that is completely a priori and must at the same time derive from such origin their authority to command. They expect nothing from the inclination of men but, rather, expect everything from the supremacy of the law and from the respect owed to the law. Without the latter expectation, these principles condemn man to self-contempt and inward abhorrence.

Hence everything empirical is not only quite unsuitable as a contribution to the principle of morality, but is even highly detrimental to the purity of morals. For the proper and inestimable worth of an absolutely good will consists precisely in the fact that the principle of action is free of all influences from contingent grounds, which only experience can furnish. This lax or even mean way of thinking which seeks its principle among empirical motives and laws cannot too much or too often be warned against, for human reason in its weariness is glad to rest upon this pillow. In a dream of sweet illusions (in which not Juno but a cloud is embraced) there is substituted for morality some bastard patched up from limbs of quite varied ancestry and looking like anything one wants to see in it but not looking like virtue to him who has once beheld her in her true form.[11]

Therefore, the question is this: is it a necessary law for all rational beings always to judge their actions according to such maxims as they can themselves will that such should serve as universal laws? If there is such a law, then it must already be connected (completely a priori) with the concept of the will of a rational being in general. But in order to discover this connection we must, however reluctantly, take a step into metaphysics, although into a region of it different from speculative philosophy, i.e., we must enter the metaphysics of morals. In practical philosophy the concern is not with [427] accepting grounds for what happens but with accepting laws of what ought to happen, even though it never does happen—that is, the concern is with objectively practical laws. Here there is no need to inquire into the grounds

11. To behold virtue in her proper form is nothing other than to present morality stripped of all admixture of what is sensuous and of every spurious adornment of reward or self-love. How much she then eclipses all else that appears attractive to the inclinations can be easily seen by everyone with the least effort of his reason, if it be not entirely ruined for all abstraction.

as to why something pleases or displeases, how the pleasure of mere sensation differs from taste, and whether taste differs from a general satisfaction of reason, upon what does the feeling of pleasure and displeasure rest, and how from this feeling desires and inclinations arise, and how, finally, from these there arise maxims through the cooperation of reason. All of this belongs to an empirical psychology, which would constitute the second part of the doctrine of nature, if this doctrine is regarded as the philosophy of nature insofar as this philosophy is grounded on empirical laws. But here the concern is with objectively practical laws, and hence with the relation of a will to itself insofar as it is determined solely by reason. In this case everything related to what is empirical falls away of itself, because if reason entirely by itself determines conduct (and the possibility of such determination we now wish to investigate), then reason must necessarily do so a priori.

The will is thought of as a faculty of determining itself to action in accordance with the representation of certain laws, and such a faculty can be found only in rational beings. Now what serves the will as the objective ground of its self-determination is an end; and if this end is given by reason alone, then it must be equally valid for all rational beings. On the other hand, what contains merely the ground of the possibility of the action, whose effect is an end, is called the means. The subjective ground of desire is the incentive; the objective ground of volition is the motive. Hence there arises the distinction between subjective ends, which rest on incentives, and objective ends, which depend on motives valid for every rational being. Practical principles are formal when they abstract from all subjective ends; they are material, however, when they are founded upon subjective ends, and hence upon certain incentives. The ends which a rational being arbitrarily proposes to himself as effects of this action (material ends) are all merely relative, for only their relation to a specially constituted faculty of desire in the subject gives them their worth. Consequently, such worth cannot provide any universal principles, which are valid and necessary for all rational beings and, furthermore, are valid for [428] every volition, i.e., cannot provide any practical laws. Therefore, all such relative ends can be grounds only for hypothetical imperatives.

But let us suppose that there were something whose existence has in itself an absolute worth, something which as an end in itself could be a ground of determinate laws. In it, and in it alone, would there be the ground of a possible categorical imperative, i.e., of a practical law.

Now I say that man, and in general every rational being, exists as an end in himself and not merely as a means to be arbitrarily used by this or that will. He must in all his actions, whether directed to himself or to other rational beings, always be regarded at the same time as an end. All the objects of inclinations have only a conditioned value; for if there were not these inclinations and the needs founded on them, then their object would be without value. But the inclinations themselves, being sources of needs, are so far from having an absolute value such as to render them desirable for their own sake that the universal wish of every rational being must be, rather, to be wholly free from them. Accordingly, the value of any object obtainable by our action is always conditioned. Beings whose existence depends not on our will but on nature have, nevertheless, if they are not rational beings, only a relative value as means and are therefore called things. On the other hand, rational beings are called persons inasmuch as their nature already marks them out as ends in themselves, i.e., as something which is not to be used merely as means and hence there is imposed thereby a limit on all arbitrary use of such beings, which are thus objects of respect. Persons are, therefore, not merely subjective ends, whose existence as an effect of our actions has a value for us; but such beings are objective ends, i.e., exist as ends in themselves. Such an end is one for which there can be substituted no other end to which such beings should serve merely as means, for otherwise nothing at all of absolute value would be found anywhere. But if all value were conditioned and hence contingent, then no supreme practical principle could be found for reason at all.

If then there is to be a supreme practical principle and, as far as the human will is concerned, a categorical imperative, then it must be such that from the conception of what is necessarily an end for everyone because this end is an end in itself it constitutes an objective principle of [429] the will and can hence serve as a practical law. The ground of such a principle is this: rational nature exists as an end in itself. In this way man necessarily thinks of his own existence; thus far is it a subjective principle of human actions. But in this way also does every other rational being think of his existence on the same rational ground that holds also for me;[12] hence it is at the same time an objective principle, from which, as a supreme practical ground, all laws of the will must be able to be derived. The practical imperative will therefore be the following: Act in such a way that you treat humanity, whether in your own person or in the person of another,

12. This proposition I here put forward as a postulate. The grounds for it will be found in the last section.

always at the same time as an end and never simply as a means. We now want to see whether this can be carried out in practice.

Let us keep to our previous examples.

First, as regards the concept of necessary duty to oneself, the man who contemplates suicide will ask himself whether his action can be consistent with the idea of humanity as an end in itself. If he destroys himself in order to escape from a difficult situation, then he is making use of his person merely as a means so as to maintain a tolerable condition till the end of his life. Man, however, is not a thing and hence is not something to be used merely as a means; he must in all his actions always be regarded as an end in himself. Therefore, I cannot dispose of man in my own person by mutilating, damaging, or killing him. (A more exact determination of this principle so as to avoid all misunderstanding, e.g., regarding the amputation of limbs in order to save oneself, or the exposure of one's life to danger in order to save it, and so on, must here be omitted; such questions belong to morals proper.)

Second, as concerns necessary or strict duty to others, the man who intends to make a false promise will immediately see that he intends to make use of another man merely as a means to an end which the latter does not likewise hold. For the man whom I want to use for my own purposes by such a promise cannot possibly concur with my way of acting toward him [430] and hence cannot himself hold the end of this action. This conflict with the principle of duty to others becomes even clearer when instances of attacks on the freedom and property of others are considered. For then it becomes clear that a transgressor of the rights of men intends to make use of the persons of others merely as a means, without taking into consideration that, as rational beings, they should always be esteemed at the same time as ends, i.e., be esteemed only as beings who must themselves be able to hold the very same action as an end.[13]

Third, with regard to contingent (meritorious) duty to oneself, it is not enough that the action does not conflict with humanity in our

13. Let it not be thought that the trivial *quod tibi non vis fieri, etc.* [do not do to others what you do not want done to yourself] can here serve as a standard or principle. For it is merely derived from our principle, although with several limitations. It cannot be a universal law, for it contains the ground neither of duties to oneself nor of duties of love toward others (for many a man would gladly consent that others should not benefit him, if only he might be excused from benefiting them). Nor, finally, does it contain the ground of strict duties toward others, for the criminal would on this ground be able to dispute with the judges who punish him; and so on.

own person as an end in itself; the action must also harmonize with this end. Now there are in humanity capacities for greater perfection which belong to the end that nature has in view as regards humanity in our own person. To neglect these capacities might perhaps be consistent with the maintenance of humanity as an end in itself, but would not be consistent with the advancement of this end.

Fourth, concerning meritorious duty to others, the natural end that all men have is their own happiness. Now humanity might indeed subsist if nobody contributed anything to the happiness of others, provided he did not intentionally impair their happiness. But this, after all, would harmonize only negatively and not positively with humanity as an end in itself, if everyone does not also strive, as much as he can, to further the ends of others. For the ends of any subject who is an end in himself must as far as possible be my ends also, if that conception of an end in itself is to have its full effect in me.

This principle of humanity and of every rational nature generally as an end in itself is the supreme limiting condition of every man's freedom of [431] action. This principle is not borrowed from experience, first, because of its universality, inasmuch as it applies to all rational beings generally, and no experience is capable of determining anything about them; and, second, because in experience (subjectively) humanity is not thought of as the end of men, i.e., as an object that we of ourselves actually make our end which as a law ought to constitute the supreme limiting condition of all subjective ends (whatever they may be); and hence this principle must arise from pure reason [and not from experience]. That is to say that the ground of all practical legislation lies objectively in the rule and in the form of universality, which (according to the first principle) makes the rule capable of being a law (say, for example, a law of nature). Subjectively, however, the ground of all practical legislation lies in the end; but (according to the second principle) the subject of all ends is every rational being as an end in himself. From this there now follows the third practical principle of the will as the supreme condition of the will's conformity with universal practical reason, viz., the idea of the will of every rational being as a will that legislates universal law.

According to this principle all maxims are rejected which are not consistent with the will's own legislation of universal law. The will is thus not merely subject to the law but is subject to the law in such a way that it must be regarded also as legislating for itself and only on this account as being subject to the law (of which it can regard itself as the author).

In the previous formulations of imperatives, viz., that based on the conception of the conformity of actions to universal law in a way similar to a natural order and that based on the universal prerogative of rational beings as ends in themselves, these imperatives just because they were thought of as categorical excluded from their legislative authority all admixture of any interest as an incentive. They were, however, only assumed to be categorical because such an assumption had to be made if the concept of duty was to be explained. But that there were practical propositions which commanded categorically could not itself be proved, nor can it be proved anywhere in this section. But one thing could have been done, viz., to indicate that in willing from duty the renunciation of all interest is the specific mark distinguishing a categorical imperative from a hypothetical one and that such renunciation was expressed in the [432] imperative itself by means of some determination contained in it. This is done in the present (third) formulation of the principle, namely, in the idea of the will of every rational being as a will that legislates universal law.

When such a will is thought of, then even though a will which is subject to law may be bound to this law by means of some interest, nevertheless a will that is itself a supreme lawgiver is not able as such to depend on any interest. For a will which is so dependent would itself require yet another law restricting the interest of its self-love to the condition that such interest should itself be valid as a universal law.

Thus the principle that every human will as a will that legislates universal law in all its maxims,[14] provided it is otherwise correct, would be well suited to being a categorical imperative in the following respect: just because of the idea of legislating universal law such an imperative is not based on any interest, and therefore it alone of all possible imperatives can be unconditional. Or still better, the proposition being converted, if there is a categorical imperative (i.e., a law for the will of every rational being), then it can only command that everything be done from the maxim of such a will as could at the same time have as its object only itself regarded as legislating universal law. For only then are the practical principle and the imperative which the will obeys unconditional, inasmuch as the will can be based on no interest at all.

When we look back upon all previous attempts that have been made to discover the principle of morality, there is no reason now to

14. I may here be excused from citing instances to elucidate this principle inasmuch as those which were first used to elucidate the categorical imperative and its formula can all serve the same purpose here.

wonder why they one and all had to fail. Man was viewed as bound to laws by his duty; but it was not seen that man is subject only to his own, yet universal, legislation and that he is bound only to act in accordance with his own will, which is, however, a will purposed by nature to legislate universal laws. For when man is thought as being merely subject to a law (whatever it might be), then the law had to carry with it some interest [433] functioning as an attracting stimulus or as a constraining force for obedience, inasmuch as the law did not arise as a law from his own will. Rather, in order that his will conform with law, it had to be necessitated by something else to act in a certain way. By this absolutely necessary conclusion, however, all the labor spent in finding a supreme ground for duty was irretrievably lost; duty was never discovered, but only the necessity of acting from a certain interest. This might be either one's own interest or another's, but either way the imperative had to be always conditional and could never possibly serve as a moral command. I want, therefore, to call my principle the principle of the autonomy of the will, in contrast with every other principle, which I accordingly count under heteronomy.

The concept of every rational being as one who must regard himself as legislating universal law by all his will's maxims, so that he may judge himself and his actions from this point of view, leads to another very fruitful concept, which depends on the aforementioned one, viz., that of a kingdom of ends.

By "kingdom" I understand a systematic union of different rational beings through common laws. Now laws determine ends as regards their universal validity; therefore, if one abstracts from the personal differences of rational beings and also from all content of their private ends, then it will be possible to think of a whole of all ends in systematic connection (a whole both of rational beings as ends in themselves and also of the particular ends which each may set for himself); that is, one can think of a kingdom of ends that is possible on the aforesaid principles.

For all rational beings stand under the law that each of them should treat himself and all others never merely as means but always at the same time as an end in himself. Hereby arises a systematic union of rational beings through common objective laws, i.e., a kingdom that may be called a kingdom of ends (certainly only an ideal), inasmuch as these laws have in view the very relation of such beings to one another as ends and means.

A rational being belongs to the kingdom of ends as a member when he legislates in it universal laws while also being himself subject to these laws. He belongs to it as sovereign, when as legislator he is himself subject to the will of no other.

[434] A rational being must always regard himself as legislator in a kingdom of ends rendered possible by freedom of the will, whether as member or as sovereign. The position of the latter can be maintained not merely through the maxims of his will but only if he is a completely independent being without needs and with unlimited power adequate to his will.

Hence morality consists in the relation of all action to that legislation whereby alone a kingdom of ends is possible. This legislation must be found in every rational being and must be able to arise from his will, whose principle then is never to act on any maxim except such as can also be a universal law and hence such as the will can thereby regard itself as at the same time the legislator of universal law. If now the maxims do not by their very nature already necessarily conform with this objective principle of rational beings as legislating universal laws, then the necessity of acting on that principle is called practical necessitation, i.e., duty. Duty does not apply to the sovereign in the kingdom of ends, but it does apply to every member and to each in the same degree.

The practical necessity of acting according to this principle, i.e., duty, does not rest at all on feelings, impulses, and inclinations, but only on the relation of rational beings to one another, a relation in which the will of a rational being must always be regarded at the same time as legislative, because otherwise he could not be thought of as an end in himself. Reason, therefore, relates every maxim of the will as legislating universal laws to every other will and also to every action toward oneself; it does so not on account of any other practical motive or future advantage but rather from the idea of the dignity of a rational being who obeys no law except what he at the same time enacts himself.

In the kingdom of ends everything has either a price or a dignity. Whatever has a price can be replaced by something else as its equivalent; on the other hand, whatever is above all price, and therefore admits of no equivalent, has a dignity.

Whatever has reference to general human inclinations and needs has a market price; whatever, without presupposing any need, accords with a [435] certain taste, i.e., a delight in the mere unpurposive play of our mental powers, has an affective price; but that which constitutes the condition under which alone something can be an end in itself has not merely a relative worth, i.e., a price, but has an intrinsic worth, i.e., dignity.

Now morality is the condition under which alone a rational being can be an end in himself, for only thereby can he be a legislating member in the kingdom of ends. Hence morality and humanity, insofar as it is capable of morality, alone have dignity. Skill and diligence in work have a market price; wit, lively imagination, and humor have an affective price; but fidelity to promises and benevolence based on principles (not on instinct) have intrinsic worth. Neither nature nor art contain anything which in default of these could be put in their place; for their worth consists, not in the effects which arise from them, nor in the advantage and profit which they provide, but in mental dispositions, i.e., in the maxims of the will which are ready in this way to manifest themselves in action, even if they are not favored with success. Such actions also need no recommendation from any subjective disposition or taste so as to meet with immediate favor and delight; there is no need of any immediate propensity or feeling toward them. They exhibit the will performing them as an object of immediate respect; and nothing but reason is required to impose them upon the will, which is not to be cajoled into them, since in the case of duties such cajoling would be a contradiction. This estimation, therefore, lets the worth of such a disposition be recognized as dignity and puts it infinitely beyond all price, with which it cannot in the least be brought into competition or comparison without, as it were, violating its sanctity.

What then is it that entitles the morally good disposition, or virtue, to make such lofty claims? It is nothing less than the share which such a disposition affords the rational being of legislating universal laws, so that he is fit to be a member in a possible kingdom of ends, for which his own nature has already determined him as an end in himself and therefore as a legislator in the kingdom of ends. Thereby is he free as regards all laws of nature, and he obeys only those laws which he gives to himself. Accordingly, his maxims can belong to a universal legislation to which he at the same time subjects himself. For nothing can have any worth other than what the [436] law determines. But the legislation itself which determines all worth must for that very reason have dignity, i.e., unconditional and incomparable worth; and the word "respect" alone provides a suitable expression for the esteem which a rational being must have for it. Hence autonomy is the ground of the dignity of human nature and of every rational nature.

The aforementioned three ways of representing the principle of morality are at bottom only so many formulas of the very same law: one of them by itself contains a combination of the other two. Nevertheless, there is a difference in them, which is subjectively rather than objectively practical, viz., it is intended to bring an idea of reason closer to intuition (in accordance with a certain analogy) and thereby closer to feeling. All maxims have, namely,

1. A form, which consists in universality; and in this respect the formula of the moral imperative is expressed thus: maxims must be so chosen as if they were to hold as universal laws of nature.

2. A matter, viz., an end; and here the formula says that a rational being, inasmuch as he is by his very nature an end and hence an end in himself, must serve in every maxim as a condition limiting all merely relative and arbitrary ends.

3. A complete determination of all maxims by the formula that all maxims proceeding from his own legislation ought to harmonize with a possible kingdom of ends as a kingdom of nature.[15] There is a progression here through the categories of the *unity* of the form of the will (its universality), the *plurality* of its matter (its objects, i.e., its ends), and the *totality* or completeness of its system of ends. But one does better if in moral judgment he follows the rigorous method and takes as his basis the [437] universal formula of the categorical imperative: Act according to that maxim which can at the same time make itself a universal law. But if one wants also to secure acceptance for the moral law, it is very useful to bring one and the same action under the three aforementioned concepts and thus, as far as possible, to bring the moral law nearer to intuition.

We can now end where we started in the beginning, viz., the concept of an unconditionally good will. That will is absolutely good which cannot be evil, i.e., whose maxim, when made into a universal law, can never conflict with itself. This principle is therefore also its supreme law: Act always according to that maxim whose universality as a law you can at the same time will. This is the only condition under which a will can never be in conflict with itself, and such an imperative is categorical. Inasmuch as the validity of the will as a universal law for possible actions is analogous to the universal connection of the existence of things in accordance with universal laws, which is the formal aspect of nature in general, the categorical imperative can also be expressed thus: Act according to maxims which can at the same time have for their object themselves as universal laws of nature. In this way there is provided the formula for an absolutely good will.

15. Teleology considers nature as a kingdom of ends; morals regards a possible kingdom of ends as a kingdom of nature. In the former the kingdom of ends is a theoretical idea for explaining what exists. In the latter it is a practical idea for bringing about what does not exist but can be made actual by our conduct, i.e., what can be actualized in accordance with this very idea.

Rational nature is distinguished from the rest of nature by the fact that it sets itself an end. This end would be the matter of every good will. But in the idea of an absolutely good will—good without any qualifying condition (of attaining this or that end)—complete abstraction must be made from every end that has to come about as an effect (since such would make every will only relatively good). And so the end must here be conceived, not as an end to be effected, but as an independently existing end. Hence it must be conceived only negatively, i.e., as an end which should never be acted against and therefore as one which in all willing must never be regarded merely as means but must always be esteemed at the same time as an end. Now this end can be nothing but the subject of all possible ends themselves, because this subject is at the same time the subject of a possible absolutely good will; for such a will cannot without contradiction be subordinated to any other object. The principle: So act in [438] regard to every rational being (yourself and others) that he may at the same time count in your maxim as an end in himself, is thus basically the same as the principle: Act on a maxim which at the same time contains in itself its own universal validity for every rational being. That in the use of means for every end my maxim should be restricted to the condition of its universal validity as a law for every subject says just the same as that a subject of ends, i.e., a rational being himself, must be made the ground for all maxims of actions and must thus be used never merely as means but as the supreme limiting condition in the use of all means, i.e., always at the same time as an end.

Now there follows incontestably from this that every rational being as an end in himself must be able to regard himself with reference to all laws to which he may be subject as being at the same time the legislator of universal law, for just this very fitness of his maxims for the legislation of universal law distinguishes him as an end in himself. There follows also that his dignity (prerogative) of being above all the mere things of nature implies that his maxims must be taken from the viewpoint that regards himself, as well as every other rational being, as being legislative beings (and hence are they called persons). In this way there is possible a world of rational beings (*mundus intelligibilis*) as a kingdom of ends, because of the legislation belonging to all persons as members. Therefore, every rational being must so act as if he were through his maxim always a legislating member in the universal kingdom of ends. The formal principle of these maxims is this: So act as if your maxims were to serve at the same time as a universal law (for all rational beings). Thus a kingdom of ends is possible only on the analogy of a kingdom of nature; yet the former is possible only through maxims, i.e., self-imposed rules, while the latter is possible only through laws of efficient causes necessitated from without. Regardless of this difference and even though nature as a whole is viewed as a machine, yet insofar as nature stands in a relation to rational beings as its ends, it is on this account given the name of a kingdom of nature. Such a kingdom of ends would actually be realized through maxims whose rule is prescribed to all rational beings by the categorical imperative, if these maxims were universally obeyed. But even if a rational being himself strictly obeys such a maxim, he cannot for that reason count on everyone else's being true to it, nor can he expect the kingdom of nature and its purposive order to be in harmony with him as a fitting member of a kingdom of ends made possible by himself, i.e., he cannot expect the kingdom of nature to favor his expectation of happiness. [439] Nevertheless, the law: Act in accordance with the maxims of a member legislating universal laws for a merely possible kingdom of ends, remains in full force, since it commands categorically. And just in this lies the paradox that merely the dignity of humanity as rational nature without any further end or advantage to be thereby gained—and hence respect for a mere idea—should yet serve as an inflexible precept for the will; and that just this very independence of the maxims from all such incentives should constitute the sublimity of maxims and the worthiness of every rational subject to be a legislative member in the kingdom of ends, for otherwise he would have to be regarded as subject only to the natural law of his own needs. And even if the kingdom of nature as well as the kingdom of ends were thought of as both united under one sovereign so that the latter kingdom would thereby no longer remain a mere idea but would acquire true reality, then indeed the kingdom of ends would gain the addition of a strong incentive, but never any increase in its intrinsic worth. For this sole absolute legislator must, in spite of all this, always be thought of as judging the worth of rational beings solely by the disinterested conduct prescribed to themselves by means of this idea alone. The essence of things is not altered by their external relations; and whatever without reference to such relations alone constitutes the absolute worth of man is also what he must be judged by, whoever the judge may be, even the Supreme Being. Hence morality is the relation of actions to the autonomy of the will, i.e., to the possible legislation of universal law by means of the maxims of the will. That action which is compatible with the autonomy of the will is permitted; that which is not compatible is forbidden. That will whose maxims are necessarily in accord with the laws of autonomy is a holy, or absolutely good, will. The dependence of a will which is not absolutely good upon the principle of autonomy (i.e., moral necessitation) is obligation, which cannot therefore be applied to a holy will. The objective necessity of an action from obligation is called duty.

From what has just been said, there can now easily be explained how it happens that, although in the concept of duty we think of subjection to the [440] law, yet at the same time we thereby ascribe a certain dignity and sublimity to the person who fulfills all his duties. For not insofar as he is subject to the moral law does he have sublimity, but rather has it only insofar as with regard to this very same law he is at the same time legislative, and only thereby is he subject to the law. We have also shown above how neither fear nor inclination, but solely respect for the law, is the incentive which can give an action moral worth. Our own will, insofar as it were to act only under the condition of its being able to legislate universal law by means of its maxims—this will, ideally possible for us, is the proper object of respect. And the dignity of humanity consists just in its capacity to legislate universal law, though with the condition of humanity's being at the same time itself subject to this very same legislation.

9

Marx and Alienation: Our Flawed Participation in Life

Karl Marx is the one philosopher surveyed in this book who is closely associated with a political position. He is easily identified with communism. This, however, is not as clear as one might think. What developed as "communism" in the Soviet Union and Eastern Europe and in China would have been thoroughly scorned by Marx. If Marx, who lived in the mid-nineteenth century, had traveled in a time machine to visit the Soviet Union, he would have been sent to Siberia. Part of his ideal of communism, besides community ownership of resources, was some degree of economic equality among people. The Soviet Union fell very short of this: factory managers earned far more than the workers.

Marx's writings are more complex and varied than most people might suppose. At the core was his concern with the connection between economic matters (including how goods were produced and sold) and the nature of a society. Marx was also concerned with social classes. These included the bourgeoisie (relatively prosperous people, some of whom might have investments) and the proletariat (ordinary workers). In Marx's view, the proletariat was oppressed in capitalist society. His appeal to workers of the world to unite, in order to escape their chains, was widely quoted.

In recent decades there has been increased interest in Marx's earliest work, much of which centered on the idea of "alienation." Alienation involves psychological discomfort because you are not thoroughly involved in your work in a way that yields real satisfaction with its process and results and the recognition of your role. Think of someone who functions in an assembly line, again and again adjusting one thing in a complicated object. Such a person is robbed of any chance for pride or for feeling that she or he was the maker of that object. Marx clearly believed that the proletariat should have more money, more power, and more respect. But even more than this, he believed that work conditions had to be adjusted so that people had a satisfactory psychological connection with their work.

Alienated Labor

We have proceeded from the presuppositions of political economy. We have accepted its language and its laws. We presupposed private property, the separation of labor, capital, and land, hence of wages, profit of capital and rent, likewise the division of labor, competition, the concept of exchange value, etc. From political economy itself, in its own words, we have shown that the worker sinks to the level of a commodity, the most miserable commodity; that the misery of the worker is inversely proportional to the power and volume of his production; that the necessary result of competition is the accumulation of capital in a few hands and thus the revival of monopoly in a more frightful form; and finally that the distinction between capitalist and landowner, between agricultural laborer and industrial worker, disappears and the whole society must divide into the two classes of *proprietors* and propertyless *workers.*

Political economy proceeds from the fact of private property. It does not explain private property. It grasps the actual, *material* process of private property in abstract and general formulae which it then takes as *laws.* It does not *comprehend* these laws, that is, does not prove them as proceeding from the nature of private property. Political economy does not disclose the reason for the division between capital and labor, between capital and land. When, for example, the relation of wages to profits is determined, the ultimate basis is taken to be the interest of the capitalists; that is, political economy assumes what it should develop. Similarly, competition is referred to at every point and explained from external circumstances. Political economy teaches us nothing about the extent to which these external, apparently accidental circumstances are simply the expression of a necessary development. We have seen how political economy regards exchange itself as an accidental fact. The only wheels which political economy puts in motion are *greed* and the *war among the greedy, competition.*

Just because political economy does not grasp the interconnections within the movement, the doctrine of competition could stand opposed to the doctrine of monopoly, the doctrine of freedom of craft to that of the guild, the doctrine of the division of landed property to that of the great estate. Competition, freedom of craft, and division of landed property were developed and conceived only as accidental,

From Marx, *Selected Writings,* ed. Laurence Simon (Indianapolis: Hackett Publishing Co., 1994). Translation by Loyd D. Easton and Kurt H. Guddat. Reprinted by permission of the publisher.

deliberate, forced consequences of monopoly, the guild, and feudal property, rather than necessary, inevitable, natural consequences.

We now have to grasp the essential connection among private property, greed, division of labor, capital and landownership, and the connection of exchange with competition, of value with the devaluation of men, of monopoly with competition, etc., and of this whole alienation with the *money*-system.

Let us not put ourselves in a fictitious primordial condition like a political economist trying to clarify things. Such a primordial state clarifies nothing. It merely pushes the question into a gray, misty distance. It acknowledges as a fact or event what it should deduce, namely, the necessary relation between two things, for example, between division of labor and exchange. In such a manner theology explains the origin of evil by the fall of man. That is, it asserts as a fact in the form of history what it should explain.

We proceed from a *present* fact of political economy.

The worker becomes poorer the more wealth he produces, the more his production increases in power and extent. The worker becomes a cheaper commodity the more commodities he produces. The *increase in value* of the world of things is directly proportional to the *decrease in value* of the human world. Labor not only produces commodities. It also produces itself and the worker as a *commodity,* and indeed in the same proportion as it produces commodities in general.

This fact simply indicates that the object which labor produces, its product, stands opposed to it as an *alien thing,* as a *power independent* of the producer. The product of labor is labor embodied and made objective in a thing. It is the *objectification* of labor. The realization of labor is its objectification. In the viewpoint of political economy this realization of labor appears as the *diminution* of the worker, the objectification as the *loss of and subservience to the object,* and the appropriation as *alienation* [*Entfremdung*], as externalization [*Entäusserung*].

So much does the realization of labor appear as diminution that the worker is diminished to the point of starvation. So much does objectification appear as loss of the object that the worker is robbed of the most essential objects not only of life but also of work. Indeed, work itself becomes a thing of which he can take possession only with the greatest effort and with the most unpredictable interruptions. So much does the appropriation of the object appear as alienation that the more objects the worker produces, the fewer he can own and the more he falls under the dominion of his product, of capital.

All these consequences follow from the fact that the worker is related to the *product of his labor* as to an *alien* object. For it is clear according to this premise: The more the worker exerts himself, the more powerful becomes the alien objective world which he fashions against himself, the poorer he and his inner world become, the less there is that belongs to him. It is the same in religion. The more man attributes to God, the less he retains in himself. The worker puts his life into the object; then it no longer belongs to him but to the object. The greater this activity, the poorer is the worker. What the product of his work is, he is not. The greater this product is, the smaller he is himself. The *externalization* of the worker in his product means not only that his work becomes an object, an *external* existence, but also that it exists *outside him* independently, alien, an autonomous power, opposed to him. The life he has given to the object confronts him as hostile and alien.

Let us now consider more closely the *objectification,* the worker's production and with it the *alienation* and loss of the object, his product.

The worker can make nothing without *nature,* without the *sensuous external world.* It is the material wherein his labor realizes itself, wherein it is active, out of which and by means of which it produces.

But as nature furnishes to labor the *means of life* in the sense that labor cannot *live* without objects upon which labor is exercised, nature also furnishes the *means of life* in the narrower sense, namely, the means of physical subsistence of the *worker* himself.

The more the worker *appropriates* the external world and sensuous nature through his labor, the more he deprives himself of the *means of life* in two respects: first, that the sensuous external world gradually ceases to be an object belonging to his labor, a *means of life* of his work; secondly, that it gradually ceases to be a *means of life* in the immediate sense, a means of physical subsistence of the worker.

In these two respects, therefore, the worker becomes a slave to his objects; first, in that he receives an *object of labor,* that is, he receives *labor,* and secondly that he receives the *means of subsistence.* The first enables him to exist as a *worker* and the second as a *physical subject.* The terminus of this slavery is that he can only maintain himself as a *physical subject* so far as he is a *worker,* and only as a *physical subject* is he a worker.

(The alienation of the worker in his object is expressed according to the laws of political economy as follows: the more the worker produces, the less he has to consume; the more values he creates the more worthless and unworthy he becomes; the better shaped his product, the more misshapen is he; the more civilized his product, the more barbaric is the worker; the more powerful the work, the more powerless becomes the worker; the more intelligence the work has, the more witless is the worker and the more he becomes a slave of nature.)

Political economy conceals the alienation in the nature of labor by ignoring the direct relationship between the worker (labor) *and production.* To be sure, labor produces marvels for the wealthy but it produces deprivation for the worker. It produces palaces, but hovels for the worker. It produces beauty, but mutilation for the worker. It displaces labor through machines, but it throws some workers back into barbarous labor and turns others into machines. It produces intelligence, but for the worker it produces imbecility and cretinism.

The direct relationship of labor to its products is the relationship of the worker to the objects of his production. The relationship of the rich to the objects of production and to production itself is only a *consequence* of the first relationship and confirms it. Later we shall observe the latter aspect.

Thus, when we ask, What is the essential relationship of labor? we ask about the relationship of the *worker* to production.

Up to now we have considered the alienation, the externalization of the worker only from one side: *his relationship to the products of his labor.* But alienation is shown not only in the result but also in the *process of production,* in the *producing activity* itself. How could the worker stand in an alien relationship to the product of his activity if he did not alienate himself from himself in the very act of production? After all, the product is only the résumé of activity, of production. If the product of work is externalization, production itself must be active externalization, externalization of activity, activity of externalization. Only alienation—and externalization in the activity of labor itself—is summarized in the alienation of the object of labor.

What constitutes the externalization of labor?

First is the fact that labor is *external* to the laborer—that is, it is not part of his nature—and that the worker does not affirm himself in his work but denies himself, feels miserable and unhappy, develops no free physical and mental energy but mortifies his body and ruins his mind. The worker, therefore, feels at ease outside work, and during work he is outside himself. He is at home when he is not working and when he is working he is not at home. His work, therefore, is not voluntary, but coerced, *forced labor.* It is not the satisfaction of a need but only a *means* to satisfy other needs. Its alien character is obvious from the fact that as soon as no physical or other pressure exists, labor is avoided like the plague. External labor, labor in which man is externalized, is labor of self-sacrifice, of penance. Finally, the external nature of work for the worker appears in the fact that it is not his own but another person's, that in work he does not belong to himself but to someone else. In religion the spontaneity of human imagination, the spontaneity of the human brain and heart, acts independently of the individual as an alien, divine or devilish activity. Similarly, activity of the worker is not his own spontaneous activity. It belongs to another. It is the loss of his own self.

The result, therefore, is that man (the worker) feels that he is acting freely only in his animal functions—eating, drinking, and procreating, or at most in his shelter and finery—while in his human functions he feels only like an animal. The animalistic becomes the human and the human the animalistic.

To be sure, eating, drinking, and procreation are genuine human functions. In abstraction, however, and separated from the remaining sphere of human activities and turned into final and sole ends, they are animal functions.

We have considered labor, the act of alienation of practical human activity, in two aspects: (1) the relationship of the worker to the *product of labor* as an alien object dominating him. This relationship is at the same time the relationship to the sensuous external world, to natural objects as an alien world hostile to him; (2) the relationship of labor to the *act of production* in *labor.* This relationship is that of the worker to his own activity as alien and not belonging to him, activity as passivity, power as weakness, procreation as emasculation, the worker's *own* physical and spiritual energy, his personal life—for what is life but activity—as an activity turned against him, independent of him, and not belonging to him. *Self-alienation,* as against the alienation of the *object,* stated above.

We have now to derive a third aspect of alienated labor from the two previous ones.

Man is a species-being [*Gattungswesen*] not only in that he practically and theoretically makes his own species as well as that of other things his object, but also—and this is only another expression for the same thing—in that as present and living species he considers himself to be a universal and consequentially free being.

The life of the species in man as in animals is physical in that man (like the animal) lives by inorganic nature. And as man is more universal than the animal, the realm of inorganic nature by which he lives is more universal. As plants, animals, minerals, air, light, etc., in theory form a part of human consciousness, partly as objects of natural science, partly as objects of art—his spiritual inorganic nature or spiritual means of life which he first must prepare for enjoyment and assimilation—so they also form in practice a part of human life and human activity. Man lives physically only by these products of nature;

they may appear in the form of food, heat, clothing, housing, etc. The universality of man appears in practice in the universality which makes the whole of nature his *inorganic* body: (1) as a direct means of life, and (2) as the matter, object, and instrument of his life activity. Nature is the *inorganic body* of man, that is, nature insofar as it is not the human body. Man *lives* by nature. This means that nature is his *body* with which he must remain in perpetual process in order not to die. That the physical and spiritual life of man is tied up with nature is another way of saying that nature is linked to itself, for man is a part of nature.

In alienating (1) nature from man, and (2) man from himself, his own active function, his life activity, alienated labor also alienates the *species* from him; it makes *species-life* the means of individual life. In the first place it alienates species-life and the individual life, and secondly it turns the latter in its abstraction into the purpose of the former, also in its abstract and alienated form.

For labor, *life activity,* and *productive life* appear to man at first only as a *means* to satisfy a need, the need to maintain physical existence. Productive life, however, is species-life. It is life begetting life. In the mode of life activity lies the entire character of a species, its species-character; and free conscious activity is the species-character of man. Life itself appears only as a *means of life.*

The animal is immediately one with its life activity, not distinct from it. The animal is *its life activity.* Man makes his life activity itself into an object of will and consciousness. He has conscious life activity. It is not a determination with which he immediately identifies. Conscious life activity distinguishes man immediately from the life activity of the animal. Only thereby is he a species-being. Or rather, he is only a conscious being—that is, his own life is an object for him—since he is a species-being. Only on that account is his activity free activity. Alienated labor reverses the relationship in that man, since he is a conscious being, makes his life activity, his *essence,* only a means for his *existence.*

The practical creation of an *objective world,* the *treatment* of inorganic nature, is proof that man is a conscious species-being, that is, a being which is related to its species as to its own essence or is related to itself as a species-being. To be sure animals also produce. They build themselves nests, dwelling places, like the bees, beavers, ants, etc. But an animal produces only what is immediately necessary for itself or its young. It produces in a one-sided way while man produces universally. The animal produces under the domination of immediate physical need while man produces free of physical need and only genuinely so in freedom from such need. The animal only produces itself while man reproduces the whole of nature. The animal's product belongs immediately to its physical body while man is free when he confronts his product. The animal builds only according to the standard and the need of the species to which it belongs while man knows how to produce according to the standard of any species and at all times knows how to apply an intrinsic standard to the object. Thus man creates also according to the laws of beauty.

In the treatment of the objective world, therefore, man proves himself to be genuinely a *species-being*. This production is his active species-life. Through it nature appears as *his* work and his actuality. The object of labor is thus the *objectification of man's species-life:* he produces himself not only intellectually, as in consciousness, but also actively in a real sense and sees himself in a world he made. In taking from man the object of his production, alienated labor takes from his *species-life,* his actual and objective existence as a species. It changes his superiority to the animal to inferiority, since he is deprived of nature, his inorganic body.

By degrading free spontaneous activity to the level of a means, alienated labor makes the species-life of man a means of his physical existence.

The consciousness which man has from his species is altered through alienation, so that species-life becomes a means for him.

(3) Alienated labor hence turns the *species-existence of man,* and also nature as his mental species-capacity, into an existence *alien* to him, into the *means* of his *individual existence.* It alienates his spiritual nature, his *human essence,* from his own body and likewise from nature outside him.

(4) A direct consequence of man's alienation from the product of his work, from his life activity, and from his species-existence, is the *alienation of man* from *man.* When man confronts himself, he confronts *other* men. What holds true of man's relationship to his work, to the product of his work, and to himself, also holds of a man's relationship to other men, to their labor, and to the object of their labor.

In general, the statement that man is alienated from his species-existence means that one man is alienated from another just as each man is alienated from human nature.

The alienation of man, the relation of man to himself, is realized and expressed in the relation between man and other men.

The Communist Manifesto

A spectre is haunting Europe—the spectre of Communism. All the Powers of old Europe have entered into a holy alliance to exorcise this spectre: Pope and Czar, Metternich and Guizot, French Radicals and German police-spies.

Where is the party in opposition that has not been decried as Communistic by its opponents in power? Where the Opposition that has not hurled back the branding reproach of Communism, against the more advanced opposition parties, as well as against its reactionary adversaries?

Two things result from this fact:

I. Communism is already acknowledged by all European Powers to be itself a Power.

II. It is high time that Communists should openly, in the face of the whole world, publish their views, their aims, their tendencies, and meet this nursery tale of the Spectre of Communism with a Manifesto of the party itself.

To this end, Communists of various nationalities have assembled in London, and sketched the following Manifesto, to be published in the English, French, German, Italian, Flemish and Danish languages.

I

Bourgeois and Proletarians[1]

The history of all hitherto existing society[2] is the history of class struggles.

Freeman and slave, patrician and plebeian, lord and serf, guild-master[3] and journeyman, in a word, oppressor and oppressed, stood

1. By bourgeoisie is meant the class of modern Capitalists, owners of the means of social production and employers of wage-labour. By proletariat, the class of modern wage-labourers who, having no means of production of their own, are reduced to selling their labour-power in order to live. [*Note by Engels to the English edition of 1888.*]

2. That is, all *written* history. In 1847, the pre-history of society, the social organisation existing previous to recorded history, was all but unknown. Since then, Haxthausen discovered common ownership of land in Russia, Maurer proved it to be the social foundation from which all Teutonic races started in history, and by and by village communities were found to be, or to have been the primitive form of society everywhere from India to Ireland. The inner organisation of this primitive Communistic society was laid bare, in its typical form, by Morgan's crowning discovery of the true nature of the *gens* and its relation to the *tribe*. With the dissolution of the primeval communities society begins to be differentiated into separate and finally antagonistic classes. I have attempted to retrace this process of dissolution in *Der Ursprung der Familie, des Privateigenthums und des Staats*, 2nd edition, Stuttgart, 1886.

3. Guild-master, that is, a full member of a guild, a master within, not a head of a guild.

in constant opposition to one another, carried on an uninterrupted, now hidden, now open fight, a fight that each time ended, either in a revolutionary reconstitution of society at large, or in the common ruin of the contending classes.

In the earlier epochs of history, we find almost everywhere a complicated arrangement of society into various orders, a manifold gradation of social rank. In ancient Rome we have patricians, knights, plebeians, slaves; in the Middle Ages, feudal lords, vassals, guild-masters, journeymen, apprentices, serfs; in almost all of these classes, again, subordinate gradations.

The modern bourgeois society that has sprouted from the ruins of feudal society has not done away with class antagonisms. It has but established new classes, new conditions of oppression, new forms of struggle in place of the old ones.

Our epoch, the epoch of the bourgeoisie, possesses, however, this distinctive feature: it has simplified the class antagonisms. Society as a whole is more and more splitting up into two great hostile camps, into two great classes directly facing each other: Bourgeoisie and Proletariat.

From the serfs of the Middle Ages sprang the chartered burghers of the earliest towns. From these burgesses the first elements of the bourgeoisie were developed.

The discovery of America, the rounding of the Cape, opened up fresh ground for the rising bourgeoisie. The East-Indian and Chinese markets, the colonisation of America, trade with the colonies, the increase in the means of exchange and in commodities generally, gave to commerce, to navigation, to industry, an impulse never before known, and thereby, to the revolutionary element in the tottering feudal society, a rapid development.

The feudal system of industry, under which industrial production was monopolised by closed guilds, now no longer sufficed for the growing wants of the new markets. The manufacturing system took its place. The guild-masters were pushed on one side by the manufacturing middle class; division of labour between the different corporate guilds vanished in the face of division of labour in each single workshop.

Meantime the markets kept ever growing, the demand ever rising. Even manufacture no longer sufficed. Thereupon, steam and machinery revolutionised industrial production. The place of manufacture was taken by the giant, Modern Industry, the place of the industrial middle class by industrial millionaires, the leaders of whole industrial armies, the modern bourgeois.

Modern industry has established the world market, for which the discovery of America paved the way. This market has given an immense development to commerce, to navigation, to communication by land. This development has, in its turn, reacted on the extension of industry; and in proportion as industry, commerce, navigation, railways extended, in the same proportion the bourgeoisie developed, increased its capital, and pushed into the background every class handed down from the Middle Ages.

We see, therefore, how the modern bourgeoisie is itself the product of a long course of development, of a series of revolutions in the modes of production and of exchange.

Each step in the development of the bourgeoisie was accompanied by a corresponding political advance of that class. An oppressed class under the sway of the feudal nobility, an armed and self-governing association in the medieval commune;[4] here independent urban republic (as in Italy and Germany), there taxable "third estate" of the monarchy (as in France), afterwards, in the period of manufacture proper, serving either the semi-feudal or the absolute monarchy as a counterpoise against the nobility, and, in fact, cornerstone of the great monarchies in general, the bourgeoisie has at last, since the establishment of Modern Industry and of the world market, conquered for itself, in the modern representative State, exclusive political sway. The executive of the modern state is but a committee for managing the common affairs of the whole bourgeoisie.

The bourgeoisie, historically, has played a most revolutionary part.

The bourgeoisie, wherever it has got the upper hand, has put an end to all feudal, patriarchal, idyllic relations. It has pitilessly torn asunder the motley feudal ties that bound man to his "natural superiors," and has left remaining no other nexus between man and man than naked self-interest, than callous "cash payment." It has drowned the most heavenly ecstasies of religious fervour, of chivalrous enthusiasm, of philistine sentimentalism, in the icy water of egotistical calculation. It has resolved personal worth into exchange value, and in place of the numberless indefeasible chartered freedoms, has set up that single, unconscionable freedom—Free Trade. In one word, for exploitation,

4. "Commune" was the name taken, in France, by the nascent towns even before they had conquered from their feudal lords and masters local self-government and political rights as the "Third Estate." Generally speaking, for the economical development of the bourgeoisie, England is here taken as the typical country; for its political development, France.

veiled by religious and political illusions, it has substituted naked, shameless, direct, brutal exploitation.

The bourgeoisie has stripped of its halo every occupation hitherto honoured and looked up to with reverent awe. It has converted the physician, the lawyer, the priest, the poet, the man of science, into its paid wage-labourers.

The bourgeoisie has torn away from the family its sentimental veil, and has reduced the family relation to a mere money relation.

The bourgeoisie has disclosed how it came to pass that the brutal display of vigour in the Middle Ages, which Reactionists so much admire, found its fitting complement in the most slothful indolence. It has been the first to show what man's activity can bring about. It has accomplished wonders far surpassing Egyptian pyramids, Roman aqueducts, and Gothic cathedrals; it has conducted expeditions that put in the shade all former Exoduses of nations and crusades.

The bourgeoisie cannot exist without constantly revolutionising the instruments of production, and thereby the relations of production, and with them the whole relations of society. Conservation of the old modes of production in unaltered form, was, on the contrary, the first condition of existence for all earlier industrial classes. Constant revolutionising of production, uninterrupted disturbance of all social conditions, everlasting uncertainty and agitation distinguish the bourgeois epoch from all earlier ones. All fixed, fast-frozen relations, with their train of ancient and venerable prejudices and opinions, are swept away, all new-formed ones become antiquated before they can ossify. All that is solid melts into air, all that is holy is profaned, and man is at last compelled to face with sober senses, his real conditions of life, and his relations with his kind.

The need of a constantly expanding market for its products chases the bourgeoisie over the whole surface of the globe. It must nestle everywhere, settle everywhere, establish connexions everywhere.

The bourgeoisie has through its exploitation of the world market given a cosmopolitan character to production and consumption in every country. To the great chagrin of Reactionists, it has drawn from under the feet of industry the national ground on which it stood. All old-established national industries have been destroyed or are daily being destroyed. They are dislodged by new industries, whose introduction becomes a life and death question for all civilised nations, by industries that no longer work up indigenous raw material, but raw material drawn from the remotest zones; industries whose products are consumed, not only at home, but in every quarter of the globe. In place of the old wants, satisfied by the productions of the country, we find new wants, requiring for their satisfaction the products of distant lands and climes. In place of the old local and national seclusion and self-sufficiency, we have intercourse in every direction, universal interdependence of nations. And as in material, so also in intellectual production. The intellectual creations of individual nations become common property. National one-sidedness and narrow-mindedness become more and more impossible, and from the numerous national and local literatures, there arises a world literature.

The bourgeoisie, by the rapid improvement of all instruments of production, by the immensely facilitated means of communication, draws all, even the most barbarian, nations into civilisation. The cheap prices of commodities are the heavy artillery with which it batters down all Chinese walls, with which it forces the barbarians' intensely obstinate hatred of foreigners to capitulate. It compels all nations, on pain of extinction, to adopt the bourgeois mode of production; it compels them to introduce what it calls civilisation into their midst, i.e., to become bourgeois themselves. In one word, it creates a world after its own image.

The bourgeoisie has subjected the country to the rule of the towns. It has created enormous cities, has greatly increased the urban population as compared with the rural, and has thus rescued a considerable part of the population from the idiocy of rural life. Just as it has made the country dependent on the towns, so it has made barbarian and semi-barbarian countries dependent on the civilised ones, nations of peasants on nations of bourgeois, the East on the West.

The bourgeoisie keeps more and more doing away with the scattered state of the population, of the means of production, and of property. It has agglomerated population, centralised means of production, and has concentrated property in a few hands. The necessary consequence of this was political centralisation. Independent, or but loosely connected provinces with separate interests, laws, governments, and systems of taxation, became lumped together into one nation, with one government, one code of laws, one national class-interest, one frontier, and one customs-tariff.

The bourgeoisie, during its rule of scarce one hundred years, has created more massive and more colossal productive forces than have all preceding generations together. Subjection of Nature's forces to man, machinery, application of chemistry to industry and agriculture, steam-navigation, railways, electric telegraphs, clearing of whole continents for cultivation, canalisation of rivers, whole populations conjured out of the ground—what earlier century had even a presentiment that such productive forces slumbered in the lap of social labour?

We see then: the means of production and of exchange, on whose foundation the bourgeoisie built itself up, were generated in feudal society. At a certain stage in the development of these means of production and of exchange, the conditions under which feudal society produced and exchanged, the feudal organisation of agriculture and manufacturing industry, in one word, the feudal relations of property became no longer compatible with the already developed productive forces; they became so many fetters. They had to be burst asunder; they were burst asunder.

Into their place stepped free competition, accompanied by a social and political constitution adapted to it, and by the economic and political sway of the bourgeois class.

A similar movement is going on before our own eyes. Modern bourgeois society with its relations of production, of exchange and of property, a society that has conjured up such gigantic means of production and of exchange, is like the sorcerer, who is no longer able to control the powers of the nether world whom he has called up by his spells. For many a decade past the history of industry and commerce is but the history of the revolt of modern productive forces against modern conditions of production, against the property relations that are the conditions for the existence of the bourgeois and of its rule. It is enough to mention the commercial crises that by their political return put on its trial, each time more threateningly, the existence of the entire bourgeois society. In these crises a great part not only of the existing products, but also of the previously created productive forces, are periodically destroyed. In these crises there breaks out an epidemic that, in all earlier epochs, would have seemed an absurdity—the epidemic of over-production. Society suddenly finds itself put back into a state of momentary barbarism; it appears as if a famine, a universal war of devastation had cut off the supply of every means of subsistence; industry and commerce seem to be destroyed; and why? Because there is too much civilisation, too much means of subsistence, too much industry, too much commerce. The productive forces at the disposal of society no longer tend to further the development of the conditions of bourgeois property; on the contrary, they have become too powerful for these conditions, by which they are fettered, and so soon as they overcome these fetters, they bring disorder into the whole of bourgeois society, endanger the existence of bourgeois property. The conditions of bourgeois society are too narrow to comprise the wealth created by them. And how does the bourgeoisie get over these crises? On the one hand by enforced destruction of a mass of productive forces; on the other, by the conquest of new markets, and by the more thorough exploitation of the old ones. That is to say, by paving the way for more extensive and more destructive crises, and by diminishing the means whereby crises are prevented.

The weapons with which the bourgeoisie felled feudalism to the ground are now turned against the bourgeoisie itself.

But not only has the bourgeoisie forged the weapons that bring death to itself; it has also called into existence the men who are to wield those weapons—the modern working class—the proletarians.

In proportion as the bourgeoisie, i.e., capital, is developed, in the same proportion is the proletariat, the modern working class, developed—a class of labourers, who live only so long as they find work, and who find work only so long as their labour increases capital. These labourers, who must sell themselves piecemeal, are a commodity, like every other article of commerce, and are consequently exposed to all the vicissitudes of competition, to all the fluctuations of the market.

Owing to the extensive use of machinery and to division of labour, the work of the proletarians has lost all individual character, and, consequently, all charm for the workman. He becomes an appendage of the machine, and it is only the most simple, most monotonous, and most easily acquired knack, that is required of him. Hence, the cost of production of a workman is restricted, almost entirely, to the means of subsistence that he requires for his maintenance, and for the propagation of his race. But the price of a commodity, and therefore also of labour, is equal to its cost of production. In proportion, therefore, as the repulsiveness of the work increases, the wage decreases. Nay more, in proportion as the use of machinery and division of labour increases, in the same proportion the burden of toil also increases, whether by prolongation of the working hours, by increase of the work exacted in a given time, or by increased speed of machinery, etc.

Modern Industry has converted the little workshop of the patriarchal master into the great factory of the industrial capitalist. Masses of labourers, crowded into the factory, are organised like soldiers. As privates of the industrial army they are placed under the command of a perfect hierarchy of officers and sergeants. Not only are they slaves of the bourgeois class, and of the bourgeois State; they are daily and hourly enslaved by the machine, by the overlooker, and, above all, by the individual bourgeois manufacturer himself. The more openly this despotism proclaims gain to be its end and aim, the more petty, the more hateful, and the more embittering it is.

The less the skill and exertion of strength implied in manual labour, in other words, the more modern industry becomes developed, the more is the labour of men superseded by that of women. Differences of age and sex have no longer any distinctive social validity for the working class. All are instruments of labour, more or less expensive to use, according to their age and sex.

No sooner is the exploitation of the labourer by the manufacturer, so far, at an end, and he receives his wages in cash, than he is set upon by the other portions of the bourgeoisie, the landlord, the shopkeeper, the pawnbroker, etc.

The lower strata of the middle class—the small tradespeople, shopkeepers, and retired tradesmen generally, the handicraftsmen and peasants—all these sink gradually into the proletariat, partly because their diminutive capital does not suffice for the scale on which Modern Industry is carried on, and is swamped in the competition with the large capitalists, partly because their specialised skill is rendered worthless by new methods of production. Thus the proletariat is recruited from all classes of the population.

The proletariat goes through various stages of development. With its birth begins its struggle with the bourgeoisie. At first the contest is carried on by individual labourers, then by the workpeople of a factory, then by the operative of one trade, in one locality, against the individual bourgeois who directly exploits them. They direct their attacks not against the bourgeois conditions of production, but against the instruments of production themselves; they destroy imported wares that compete with their labour, they smash to pieces machinery, they set factories ablaze, they seek to restore by force the vanished status of the workman of the Middle Ages.

At this stage the labourers still form an incoherent mass scattered over the whole country, and broken up by their mutual competition. If anywhere they unite to form more compact bodies, this is not yet the consequence of their own active union, but of the union of the bourgeoisie, which class, in order to attain its own political ends, is compelled to set the whole proletariat in motion, and is moreover yet, for a time, able to do so. At this stage, therefore, the proletarians do not fight their enemies, but the enemies of their enemies, the remnants of absolute monarchy, the landowners, the non-industrial bourgeois, the petty bourgeoisie. Thus the whole historical movement is concentrated in the hands of the bourgeoisie; every victory so obtained is a victory for the bourgeoisie.

But with the development of industry the proletariat not only increases in number; it becomes concentrated in greater masses, its strength grows, and it feels that strength more. The various interests and conditions of life within the ranks of the proletariat are more and more equalised, in proportion as machinery obliterates all distinctions of labour, and nearly everywhere reduces wages to the same low level. The growing competition among the bourgeois, and the resulting commercial crises, make the wages of the workers ever more fluctuating. The unceasing improvement of machinery, ever more rapidly developing, makes their livelihood more and more precarious; the collisions between individual workmen and individual bourgeois take more and more the character of collisions between two classes. Thereupon the workers begin to form combinations (Trades' Unions) against the bourgeois; they club together in order to keep up the rate of wages; they found permanent associations in order to make provision beforehand for these occasional revolts. Here and there the contest breaks out into riots.

Now and then the workers are victorious, but only for a time. The real fruit of their battles lies, not in the immediate result, but in the ever-expanding union of the workers. This union is helped on by the improved means of communication that are created by modern industry and that place the workers of different localities in contact with one another. It was just this contact that was needed to centralise the numerous local struggles, all of the same character, into one national struggle between classes. But every class struggle is a political struggle. And that union, to attain which the burghers of the Middle Ages, with their miserable highways, required centuries, the modern proletarians, thanks to railways, achieve in a few years.

This organisation of the proletarians into a class, and consequently into a political party, is continually being upset again by the competition between the workers themselves. But it ever rises up again, stronger, firmer, mightier. It compels legislative recognition of particular interests of the workers, by taking advantage of the divisions among the bourgeoisie itself. Thus, the ten-hours' bill in England was carried.

Altogether collisions between the classes of the old society further, in many ways, the course of development of the proletariat. The bourgeoisie finds itself involved in a constant battle. At first with the aristocracy; later on, with those portions of the bourgeoisie itself, whose interests have become antagonistic to the progress of industry; at all time with the bourgeoisie of foreign countries. In all these battles it sees itself compelled to appeal to the proletariat, to ask for its help, and thus, to drag it into the political arena. The bourgeoisie itself, therefore, supplies the proletariat with its own elements of political and general education, in other words, it furnishes the proletariat with weapons for fighting the bourgeoisie.

Further, as we have already seen, entire sections of the ruling classes are, by the advance of industry, precipitated into the proletariat, or are at least threatened in their conditions of existence. These also supply the proletariat with fresh elements of enlightenment and progress.

Finally, in times when the class struggle nears the decisive hour, the progress of dissolution going on within the ruling class, in fact within the whole range of old society, assumes such a violent, glaring character, that a small section of the ruling class cuts itself adrift, and joins the revolutionary class, the class that holds the future in its hands. Just as, therefore, at an earlier period, a section of the nobility went over to the bourgeoisie, so now a portion of the bourgeoisie goes over to the proletariat, and in particular, a portion of the bourgeois ideologists, who have raised themselves to the level of comprehending theoretically the historical movement as a whole.

Of all the classes that stand face to face with the bourgeoisie today, the proletariat alone is a really revolutionary class. The other classes decay and finally disappear in the face of Modern Industry; the proletariat is its special and essential product.

The lower middle class, the small manufacturer, the shopkeeper, the artisan, the peasant, all these fight against the bourgeoisie, to save from extinction their existence as fractions of the middle class. They are therefore not revolutionary, but conservative. Nay more, they are reactionary, for they try to roll back the wheel of history. If by chance they are revolutionary, they are so only in view of their impending transfer into the proletariat, they thus defend not their present, but their future interests, they desert their own standpoint to place themselves at that of the proletariat.

The "dangerous class," the social scum, that passively rotting mass thrown off by the lowest layers of the old society may, here and there, be swept into the movement by a proletarian revolution; its conditions of life, however, prepare it far more for the part of a bribed tool of reactionary intrigue.

In the conditions of the proletariat, those of old society at large are already virtually swamped. The proletarian is without property; his relation to his wife and children has no longer anything in common with the bourgeois family relations; modern industrial labour, modern subjection to capital, the same in England as in France, in America as in Germany, has stripped him of every trace of national character. Law, morality, religion, are to him so many bourgeois prejudices, behind which lurk in ambush just as many bourgeois interests.

All the preceding classes that got the upper hand, sought to fortify their already acquired status by subjecting society at large to their conditions of appropriation. The proletarians cannot become masters of the productive forces of society, except by abolishing their own previous mode of appropriation, and thereby also every other previous mode of appropriation. They have nothing of their own to secure and to fortify; their mission is to destroy all previous securities for, and insurances of, individual property.

All previous historical movements were movements of minorities, or in the interest of minorities. The proletarian movement is the self-conscious, independent movement of the immense majority, in the interest of the immense majority. The proletariat, the lowest stratum of our present society, cannot stir, cannot raise itself up, without the whole superincumbent strata of official society being sprung into the air.

Though not in substance, yet in form, the struggle of the proletariat with the bourgeoisie is at first a national struggle. The proletariat of each country must, of course, first of all settle matters with its own bourgeoisie.

In depicting the most general phases of the development of the proletariat, we traced the more or less veiled civil war, raging within existing society, up to the point where that war breaks out into open revolution, and where the violent overthrow of the bourgeoisie lays the foundation for the sway of the proletariat.

Hitherto, every form of society has been based, as we have already seen, on the antagonism of oppressing and oppressed classes. But in order to oppress a class, certain conditions must be assured to it under which it can, at least, continue its slavish existence. The serf, in the period of serfdom, raised himself to membership in the commune, just as the petty bourgeois, under the yoke of the feudal absolutism, managed to develop into a bourgeois. The modern labourer, on the contrary, instead of rising with the process of industry, sinks deeper and deeper below the conditions of existence of his own class. He becomes a pauper, and pauperism develops more rapidly than population and wealth. And here it becomes evident, that the bourgeoisie is unfit any longer to be the ruling class in society, and to impose its conditions of existence upon society as an over-riding law. It is unfit to rule because it is incompetent to assure an existence to its slave within his slavery, because it cannot help letting him sink into such a state, that it has to feed him, instead of being fed by him. Society can no longer live under this bourgeoisie, in other words, its existence is no longer compatible with society.

The essential condition for the existence, and for the sway of the bourgeois class, is the formation and augmentation of capital; the condition for capital is wage-labour. Wage-labour rests exclusively on competition between the labourers. The advance of industry, whose involuntary promoter is the bourgeoisie, replaces the isolation of the labourers, due to competition, by the revolutionary combination, due to association. The development of Modern Industry, therefore, cuts from under its feet the very foundation on which the bourgeoisie produces and appropriates products. What the bourgeoisie therefore produces, above all, are its own grave-diggers. Its fall and the victory of the proletariat are equally inevitable.

II

Proletarians and Communists

In what relation do the Communists stand to the proletarians as a whole?

The Communists do not form a separate party opposed to the other working-class parties.

They have no interests separate and apart from those of the proletariat as a whole.

They do not set up any sectarian principles of their own, by which to shape and mould the proletarian movement.

The Communists are distinguished from the other working-class parties by this only: 1. In the national struggles of the proletarians of the different countries, they point out and bring to the front the common interests of the entire proletariat, independently of all nationality. 2. In the various stages of development which the struggle of the working class against the bourgeoisie has to pass through, they always and everywhere represent the interests of the movement as a whole.

The Communists, therefore, are on the one hand, practically, the most advanced and resolute section of the working-class parties of every country, that section which pushes forward all others; on the other hand, theoretically, they have over the great mass of the proletariat the advantage of clearly understanding the line of march, the conditions, and the ultimate general results of the proletarian movement.

The immediate aim of the Communists is the same as that of all other proletarian parties: formation of the proletariat into a class, overthrow of the bourgeois supremacy, conquest of political power by the proletariat.

The theoretical conclusions of the Communists are in no way based on ideas or principles that have been invented, or discovered by this or that would-be universal reformer.

They merely express, in general terms, actual relations springing from an existing class struggle, from a historical movement going on under our very eyes. The abolition of existing property relations is not at all a distinctive feature of communism.

All property relations in the past have continually been subject to historical change consequent upon the change in historical conditions.

The French Revolution, for example, abolished feudal property in favour of bourgeois property.

The distinguishing feature of Communism is not the abolition of property generally, but the abolition of bourgeois property. But modern bourgeois private property is the final and most complete expression of the system of producing and appropriating products, that is based on class antagonisms, on the exploitation of the many by the few.

In this sense, the theory of the Communists may be summed up in the single sentence: Abolition of private property.

We Communists have been reproached with the desire of abolishing the right of personally acquiring property as the fruit of a man's own labour, which property is alleged to be the groundwork of all personal freedom, activity, and independence.

Hard-won, self-acquired, self-earned property! Do you mean the property of the petty artisan and of the small peasant, a form of property that preceded the bourgeois form? There is no need to abolish that; the development of industry has to a great extent already destroyed it, and is still destroying it daily.

Or do you mean modern bourgeois private property?

But does wage-labour create any property for the labourer? Not a bit. It creates capital, i.e., that kind of property which exploits wage-labour, and which cannot increase except upon condition of begetting a new supply of wage-labour for fresh exploitation. Property, in its present form, is based on the antagonism of capital and wage-labour. Let us examine both sides of this antagonism.

To be a capitalist is to have not only a purely personal, but a social *status* in production. Capital is a collective product, and only by the united action of many members, nay, in the last resort, only by the united action of all members of society, can it be set in motion.

Capital is, therefore, not only personal, it is a social power.

When, therefore, capital is converted into common property, into the property of all members of society, personal property is not thereby transformed into social property. It is only the social character of the property that is changed. It loses its class character.

Let us now take wage-labour.

The average price of wage-labour is the minimum wage, i.e., that quantum of the means of subsistence, which is absolutely requisite to keep the labourer in bare existence as a labourer. What, therefore, the wage-labourer appropriates by means of his labour, merely suffices to prolong and reproduce a bare existence. We by no means intend to abolish this personal appropriation of the products of labour, an appropriation that is made for the maintenance and reproduction of human life, and that leaves no surplus wherewith to command the labour of others. All that we want to do away with is the miserable character of this appropriation, under which the labourer lives merely to increase capital, and is allowed to live only insofar as the interest of the ruling class requires it.

In bourgeois society, living labour is but a means to increase accumulated labour. In Communist society, accumulated labour is but a means to widen, to enrich, to promote the existence of the labourer.

In bourgeois society, therefore, the past dominates the present; in Communist society, the present dominates the past. In bourgeois society capital is independent and has individuality, while the living person is dependent and has no individuality.

And the abolition of this state of things is called by the bourgeois abolition of individuality and freedom! And rightly so. The abolition of bourgeois individuality, bourgeois independence, and bourgeois freedom is undoubtedly aimed at.

By freedom is meant, under the present bourgeois conditions of production, free trade, free selling and buying.

But if selling and buying disappears, free selling and buying disappears also. This talk about free selling and buying, and all the other "brave words" of our bourgeoisie about freedom in general, have a meaning, if any, only in contrast with restricted selling and buying, with the fettered traders of the Middle Ages, but have no meaning when opposed to the Communistic abolition of buying and selling, of the bourgeois conditions of production, and of the bourgeoisie itself.

You are horrified at our intending to do away with private property. But in your existing society, private property is already done away with for nine-tenths of the population; its existence for the few is solely due to its non-existence in the hands of those nine-tenths. You reproach us, therefore, with intending to do away with a form of property, the necessary condition for whose existence is the non-existence of any property for the immense majority of society.

In one word, you reproach us with intending to do away with your property. Precisely so; that is just what we intend.

From the moment when labour can no longer be converted into capital, money, or rent, into a social power capable of being monopolised, i.e., from the moment when individual property can no longer be transformed into bourgeois property, into capital, from that moment, you say, individuality vanishes.

You must, therefore, confess that by "individual" you mean no other person than the bourgeois, than the middle-class owner of property. This person must, indeed, be swept out of the way, and made impossible.

Communism deprives no man of the power to appropriate the products of society; all that it does is to deprive him of the power to subjugate the labour of others by means of such appropriation.

It has been objected that upon the abolition of private property, all work will cease, and universal laziness will overtake us.

According to this, bourgeois society ought long ago to have gone to the dogs through sheer idleness; for those of its members who work, acquire nothing, and those who acquire anything, do not work. The whole of this objection is but another expression of the tautology: that there can no longer be any wage-labour when there is no longer any capital.

All objections urged against the Communistic mode of producing and appropriating material products, have, in the same way, been urged against the Communistic mode of producing and appropriating intellectual products. Just as, to the bourgeois, the disappearance of class property is the disappearance of production itself, so the disappearance of class culture is to him identical with the disappearance of all culture.

That culture, the loss of which he laments, is, for the enormous majority, a mere training to act as a machine.

But don't wrangle with us so long as you apply, to our intended abolition of bourgeois property, the standard of your bourgeois notions of freedom, culture, law, etc. Your very ideas are but the outgrowth of the conditions of your bourgeois production and bourgeois property, just as your jurisprudence is but the will of your class made into a law for all, a will, whose essential character and direction are determined by the economical conditions of existence of your class.

The selfish misconception that induces you to transform into eternal laws of nature and of reason, the social forms springing from your present mode of production and form of property—historical relations that rise and disappear in the progress of production—this misconception you share with every ruling class that has preceded you. What you see clearly in the case of ancient property, what you admit in the case of feudal property, you are of course forbidden to admit in the case of your own bourgeois form of property.

Abolition of the family! Even the most radical flare up at this infamous proposal of the Communists.

On what foundation is the present family, the bourgeois family, based? On capital, on private gain. In its completely developed form this family exists only among the bourgeoisie. But this state of things finds its complement in the practical absence of the family among the proletarians, and in public prostitution.

The bourgeois family will vanish as a matter of course when its complement vanishes, and both will vanish with the vanishing of capital.

Do you charge us with wanting to stop the exploitation of children by their parents? To this crime we plead guilty.

But, you will say, we destroy the most hallowed of relations, when we replace home education by social.

And your education! Is not that also social, and determined by the social conditions under which you educate, by the intervention, direct or indirect, of society, by means of schools, etc.? The Communists have not invented the intervention of society in education; they do but seek to alter the character of that intervention, and to rescue education from the influence of the ruling class.

The bourgeois clap-trap about the family and education, about the hallowed co-relation of parents and child, becomes all the more disgusting, the more, by the action of Modern Industry, all family ties among the proletarians are torn asunder, and their children transformed into simple articles of commerce and instruments of labour.

But you Communists would introduce community of women, screams the bourgeoisie in chorus.

The bourgeois sees in his wife a mere instrument of production. He hears that the instruments of production are to be exploited in common, and, naturally, can come to no other conclusion than that the lot of being common to all will likewise fall to the women.

He has not even a suspicion that the real point aimed at is to do away with the status of women as mere instruments of production.

For the rest, nothing is more ridiculous than the virtuous indignation of our bourgeois at the community of women which, they pretend, is to be openly and officially established by the Communists. The Communists have no need to introduce community of women; it has existed almost from time immemorial.

Our bourgeois, not content with having wives and daughters of their proletarians at their disposal, not to speak of common prostitutes, take the greatest pleasure in seducing each other's wives.

Bourgeois marriage is in reality a system of wives in common and thus, at the most, what the Communists might possibly be reproached with, is that they desire to introduce, in substitution for a hypocritically concealed, an openly legalised community of women. For the rest, it is self-evident that the abolition of the present system of production must bring with it the abolition of the community of women springing from that system, i.e., of prostitution both public and private.

The Communists are further reproached with desiring to abolish countries and nationality.

The working men have no country. We cannot take from them what they have not got. Since the proletariat must first of all acquire political supremacy, must rise to be the leading class of the nation, must constitute itself *the* nation, it is so far, itself national, though not in the bourgeois sense of the word.

National differences and antagonism between peoples are daily more and more vanishing, owing to the development of the bourgeoisie, to freedom of commerce, to the world market, to uniformity in the mode of production and in the conditions of life corresponding thereto.

The supremacy of the proletariat will cause them to vanish still faster. United action, of the leading civilised countries at least, is one of the first conditions for the emancipation of the proletariat.

In proportion as the exploitation of one individual by another is put an end to, the exploitation of one nation by another will also be put an end to. In proportion as the antagonism between classes within the nation vanishes, the hostility of one nation to another will come to an end.

The charges against Communism made from a religious, a philosophical, and, generally, from an ideological standpoint, are not deserving of serious examination.

Does it require deep intuition to comprehend that man's ideas, views, and conception, in one word, man's consciousness, changes with every change in the conditions of his material existence, in his social relations and in his social life?

What else does the history of ideas prove, than that intellectual production changes its character in proportion as material production is changed? The ruling ideas of each age have ever been the ideas of its ruling class.

When people speak of the ideas that revolutionise society, they do but express the fact, that within the old society, the elements of a new one have been created, and that the dissolution of the old ideas keeps even pace with the dissolution of the old conditions of existence.

When the ancient world was in its last throes, the ancient religions were overcome by Christianity. When Christian ideas succumbed in the 18th century to rationalist ideas, feudal society fought its death battle with the then revolutionary bourgeoisie. The ideas of religious liberty and freedom of conscience merely gave expression to the sway of free competition within the domain of knowledge.

"Undoubtedly," it will be said, "religious, moral, philosophical and juridical ideas have been modified in the course of historical development. But religion, morality, philosophy, political science, and law, constantly survived this change.

"There are, besides, eternal truths, such as Freedom, Justice, etc., that are common to all states of society. But Communism abolishes eternal truths, it abolishes all religion and all morality, instead of constituting them on a new basis; it therefore acts in contradiction to all past historical experience."

What does this accusation reduce itself to? The history of all past society has consisted in the development of class antagonisms, antagonisms that assumed different forms at different epochs.

But whatever form they may have taken, one fact is common to all past ages, viz., the exploitation of one part of society by the other. No wonder, then, that the social consciousness of past ages, despite all the multiplicity and variety it displays, moves within certain common forms, or general ideas, which cannot completely vanish except with the total disappearance of class antagonisms.

The Communist revolution is the most radical rupture with traditional property relations; no wonder that its development involves the most radical rupture with traditional ideas.

But let us have done with the bourgeois objections to Communism.

We have seen above, that the first step in the revolution by the working class is to raise the proletariat to the position of ruling class, to win the battle of democracy.

The proletariat will use its political supremacy to wrest, by degree, all capital from the bourgeoisie, to centralise all instruments of production in the hands of the State, i.e., of the proletariat organised as the ruling class; and to increase the total productive forces as rapidly as possible.

Of course, in the beginning, this cannot be effected except by means of despotic inroads on the rights of property, and on the conditions of bourgeois production; by means of measures, therefore, which appear economically insufficient and untenable, but which, in the course of the movement, outstrip themselves, necessitate further inroads upon the old social order, and are unavoidable as a means of entirely revolutionising the mode of production.

These measures will of course be different in different countries.

Nevertheless in most advanced countries, the following will be pretty generally applicable.

1. Abolition of property in land and application of all rents of land to public purposes.

2. A heavy progressive or graduated income tax.

3. Abolition of all rights of inheritance.

4. Confiscation of the property of all emigrants and rebels.

5. Centralisation of credit in the hands of the State, by means of a national bank with State capital and an exclusive monopoly.

6. Centralisation of the means of communication and transport in the hands of the State.

7. Extension of factories and instruments of production owned by the State; the bringing into cultivation of waste-lands, and the improvement of the soil generally in accordance with a common plan.

8. Equal liability of all to labour. Establishment of industrial armies, especially for agriculture.

9. Combination of agriculture with manufacturing industries; gradual abolition of the distinction between town and country, by a more equable distribution of the population over the country.

10. Free education for all children in public schools. Abolition of children's factory labour in its present form. Combination of education with industrial production, etc., etc.

When, in the course of development, class distinctions have disappeared, and all production has been concentrated in the hands of a vast association of the whole nation, the public power will lose its political character. Political power, properly so called, is merely the organised power of one class for oppressing another. If the proletariat during its contest with the bourgeoisie is compelled, by the force of circumstances, to organise itself as a class, if, by means of a revolution, it makes itself the ruling class, and, as such, sweeps away by force the old conditions of production, then it will, along with these conditions, have swept away the conditions for the existence of class antagonisms and of classes generally, and will thereby have abolished its own supremacy as a class.

In place of the old bourgeois society, with its classes and class antagonisms, we shall have an association, in which the free development of each is the condition for the free development of all.

10

Sartre and Kierkegaard: Radical Incompleteness as the Human Lot

Jean-Paul Sartre and Soren Kierkegaard might seem like a very odd couple. Sartre was a leading twentieth-century existentialist, very concerned with the structure of human choice. He also was devoutly irreligious. Kierkegaard was a nineteenth-century Danish Lutheran whose primary concern was religion. In most of his writing he emphasized the importance of deep faith. The degree of this extreme religiosity was not universally shared. There was a small riot at his funeral.

The two do share something though. It is an insight into a kind of fluidity or openness in the self that a person has. This involves a contrast between persons and objects, such as chairs. A chair has a definite nature: an essence. To be a chair, an object has to be something the primary function of which is to be sat upon. Some philosophers have tried to find something comparable in human beings. Aristotle, for example, held that to be a human being is to be a rational sort of animal.

Some would argue that chimpanzees sometimes are rational animals. Also some human beings are thoroughly irrational, in some cases deranged. More broadly, any individual human being may change her or his nature over time. Twenty years from now you may not be the person you are today.

This slipperiness or openness in the nature of a human being is linked to what Sartre calls "freedom." We are, he says, condemned to be free. The idea here is that many of us would like to have a definite personal nature. Some people may try, Sartre thinks, to get a feeling of this by wearing uniforms or insignias. Even so, their natures remain open and changeable—because they are condemned to be free.

Clearly Sartre regards freedom and openness as having an unappealing side, at least as far as many people are concerned. Kierkegaard, who had lived in the previous century, had anticipated this view. His response to the problem, though, was one that Sartre definitely would have rejected. Kierkegaard, in two major works (*Fear and Trembling* and *The Sickness unto Death*) contended that the emotional state that naturally resulted from one's fluidity and openness was despair (often accompanied by anxiety). Despair is unpleasant. However, Kierkegaard saw a way out. The unanchored self could anchor itself to God. A deep religious faith could enable you to mitigate the pain of having a fluid, open, and uncertain self.

In summary, Kierkegaard and Sartre agreed that personal fluidity and openness of self would normally have some negative emotional aspects. Kierkegaard, however, in his appeal to deep faith, believes that there is a way out. Sartre does not.

Being and Nothingness

VI. Being-in-Itself

We can now form a few definite conclusions about the *phenomenon of being,* which we have considered in order to make the preceding observations. Consciousness is the revealed-revelation of existents, and existents appear before consciousness on the foundation of their being. Nevertheless the primary characteristic of the being of an existent is never to reveal itself completely to consciousness. An existent can not be stripped of its being; *being* is the ever present foundation of the existent; it is *everywhere in it and nowhere*. There is no being which is not the being of a certain mode of being, none which cannot be apprehended through the mode of being which manifests being and veils it at the same time. *Consciousness can always pass beyond the existent,* not toward its being, but *toward the meaning of this being*. That is why we call it *ontic-ontological,* since a fundamental characteristic of its transcendence is to *transcend the ontic* toward the *ontological*. The *meaning* of the being of the existent insofar as it reveals itself to consciousness is the *phenomenon of being*. This meaning has itself a being, based on which it manifests itself.

It is from this point of view that we can understand the famous Scholastic argument according to which there is a vicious circle in every proposition which concerns being, since any judgment about being already implies being. But in actuality there is no vicious circle, for it is not necessary again to pass beyond the being of this meaning toward its meaning; the meaning of being is valid for the being of every phenomenon, including its own being. The phenomenon of being is not being, as we have already noted. But it indicates being and requires it—although, in truth, the ontological proof which we mentioned above is not valid *especially* or *uniquely* for it; there is *one* ontological proof valid for the whole domain of consciousness. But this proof is sufficient to justify all the information which we can derive from the phenomenon of being. The phenomenon of being, like every primary phenomenon, is immediately disclosed to consciousness. We have at each instant what Heidegger calls a pre-ontological comprehension of it; that is, one which is not accompanied by a fixing in concepts and elucidation. For us at present, then, there is no question of considering this phenomenon for the sake of trying to fix the meaning of being. We must observe always:

(1) That this elucidation of the meaning of being is valid only for the being of the phenomenon. Since the being of consciousness is radically different, its meaning will necessitate a particular elucidation, in terms of the revealed-revelation of another type of being, *being-for-itself* (*l'être-pour-soi*), which we shall define later and which is *opposed to* the *being-in-itself* (*l'être-en-soi*) of the phenomenon.

The Sickness unto Death

Despair Is the Sickness unto Death

A.

Despair Is a Sickness of the Spirit, of the Self, and Accordingly Can Take Three Forms: in Despair Not to Be Conscious of Having a Self (Not Despair in the Strict Sense); in Despair Not to Will to Be Oneself; in Despair to Will to Be Oneself

A human being is spirit. But what is spirit? Spirit is the self. But what is the self? The self is a relation that relates itself to itself or is the relation's relating itself to itself in the relation; the self is not the relation but is the relation's relating itself to itself. A human being is a synthesis of the infinite and the finite, of the temporal and the eternal, of freedom and necessity, in short, a synthesis. A synthesis is a relation between two. Considered in this way, a human being is still not a self.

In the relation between two, the relation is the third as a negative unity, and the two relate to the relation and in the relation to the relation; thus under the qualification of the psychical the relation between the psychical and the physical is a relation. If, however, the relation relates itself to itself, this relation is the positive third, and this is the self.

Such a relation that relates itself to itself, a self, must either have established itself or have been established by another.

If the relation that relates itself to itself has been established by another, then the relation is indeed the third, but this relation, the third, is yet again a relation and relates itself to that which established the entire relation.

The human self is such a derived, established relation, a relation that relates itself to itself and in relating itself to itself relates itself to another. This is why there can be two forms of despair in the strict sense. If a human self had itself established itself, then there could be only one form: not to will to be oneself, to will to do away with oneself, but there could not be the form: in despair to will to be oneself. This second formulation is specifically the expression for the complete dependence of the relation (of the self), the expression for the inability of the self to arrive at or to be in equilibrium and rest by itself, but only, in relating itself to itself, by relating itself to that which has established the entire relation. Yes, this second form of despair (in despair to will to be oneself) is so far from designating merely a distinctive kind of despair that, on the contrary, all despair ultimately can be traced back to and be resolved in it. If the despairing person is aware of his despair, as he thinks he is, and does not speak meaninglessly of it as of something that is happening to him (somewhat as one suffering from dizziness speaks in nervous delusion of a weight on his head or of something that has fallen down on him, etc., a weight and a pressure that nevertheless are not something external but a reverse reflection of the internal) and now with all his power seeks to break the despair by himself and by himself alone—he is still in despair and with all his presumed effort only works himself all the deeper into deeper despair. The misrelation of despair is not a simple misrelation but a misrelation in a relation that relates itself to itself and has been established by another, so that the misrelation in that relation which is for itself [*for sig*] also reflects itself infinitely in the relation to the power that established it.

The formula that describes the state of the self when despair is completely rooted out is this: in relating itself to itself and in willing to be itself, the self rests transparently in the power that established it.

B.
The Possibility and the Actuality of Despair

Is despair an excellence or a defect? Purely dialectically, it is both. If only the abstract idea of despair is considered, without any thought of someone in despair, it must be regarded as a surpassing excellence. The possibility of this sickness is man's superiority over the animal, and this superiority distinguishes him in quite another way than does his erect walk, for it indicates infinite erectness or sublimity, that he is spirit. The possibility of this sickness is man's superiority over the animal; to be aware of this sickness is the Christian's superiority over the natural man; to be cured of this sickness is the Christian's blessedness.

Consequently, to be able to despair is an infinite advantage, and yet to be in despair is not only the worst misfortune and misery—no it is ruination. Generally this is not the case with the relation between possibility and actuality. If it is an excellence to be able to be this or that, then it is an even greater excellence to be that; in other words, to be is like an ascent when compared with being able to be. With respect to despair, however, to be is like a descent when compared with being able to be; the descent is as infinitely low as the excellence of possibility is high. Consequently, in relation to despair, not to be in despair is the ascending scale. But here again this category is equivocal. Not to be in despair is not the same as not being lame, blind, etc. If not being in despair signifies neither more nor less than not being in despair, then it means precisely to be in despair. Not to be in despair must signify the destroyed possibility of being able to be in despair; if a person is truly not to be in despair, he must at every moment destroy the possibility. This is generally not the case in the relation between actuality and possibility. Admittedly, thinkers say that actuality is annihilated possibility, but that is not entirely true; it is the consummated, the active possibility. Here, on the contrary, the actuality (not to be in despair) is the impotent, destroyed possibility, which is why it is also a negation; although actuality in relation to possibility is usually a corroboration, here it is a denial.

Despair is the misrelation in the relation of a synthesis that relates itself to itself. But the synthesis is not the misrelation; it is merely the possibility, or in the synthesis lies the possibility of the misrelation. If the synthesis were the misrelation, then despair would not exist at all, then despair would be something that lies in human nature as such. That is, it would not be despair; it would be something that happens to a man, something he suffers, like a disease to which he succumbs, or like death, which is everyone's fate. No, no, despairing lies in man himself. If he were not a synthesis, he could not despair at all, nor could he despair if the synthesis in its original state from the hand of God were not in the proper relationship.

Where, then, does the despair come from? From the relation in which the synthesis relates itself to itself, inasmuch as God, who constituted man a relation, releases it from his hand, as it were—that is, inasmuch as the relation relates itself to itself. And because the relation is spirit, is the self, upon it rests the responsibility for all despair at every moment of its existence, however much the despairing person speaks of his despair as a misfortune and however ingeniously he deceives himself and others, confusing it with that previously mentioned case of dizziness, with which despair, although qualitatively different, has much in common, since dizziness corresponds, in the category of the physical, to what despair is in the category of the spirit, and lends itself to numerous analogies to despair.

Once the misrelation, despair, has come about, does it continue as a matter of course? No, it does not continue as a matter of course; if the misrelation continues, it is not attributable to the misrelation but to the relation which relates itself to itself. That is, every time the misrelation manifests itself and every moment it exists, it must be traced back to the relation. For example, we say that someone catches sickness, perhaps through carelessness. The sickness sets in and from then on is in force and is an *actuality* whose origin recedes more and more into the *past.* It would be both cruel and inhuman to go on saying, "You, the sick person, are in the process of catching the sickness right now." That would be the same as perpetually wanting to dissolve the actuality of the sickness into its possibility. It is true that he was responsible for catching the sickness, but he did that only once; the continuation of the sickness is a simple result of his catching it that one time, and its progress cannot to be traced at every moment to him as the cause; he brought it upon himself, but it cannot say that he is *bringing* it upon himself. To despair, however, is a different matter. Every actual moment of despair is traceable to possibility; every moment he is in despair he is *bringing* it upon himself. It is always in the present tense; in relation to the actuality there is no pastness of the past: in every actual moment of despair the person in despair bears all the past as a present in possibility. The reason for this is that to despair is a qualification of spirit and relates to the eternal in man. But he cannot rid himself of the eternal—no, never in all eternity. He cannot throw it away once and for all, nothing is more impossible; at any moment that he does not have it, he must have thrown it or is throwing it away—but it comes again, that is, every moment he is in despair he is bringing his despair upon himself. For despair is not attributable to the misrelation but to the relation that relates itself to itself. A person cannot rid himself of the relation to himself any more than he can rid himself of his self, which, after all, is one and the same thing, since the self is the relation to oneself.

C.
Despair Is "The Sickness unto Death"

This concept, this sickness unto death, must, however, be understood in a particular sense. Literally it means a sickness of which the end and the result are death. Therefore we use the expression "fatal sickness" as synonymous with the sickness unto death. In this sense, despair cannot be called the sickness unto death. Christianly understood, death itself is a passing into life. Thus, from a Christian point of view, no earthly, physical sickness is the sickness unto death, for death is indeed the end of the sickness, but death is not the end. If there is to be any question of a sickness unto death in the strictest sense, it must be a sickness of which the end is death and death is the end. This is precisely what despair is.

But in another sense despair is even more definitely the sickness unto death. Literally speaking, there is not the slightest possibility that anyone will die from this sickness or that it will end in physical death. On the contrary, the torment of despair is precisely this inability to die. Thus it has more in common with the situation of a mortally ill person when he lies struggling with death and yet cannot die. Thus to be sick *unto* death is to be unable to die, yet not as if there were hope of life; no, the hopelessness is that there is not even the ultimate hope, death. When death is the greatest danger, we hope for life; but when we learn to know the even greater danger, we hope for death. When the danger is so great that death becomes the hope, then despair is the hopelessness of not even being able to die.

It is in this last sense that despair is the sickness unto death, this tormenting contradiction, this sickness of the self, perpetually to be dying, to die and yet not die, to die death. For to die signifies that it is all over, but to die death means to experience dying, and if this is experienced for one single moment, one thereby experiences it forever. If a person were to die of despair as one dies of a sickness, then the eternal in him, the self, must be able to die in the same sense as the body dies of sickness. But this is impossible; the dying of despair continually converts itself into a living. The person in despair cannot die; "no more than the dagger can slaughter thoughts" can despair consume the eternal, the self at the root of despair, whose worm does not die and whose fire is not quenched. Nevertheless, despair is veritably a self-consuming, but an impotent self-consuming that cannot do what it wants to do. What it wants to do is to consume itself, something it cannot do, and this impotence is a new form of self-consuming, in which despair is once again unable to do what it wants to do, to consume itself; this is an intensification, or the law of intensification. This is the provocativeness or the cold fire in despair, this gnawing that burrows deeper and deeper in impotent self-consuming. The inability of despair to consume him is so remote from being any kind of comfort to the person in despair that it is the very opposite. This comfort is precisely the torment, is precisely what keeps the gnawing alive and keeps life in the gnawing, for it is precisely over this that he despairs (not as having despaired): that he cannot consume himself, cannot get rid of himself, cannot reduce himself to nothing. This is the formula for despair raised to a higher power, the rising fever in this sickness of the self.

An individual in despair despairs over *something.* So it seems for a moment, but only for a moment; in the same moment the true despair or despair in its true form shows itself. In despairing over *something,* he really despaired over *himself,* and now he wants to be rid of himself. For example, when the ambitious man whose slogan is "Either Caesar or nothing" does not get to be Caesar, he despairs over it. But this also means something else: precisely because he did not get to be Caesar, he now cannot bear to be himself. Consequently he does not despair because he did not get to be Caesar but despairs over himself because he did not get to be Caesar. This self, which, if it had become Caesar, would have been in seventh heaven (a state, incidentally, that in another sense is just as despairing), this self is now utterly intolerable to him. In a deeper sense, it is not his failure to become Caesar that is intolerable, but it is this self that did not become Caesar that is intolerable; or, to put it even more accurately, what is intolerable to him is that he cannot get rid of himself. If he had become Caesar, he would despairingly get rid of himself, but he did not become Caesar and cannot despairingly get rid of himself. Essentially, he is just as despairing, for he does not have his self, is not himself. He would not have become himself by becoming Caesar but would have been rid of himself, and by not becoming Caesar he despairs over not being able to get rid of himself. Thus it is superficial for someone (who probably has never seen anyone in despair, not even himself) to say of a person in despair: He is consuming himself. But this is precisely what he in his despair [wants] and this is precisely what he to his torment cannot do, since the despair has inflamed something that cannot burn or be burned up in the self.

Consequently, to despair over something is still not despair proper. It is the beginning, or, as the physician says of an illness, it has not yet declared itself. The next is declared despair, to despair over oneself. A young girl despairs of love, that is, she despairs over the loss of her beloved, over his death or his unfaithfulness to her. This is not declared despair; no, she despairs over herself. This self of hers, which she would have been rid of or would have lost in the most blissful manner had it become "his" beloved, this self becomes a torment to her if it has to be a self without "him." This self, which would have become her treasure (although, in another sense, it would have been just as despairing), has now become to her an abominable void since "he" died, or it has become to her a nauseating reminder that she has been deceived. Just try it, say to such a girl, "You are consuming yourself," and you will hear her answer, "Oh, but the torment is simply that I cannot do that."

To despair over oneself, in despair to will to be rid of oneself—this is the formula for all despair. Therefore the other form of despair, in despair to will to be oneself, can be traced back to the first, in despair not to will to be oneself, just as we previously resolved the form, in despair not to will to be oneself, into the form, in despair to will to be oneself (see A). A person in despair despairingly wills to be himself. But if he despairingly wills to be himself, he certainly does not want to be rid of himself. Well, so it seems, but upon closer examination it is clear that the contradiction is the same. The self that he despairingly wants to be is a self that he is not (for to will to be the self that he is in truth is the very opposite of despair), that is, he wants to tear his self away from the power that established it. In spite of all his despair, however, he cannot manage to do it; in spite of all his despairing efforts, that power is the stronger and forces him to be the self he does not want to be. But this is his way of willing to get rid of himself, to rid himself of the self that he is in order to be the self that he has dreamed up. He would be in seventh heaven to be the self wants to be (although in another sense he would be just as despairing), but to be forced to be the self he does not want to be, that is his torment—that he cannot get rid of himself.

Socrates demonstrated the immortality of the soul from the fact that sickness of the soul (sin) does not consume it as sickness of the body consumes the body. Thus, the eternal in a person can be demonstrated by the fact that despair cannot consume his self, that precisely this is the torment of contradiction in despair. If there were nothing eternal in a man, he could not despair at all; if despair could consume his self, then there would be no despair at all.

Such is the nature of despair, this sickness of the self, this sickness unto death. The despairing person is mortally ill. In a completely different sense than is the case with any illness, this sickness has attacked the most vital organs, and yet he cannot die. Death is not the end of the sickness, but death is incessantly the end. To be saved from this sickness by death is an impossibility, because the sickness and its torment—and the death—are precisely this inability to die.

This is the state in despair. No matter how much the despairing person avoids it, no matter how successfully he has completely lost himself (especially the case in the form of despair that is ignorance of being in despair) and lost himself in such a manner that the loss is not at all detectable—eternity nevertheless will make it manifest that his condition was despair and will nail him to himself so that his torment will still be that he cannot rid himself of his self, and it will become obvious that he was just imagining that he had succeeded in doing so. Eternity is obliged to do this, because to have a self, to be a self, is the greatest concession, an infinite concession, given to man, but it is also eternity's claim upon him.